MANAGING ETHNIC DIVERSITY

Research in Migration and Ethnic Relations Series

Series Editor:
Maykel Verkuyten, ERCOMER
Utrecht University

The Research in Migration and Ethnic Relations series has been at the forefront of research in the field for ten years. The series has built an international reputation for cutting edge theoretical work, for comparative research especially on Europe and for nationally-based studies with broader relevance to international issues. Published in association with the European Research Centre on Migration and Ethnic Relations (ERCOMER), Utrecht University, it draws contributions from the best international scholars in the field, offering an interdisciplinary perspective on some of the key issues of the contemporary world.

Forthcoming

Media in Motion
Cultural Complexity and Migration in the Nordic Region
Edited by Elisabeth Eide and Kaarina Nikunen
ISBN 978-1-4094-0446-0

Full series list at back of book

EUROPEAN RESEARCH CENTRE
ON MIGRATION & ETHNIC RELATIONS

Managing Ethnic Diversity

Meanings and Practices from an International Perspective

REZA HASMATH
University of Toronto, Canada

ASHGATE

Published by
Ashgate Publishing Limited
Wey Court East
Union Road
Farnham
Surrey, GU9 7PT
England

Ashgate Publishing Company
Suite 420
101 Cherry Street
Burlington
VT 05401–4405
USA

www.ashgate.com

British Library Cataloguing in Publication Data
Managing ethnic diversity : meanings and practices from an
    international perspective. – (Research in migration and
    ethnic relations series)
    1. Multiculturalism. 2. Ethnic relations.
    I. Series II. Hasmath, Reza.
    305.8–dc22

Library of Congress Control Number: 2010937743

ISBN 9781409411215 (hbk)
ISBN 9781409411222 (ebk)

Printed and bound in Great Britain by the
MPG Books Group, UK

Contents

List of Tables

Notes on Contributors

Editor

Reza Hasmath (PhD, Cambridge) is a Lecturer in Sociology at the University of Toronto. His research examines the labour market experiences of ethnic minorities in North America and China. He is the author of *The Ethnic Penalty*, *A Comparative Study of Minority Development in China and Canada*, and has co-edited *China in an Era of Transition: Understanding Contemporary State and Society Actors*. He is currently completing a monograph examining ethnicity in contemporary urban China.

Authors

Margaret Adsett (PhD, Carleton) has worked for the three federal government departments that have housed Canada's multiculturalism policy since its inception, and is presently the Director of Research in the Department of Canadian Heritage – the department that is presently responsible for the policy. Margaret has a number of publications in the areas of identity, youth voter participation, intercultural relations, Quebec separatism, and the management of diversity and integration.

Stefano Fait (PhD, St. Andrews) is a member of the Centre for the Anthropological Study of Knowledge and Ethics at the University of St Andrews. His research interests include political anthropology, human rights and bioethics, racism, immigration, the social and historical studies of the biomedical sciences, and disability studies.

Augie Fleras (PhD, Victoria University of Wellington) is an Associate Professor of Sociology at the University of Waterloo. He is the author of numerous books, including *The Politics of Indigeneity: Canada and New Zealand Perspectives*, *Social Problems in Canada: Constructions, Conditions and Challenges* and *Engaging Diversity: Multiculturalism in Canada*.

Barbara Herzog-Punzenberger (Mag., Vienna) is a Lecturer in Social and Cultural Anthropology at Vienna University and a Research Fellow at the Institute for European Integration Research at the Austrian Academy of Sciences. She has published extensively on multiculturalism, education and labour market, with a particular emphasis on the second generation in Austria.

Patti Tamara Lenard (D. Phil, Oxford) is a Lecturer in Social Studies at Harvard University. She research focuses on the role of trust in democratic communities and the stresses posed to that trust by the presence of ethno-cultural diversity. In 2006, Patti held a Fulbright Fellowship to conduct research that evaluated the rates of political participations of immigrant minorities in Canada and the United States.

Rachel Marangozov (PhD, Cambridge) is currently a Senior Research Fellow at the Institute for Employment Studies in the United Kingdom. Her research looks at the corporate appropriation of cultural difference in mass advertising and how it influences the way in which multiculturalism is popularly understood among the United Kingdom public. She has produced five major publications around migration, diversity and race relations and became a regular commentator on these issues on national TV and radio.

Toula Nicolacopoulos (PhD, La Trobe) is a Lecturer in Philosophy at La Trobe University. She hold a law degree from Melbourne University and has recently published three books, *The Radical Critique of Liberalism: In Memory of a Vision*, *From Foreigner to Citizen: Greek Migrants and Social Change in White Australia* (co-authored with George Vassilacopoulos) and *Hegel and the Logical Structure of Love: An Essay on Sexualities Family and the Law* (co-authored with George Vassilacopoulos).

Govind Rao (PhD, York) is a Lecturer in Political Science at McMaster University. He has co-edited the volume *Analyzing and Evaluating Intervention: The War in Zaire/Congo 1996–7*.

Suzanna Reiss (PhD, NYU) is an Assistant Professor of United States Foreign Relations in the Department of History at the University of Hawai'i at Manoa, and a Fellow at the Charles Warren Center for Studies in American History at Harvard University. After completing her PhD, she lectured in History at Princeton University before assuming her current position. Her teaching and research looks at questions of US imperialism, the history of capitalism, US-Latin American and Caribbean relations, and the political economy of the African Diaspora.

Andrew M. Robinson (PhD, Western Ontario) is an Associate Professor of Contemporary Studies at Wilfrid Laurier University's where he has initiated an undergraduate Combined Honours program in Human Rights and Human Diversity. His most recent book is *Multiculturalism and the Foundations of Meaningful Life*.

George Vassilacopoulos (PhD, La Trobe) is a Lecturer in Philosophy at La Trobe University. He recently published with Toula Nicolacopoulos *From Foreigner to*

Citizen: Greek Migrants and Social Change in White Australia and *Hegel and the Logical Structure of Love: An Essay on Sexualities Family and the Law*.

Ming-Bao Yue (PhD, Stanford) is an Associate Professor of twentieth Chinese literature and culture in the Department of East Asian Languages and Literatures at the University of Hawai'i at Manoa. She has published widely on the construction of Chinese identities/culture in various national and diasporic contexts. She is completing her book manuscript *Migrating Chinese Identities: Essays on Global Culture, Diaspora and New Ethnicities*.

Chapter 1

The Complexities of Ethnic Diversity

Reza Hasmath

The complexities of ethnic diversity have caused much debate and ink to flow. At the onset, the concept of ethnicity lacks a clear theoretical framework and is often bemused by contradictory and limited empirical scope. In fact, the term 'ethnic' itself is a contentious one refashioning new significance in the twentieth century. The term derived from the classical Greek word *ethnos*, referring to 'pagan' or 'heathen', and was popularized by the New Testament appearing 167 times. In Catholic Europe, the term *ethnos* was primarily used in this sense from the mid-fourteenth century until mid-/late-nineteenth century, when it gradually began to refer to 'racial' characteristics.[1]

In the twentieth century, an understanding of ethnicity and ethnic groups has taken divergent paths. At one extreme, particularly in nations with a rich Communist history such as Russia, China and various Eastern European nations, ethnicity has been heavily influenced by a Soviet model which politicized and institutionalized the identification and categorization of ethnic minority groups. A *natsionalnost* or minority 'nationality' was officially characterized by the State following a "four commons" criterion: (1) a distinct language; (2) a recognized indigenous homeland and a common territory; (3) a common economic life; and, (4) a strong sense of identity and distinctive customs, ranging from dress, religion, foods. As discussed further in Chapter Six, this has resulted in 55 official ethnic minority groups being recognized in China, in spite of a potential pool of more than 400 ethnic minority groups. Operationally, this form of fixed identification essentially narrows the ability of the individual to define themselves outside the boundaries of State accepted ethnic group categories.

A corollary of this idea is the classification of ethnicity by nation of birth, as practiced in Austria, France, Germany and Italy. An ethnic minority is thus born into a particular ethnic category based on national boundaries and is seen a member of that group for life. Further, given one's ethnicity is bounded by national boundaries the relative freedom to classify one's ethnicity by sub-national areas

---

1   The term 'race' in the modern context has questionable descriptive and analytical value. While the term continues to appear in literature and discourse on ethnicity, there are two principal reasons why it may potentially be flawed to speak about 'races'. First, there has always been interbreeding between human populations that it would be meaningless to talk of fixed boundaries between 'races'. Second, as Cavalli-Sforza et al. (1994) argue, the distribution of hereditary physical traits does not follow clear delineations.

(e.g. Scottish) or religious-oriented groups (e.g. Sikh) is subdued. For example, if a Kurdish person is born in Turkey and migrates to Austria after the age of six, they will subsequently be classified as Turkish rather than Kurdish for the remainder of their natural life.

Finally, in classic post-World War Two immigrant reception societies such as Canada and Australia, 'ethnics' initially evolved into a polite term referring to first-wave immigrants, from 1945 to the late 1960s – most prominently the Italians, Portuguese, Greeks – who were often considered 'different' on cultural grounds relative to the Charter groups (non-Aboriginal, non-British and in the case of Canada, non-French). By the second-wave of immigration from the late 1960s to late 1990s, marked by changes in immigration policies that removed overt favour for family sponsorship and subsequent patterns of chain migration of Western European backgrounds, the 'visible ethnic minority' demographics increased steadily.[2] Today, 9.2 percent of Australia's population (the majority comprising of Asian ancestries) and 13.4 percent of Canada's population (a mix of Asian, Latin American and Caribbean ancestries) are visible ethnic minorities, who have colloquial taken on the mantle of 'ethnics'.

Due partially to a legacy of recent mass-immigration, both Canada and Australia practice self-identification of ethnicity. This is perhaps the most accepted normative form of identifying membership into an ethnic group as it provides the freedom of the individual to define him or herself.[3] Given our nominal repertoire of identities, individuals in this form of identification are able to choose the ethnic group category(-ics) that define them. Moreover, the advantages of self-identification versus a fixed style is evident for immigrant receptive societies – it encourages migrants to receive a strong message that they are welcome to their host nation; and to promote a multiculturalist tenet of pride in one's ancestry, which has become a stronger part of prevailing multicultural ideologies as demonstrated throughout the chapters, self-identification based on people's ancestries is promoted. In the process however, there is a risk of confusing ancestry with ethnicity, so that everyone's 'true' ethnic identity is presumed to be rooted as a fixed concrete entity.

---

2   In the Canadian case, changes in immigration policy were timed with the formalization of multiculturalism policy. In 1966, a new immigration policy based on a points system involving factors including age and occupational qualification, replaced the older system which stressed sponsorship. Not coincidentally, only a year prior to changes in the immigration policy the Canadian government commissioned the *Preliminary Report of the Royal Commission on Bilingualism and Biculturalism*, which is commonly referred to as the first use of multiculturalism as a social policy for managing ethnic differences.

3   No one is completely free to self-define his/her ethnic membership. Constraints may be imposed by numerous circumstances, family and genetic markers to name a few. The point nevertheless remains that within reason, self-identification of ethnicity provides a relative freedom to choose one's ethnic membership both in a legal sense and in daily life.

Table 1.1   Ethnic Categorization and First Generation Classification

	Ethnic Categorization	First Generation Classification
Australia	Self-Identification	Foreign born
Austria	Nation of Birth	Foreign born, after age 6
Canada	Self-Identification	Foreign born, after age 4
China	Fixed Identification	n/a
France	Nation of Birth or Parents' Nation of Birth	Foreign born, after age 5
Germany	Nation of Birth	Foreign born, after age 6
Italy	Nation of Birth	Foreign born
New Zealand	Self-Identification	Foreign born
Taiwan	Fixed Identification	n/a
United Kingdom	Self-Identification	Foreign born, after age 6

Definitions and Scope

Suffice to say, 'ethnic groups' and 'ethnicity' have cogently become commonly used to the extent that most individuals using these terms find definitions unnecessary, political toiling and census reporting notwithstanding.[4] As Cohen (1978) insightfully pointed out – and still holds true today – the literature takes for granted that 'ethnic groups' and 'ethnicity' refer to a set of named groupings singled out by the researcher as ethnic units. Ethnic membership in these named groupings is thereafter shown to have an effect or correlation with one or more dependent variable(s). In this respect, ethnicity is used as a significant structural phenomenon, but this does not constitute a definition.

In the most simplistic form, sociologists and anthropologists view ethnicity in two lights, which are not necessarily mutually exclusive. The first, as a primordial occurrence that is unchanging and universal, meaning certain ethnic traits can be ascribed at birth, for example one's skin pigmentation (see note one for potential objections). The second understanding sees ethnicity as socially constructed, forged on the basis of a particular history. In other words, ethnic identity is achieved after birth, for instance, a member of an ethnic group may be identified by the language spoken (Fishman 1980); by ancestry – either by place of birth or the ancestors of the individuals forming the group (Schermerhorn 1970); by religious affiliation (Goldman 2000); and more broadly, by cultural artefacts, i.e. foods, traditions. The majority of ethnic group identities are not based on ascribed traits, but rather on shared values, beliefs and concerns that are open to acquisition by social conditions. As a consequence, the characteristics that define ethnic groups may vary by context. For example, Thai may be considered an ethnic minority in

---

4   When Isajiw (1974) examined sixty-five studies of ethnicity in sociology and anthropology he found only thirteen defined the term.

Australia, yet in another context, in Thailand, Thai can constitute a combination of several ethnic groups in the south-east Asian nation.

The concept of ethnicity can become so complex that Max Weber even suggested abandoning it altogether. Ironically, it is Weber's definition of ethnic groups that became the standard bearer for generations of sociologists. He posited an ethnic group constitutes,

> those human groups that entertain a subjective belief in their common descent because of similarities of physical type or of customs, or of both, or because of memories of colonization or migration (Weber 1968, 389).

For Weber, ethnicity is seen as a combination of common customs, language and values based on a sense of descent extending beyond kinship. He notes that the

> persistent effect of the old ways ... continue as a source of native country sentiment among emigrants even when they have become so thoroughly adjusted to the new country (Weber 1997, 18).

In anthropological terms, Barth (1969, 10–11) defines an ethnic group as a designated population that has four elements: (1) has a biologically self-perpetuating population; (2) shares fundamental cultural values and forms; (3) has a field of communication and interaction; and, (4) has a membership that identifies itself and is identified by others, as constituting a category different from other categories of the same order. Barth criticizes past anthropology for isolating the ethnic unit conceptually so that its cultural and social forms are seen as remote outcomes of local ecological adaptation, via a history of "adaptation by invention and selective borrowing". In this line of thinking, this history has produced separate 'peoples', each with their own culture. To move beyond this conceptual reification of ethnic groups, Barth suggests using a general identity determined in large part by origin and background. Instead of assuming ethnic groups have fixed organizational characteristics, ethnic groups are thus scaled subjectively, utilizing modes of identification based on interactions between and among groups.

From Group Characteristics to Social and Political Processes

In large part, the work of Barth provided an impetus to shift the focus of studies on ethnic diversity from group characteristics to analyzing social and political processes. In this mode of thinking, ethnicity is seen as a particular social and political relationship between agents who consider themselves as being culturally distinctive from members of other groups. As Eriksen (2002) puts it, when cultural differences actively make a difference in interactions between members of groups, the social and political relationships have an ethnic element. In other words, ethnicity refers to aspects of both gain and loss in a burgeoning social and political interaction.

In this spirit, innumerable theories of ethnicity have been developed serving varying analytical purposes, including primordialist theory (see Geertz 1973; Shils 1957); modernization theory (see Hettne 1996); neo-Marxist or a class approach to ethnicity – including class segmentation (see Reich et al. 1973); split-labor

Table 1.2   Population and Minority Demographics

	Population	Minority Total	Largest Three Minority Groups			Source
Australia*	20,544,064	9.2 %[+]	Chinese 3.37 %	Indian 1.18 %	Lebanese 0.92 %	2006 Census
Austria	8,199,783	9.8 %	Southern Slavic 4.0 %	Turkish 1.6 %	Germans 0.9 %	2006 Census
Canada*	29,639,035	13.4 %[+]	Chinese 3.7 %	East Indian 2.4 %	Filipino 1.1 %	2001 Census
China	1,137,386,112	8.5 %	Zhuang 1.3 %	Manchu 0.9 %	Hui 0.8 %	2000 Census
France	61,399,541 (2006)	~ 16.0 %	North African ~ 7.0 %	Other European ~ 7.0 %	Others ~ 2.0 %	Various Survey Estimates[#]
Germany	82,220,000	9.0 % 19.0 % (w/Immigrant Backgrounds)	Turkish 2.1 %	Serb 0.6 %	Italian 6.7 %	2005 Micro-Census
Italy	58,802,902	5.0 %	Other European 2.5 %	African 1.5 %	Others 1.0 %	2006 Census
New Zealand	4,143,279	29.4 % 9.4 % (excludes Aboriginal groups)	Maori 13.7 %	Asians 8.1 %	Pacific Islanders 6.4 %	2006 Census
Taiwan	22,858,872 (2007)	~ 2.1 %[^]	Hokkien ~ 70 %	Hakka ~ 15 %	Mainland Chinese ~ 13 %	Various Survey Estimates[#]
United Kingdom	58,789,194	7.9 %	African 2.0 %	Indian 1.8 %	Pakistani 1.3 %	2001 Census

* Largest visible ethnic minority groups
+ Excludes Aboriginal and Native groups
# Official statistics not collected
^ Only the 13 aboriginal groups are officially classified as minority groups

market (see Bonacich 1972); internal colonialism (see Gonzalez-Casanova 1965); and, world systems theory (see Wallerstein 1979). These theories ultimately point to different mechanisms and accuse different actors of using ethnic division to their advantage. At a more basic level, all of the approaches nevertheless agree that ethnicity has something to do with the classification of people and group relationships. They emphasize the sharing of social ties by reference to common origins and a historical past (whether real or perceived); shared cultural heritage; and/or language. But then they introduce a power factor, and this is where it gets muddy.

Ethnicity can be seen as one of several outcomes of group interactions in which there is differential power between non-minority and minority groups. An excellent way to conceptualize this idea is to look at the interplay of size and access to power to determine whether ethnic groups are dominant or subordinate. Accordingly, if an ethnic group has both power and size, it is the *dominant majority*. If it has power, but not size, they are the *dominant elite*. If it has size, but does not have power, it is classified as *mass subjects*. And finally, if the group has neither size nor power, it is classified as a *minority group*. It is important to note each of the four types of stratified groups can be multi-ethnic or homogeneous. As such, any of the group types could comprise of several ethnic groups or just one. Through situations of social change and increased mobility they may start to crosscut one another so that members of all ethnic groups are found in all strata.

In sum, ethnicity can be a useful concept to analyze contact and mutual accommodation between groups, as well as, the strategic positions of group power within the structure of modern society. This characterization opens the door to discuss the management of ethnic diversity by looking at power relations, and the management of social, political and economic resources among, and between dominant and minority groups. The objective of this book is thus to examine how ethnic diversity is managed across various national contexts – how do these manifestations and meanings of ethnic diversity vary from place to place? And to what extent are there contradictions and inconsistencies, with respect to public policy and political philosophies versus practices on the ground?

Managing Ethnic Diversity

Nearly 2,350 years ago, Alexander the Great was credited for successfully practicing one of the first mass-scale policies of cultural fusion after his numerous conquests in the Middle East and Asia Minor. His ethno-management successfully fused Macedonian, Greek and Persian cultures into court; the integration of a multi-ethnic army; the retention of local rulers; and, a legacy of tolerance for non-Greek practices. What makes the management of ethnic diversity more complex than in antiquity is rooted in the fact that the modern discourse on ethnicity has contributed to a new form of 'ethnic' self-awareness, notably about 'home country' origins and traditions. This has led to the continuation of ethnic networks which provide a large space for local ethnic communities and economies to prosper. Major cosmopolitan cities have neighbourhoods dominated by people with the same origin as themselves and continue to regard themselves, for example, as 'Chinese' or 'Nigerian' in addition to being Canadian, Australian or British – two generations or more after their ancestors left their 'home country'. This may be the result of ethnic organization and identity reacting to the process of modernization itself. As Friedman (1990, 311) puts it, "ethnic fragmentation and modernist homogenization are not two arguments, two opposing views of what is happening in the world today, but two constitutive trends of global reality". Through situations of social change and increased mobility they may start to crosscut one another so that members of all ethnic groups are found in all strata.

Against this propitious background, questions about the modern management of ethnic diversity in traditional and non-traditionally viewed multi-ethnic nations have come to the forefront. In traditionally viewed, multi-ethnic nations such as Canada, Australia and the United Kingdom, where a prevailing multiculturalism policy is practiced, questions about whether this policy can lead to the advancement of group rights are pondered. For instance, Patti Tamara Lenard (Chapter 2) questions whether an increase in ethno-cultural diversity contributes to a decline in the trust necessary to sustain redistributive policies, as well as active participation? In effect, for Lenard, it is essential that we ask whether multicultural policies can serve to build or strengthen trust relations in ethno-culturally diverse societies. Relatedly, Andrew Robinson (Chapter 3) asks whether there is truly a single basis upon which varied cultural accommodations can be justified. And, if there is such a basis, can it inform normative principles to guide the design of accommodations and the adjudication of the inter- and intra-communal conflicts that will inevitably arise. Robinson's chapter suggests that such a basis is available if the foundational value of a meaningful life is properly articulated. By illustrating how the values of personal autonomy and communal identification are capable both of working together to support meaningful life and also, conflicting to undermine it, his conception of meaningful life is used to develop normative principles that can define the parameters of a workable and justifiable multiculturalism.

It will be ill-advised to consider the contemporary management of ethnic diversity without considering the various philosophical and historical legacies that have contributed to the present reality. While Lenard and Robinson utilize a political philosophical reductionism to ascertain potential consequences of multiculturalism, Adsett (Chapter 4) adopts a historical approach suggesting multiculturalism in Canada is an outcome of British liberal political philosophy, especially that of John Stuart Mill, and could never have been accepted in Canada without the shared understanding of the meaning of liberty, equality and community that comes from that philosophical tradition. This thesis is further supported by looking at the French understanding of these three concepts, which come primarily from the philosophical works of Jean-Jacques Rousseau; and which she demonstrates, render impossible a French version of multiculturalism. Today, the differences in ethno-management are evident. Both Canada and the

United Kingdom manage ethnic diversity by stressing integration and equality, *inter alia*, by an incorporatist approach codified in legal apparatus – primarily the 1988 Multiculturalism Act in Canada; and the 1976 Race Relations Act in the United Kingdom. In respect to the United Kingdom, Marangozov (Chapter 10) further points out that in the post-colonial period, Britain made significant efforts to integrate immigrant communities through non-discriminatory treatment in health care, social security and the franchise. This potentially, is a sharp contrast to the immigrant experience in France, where the French conception of ethnic management is not conducive to the overt acceptance of diversity in the public sphere – or so it is argued in Chapter 4.

This begs the question, is our understanding of managing ethnic diversity, via multiculturalism policy or otherwise, localized? Is it based primarily on local political and social histories? We find proof about the localization of managing diversity by looking at Suzanna Reiss' and Reza Hasmath's chapters. Reiss' (Chapter 5) looks at the practice of Canadian multiculturalism through the lens of the Caribbean population. For Reiss, multiculturalism provided a way for Canada to perpetuate a myth of ethno-racial tolerance while obscuring issues of race subsumed by its official policy of accepting ethno-cultural diversity. In addition, she argues that while ethno-cultural events such as Caribana embodied for some the libratory potential of cultural affirmation, an official policy of multiculturalism clearly relegated issues of ethnicity to a strictly cultural rather than political realm; removing culture from its socio-economic context in an effort to avoid any serious challenge to the status quo. Interestingly, this message is echoed in the case of China presented in Chapter 6. The institutionalization of ethnic relations in China appears to have a double-edged sword. On the one hand, celebratory festivals and events showcasing ethnic traditions and culture serve as a mechanism to promote minority groups to the mainstream.

Yet, an attendant concern is that the socio-economic struggles of many ethnic minority groups are being masked when a celebratory version of their culture and traditions is presented.

Attempting to re-center the socio-economic context in the multiculturalism debate, Chapter 7 examines the educational attainment and occupational outcomes of ethnic minorities in Toronto and Taipei. The chapter suggests the existence of an ethnic penalty in the labour market – that is, minorities are seemingly under-represented in the managerial and professional class when accounting for their education.

We start to see Canada's contemporary patterns in managing ethnic diversity reappearing in Australia and New Zealand. Australia and New Zealand, like Canada, has transformed itself from a predominantly 'white settler' society into a socially cohesive multi-ethnic nation through the implementation of an extensive mass migration program that was followed by the adoption of multiculturalism as state policy. Toula Nicolacopoulos and George Vassilacopoulos (Chapter 9) argue that the Australian concept of multiculturalism has acquired a covert meaning via its implication in what they term the 'onto-pathology of white

Australia' and the latter's reliance upon 'the perpetual foreigners-within'. The basic idea is that far from doing away with migrants' ascription of their perpetual foreigner status, multiculturalism reinforces the social positioning of specific ethnic minority groups as the perpetual foreigners-within. In extricating itself from a White Australia paradigm, the inception of multiculturalism inaugurated a new mythology around an open and tolerant society or so it is argued by Augie Fleras (Chapter 8). Fleras' compares Australia and New Zealand's tactics when it comes to ethnic management. Fleras' concludes by demonstrating how debates over immigration and indigeneity may account for diverse multicultural politics in the art of living together with differences in deeply divided societies.

Our journey ends in Western Europe by examining non-traditionally perceived multi-ethnic nations such as Austria, Germany and Italy, who seemingly share common difficulties implementing effective strategies for managing ethnic differences. The chapter on Austria, a nation who Barbara Herzog-Punzenberger and Govind Rao (Chapter 11) argue possesses for many years 'preconditions' for multiculturalism as a potential official policy for managing ethnic differences, but has made very few steps towards its adoption. Their chapter poses the questions: What explains a country's non-adoption of multiculturalism policy, when other factors would seem to speak in its favour? Why has the Austrian state and society remained so resistant to the idea of multiculturalism and recognition of diversity when other similar countries have adopted it? Germany appears to share many similarities with Austria. The German debate on *Leitkultur* (guiding culture) has sparked a great deal of media attention and can be considered as Germany's first sustained public attempt to come to terms with the reality of an increasingly multicultural society. Ming-Bao Yue (Chapter 12) situates this conversation and discusses potential responses to the multiculturalism debate in Germany.

The case of Austria and Germany provokes the subject of the final chapter: what happens when an assimilationist logic, stressing what people have in common, comes face to face with an ethnic identity which celebrates difference? In South Tyrol, the northernmost trilingual Italian region, Nazi-fascism and the two World Wars have caused ethnic membership to become a deeply divisive issue. The post-war agreement rested on a peculiar reinterpretation of the 'separate but equal' doctrine. The campaign slogan adopted by the local ethnic German majority used to be: "the clearer we make the distinction between us, the better we will get on with each other", roughly corresponding to the English saying 'good fences make good neighbours'. Stefano Fait examines the consequences of a 'fenced society' in the region caused largely in part by an arrangement originally designed to protect ethnic Ladins and Germans – a majority in the region but a minority nationally – from the encroachments of the Italian state.

Throughout the chapters it becomes evident that the complexities of ethnic diversity are not the exclusive domain of one academic discipline. To cast our nets more broadly, the collection of chapters is purposely interdisciplinary in the resources it draws upon and the perspectives in constructs on salient meanings and practices for managing ethnic diversity. What is particularly interesting to observe is that for various nations there are very different patterns of change in managing ethnic differences across time, and these changes are very much shaped by local factors and constraints. This is not to deny that there are some global forces at work as well, but even these appear to play out in unique ways in local contexts.

References

Barth, F. 1969. *Ethnic Groups and Boundaries*. UK: Waveland Press.

Bonacich, E. 1972. A Theory of Ethnic Antagonism: The Split Labour Market. *American Sociological Review* 37: 547–59.

Cavalli-Sforza, L.L, P. Menozzi and A. Piazza. 1994. *The History and Geography of Human Genes*. USA: Princeton University Press.

Cohen, R. 1978. Ethnicity: Problem and Focus in Anthropology. *Annual Review of Anthropology* 7: 379–403.

Eriksen, T.H. 2002. *Ethnicity and Nationalism: Anthropological Perspectives*. London: Pluto Press.

Fishman, J. 1980. Social Theory and Ethnography. In *Ethnic Diversity and Conflict in Eastern Europe*, ed. P. Sugar, 84–97. USA: ABC-CLIO.

Friedman, J. 1990. Being in the World: Localization and Globalization. In *Global Culture: Nationalism, Globalization and Modernity*, ed. M. Featherston, 311–25. London: Sage Publications.

Geertz, C. 1973. *The Interpretation of Cultures*. New York: Basic Books.

Goldman, G. 2000. Defining and Observing Minorities: An Objective Assessment. IAOS Conference, Montreux, Switzerland, 4–8 September.

Gonzalez-Casanova, P. 1965. Internal Colonialism and National Development. *Studies in Comparative International Development* 1(4): 27–37.

Hettne, B. 1996. Ethnicity and Development: An Elusive Relationship. In *Ethnicity and Development: Geographical Perspectives*, eds D. Dwyer and D. Drakakis-Smith, 15–44. UK: John Wiley & Sons.

Isajiw, W.W. 1974. Definitions of Ethnicity. *Ethnicity* 1: 111–24.

Reich, M. et al. 1973. A Theory of Labour Market Segmentation. *American Economic Review* 63: 359–65.

Schermerhorn, R.A. 1970. *Comparative Ethnic Relations*. New York: Random House.

Shils, E. 1957. Primordial, Personal, Sacred and Civil Ties. *British Journal of Sociology* 8: 130–45.

Wallerstein, I.M. 1979. *The Capitalist World Economy*. Cambridge: Cambridge University Press.

Weber, M. 1968. *Economy and Society*. Trans. G. Roth and C. Wittich. New York: Bedminster.

Weber, M. 1997. What is an Ethnic Group? In *The Ethnicity Reader: Nationalism, Multiculturalism and Migration*, eds. M. Guibernau and J. Rex, 15–32. London: Polity Press.

Chapter 2
Can Multiculturalism Build Trust?

Patti Tamara Lenard

One worry recently expressed in response to large-scale immigration in western democratic countries is that the presence of ethno-cultural diversity within a population will cause a decline in the trust that is necessary to sustain redistributive politics, as well as a commitment to active political participation. An attendant worry is that multicultural policies, which allegedly heighten the salience of ethno-cultural diversity, are responsible for the decline in the trust that sustains a commitment to social justice policies and liberal democratic political activism. Recent empirical research, however, has failed to find corroborating evidence of these claims. Although there is some evidence that ethno-cultural diversity may well lead to a decline in levels of trust among citizens, and although trust does appear linked to the support (or otherwise) of redistributive policies, evidence gathered thus far fails to illustrate "a strong, consistent relationship between ethnic context and the health of the welfare state" (Eisenberg 2004, 68). Defenders of multicultural policies, therefore, continue to advocate them as solutions to systemic discrimination against ethno-cultural minorities and as facilitators of the social and political integration of immigrants.[1]

Although advocates of multicultural policies are defending these policies with renewed confidence, in light of evidence that there appears to be no consistent relationship between adopting multicultural policies and a decline in support for the welfare state, there is a worry that is unresolved. That is, as suggested above, ethno-cultural diversity is in some instances linked to declines in levels of trust. The reason we ought to worry about the link between ethno-cultural diversity and the level of trust is this: trust is essential in sustaining a commitment to the cooperative attitudes that define and underpin liberal democratic political systems. If ethno-cultural diversity erodes trust, our liberal democracies – at least, some of the best features of liberal democratic political institutions – will be at risk. It is therefore essential that we ask not only whether multicultural policies are linked to decline in support for the welfare state (and they appear not to be so linked), but

---

1 Let me clarify how terms are being used, here. The term 'immigrant' refers to first- and second-generation immigrations to a country, and the term 'ethno-cultural minority' refers to visible minorities who are the product of immigration, as well as those who are long-term citizens of a country. I will justify the inclusion of the latter population – long-term visible minority citizens – as a target of multicultural policies in a later section of the chapter.

also whether multicultural policies can serve to build or strengthen trust relations in ethno-culturally diverse societies. This is the central question that is the focus of this chapter, which is organized as follows. The first section of the chapter delves into the nature of trust, and its role in sustaining liberal democratic systems. It then evaluates whether there is a 'trust problem' that we must worry about in the first place – it suggests that there is a problem of trust relations in environments characterized by certain patterns of ethno-cultural diversity. This discussion is followed by an account of what is entailed by trust-building strategies – I suggest that the main focus of trust-building strategies ought to be the minimization of the vulnerability connected to extending and rewarding trust. The bulk of the chapter considers whether multicultural policies – and more specifically, what sort of multicultural policies – can legitimately be included as part of a trust-building strategy. Finally, the chapter concludes that multicultural policies can only be one component of a comprehensive trust-building strategy; policies that are often described as 'nation-building' are, equally, essential to building trust in a liberal democratic community. It is worth noting at the outset that there is nothing new in the link between multicultural policies and nation-building policies – what is new, however, is an attempt to make a clear link between them via the *trust* that, the chapter will argue, is essential to liberal democratic institutions and practice. Both multicultural policies and nation-building policies are *essential* to effective trust-building in an ethno-culturally diverse democratic environment; each of them focuses on trust-building in distinct ways, as this chapter will illustrate.

Trust and Liberal Democratic Practices

As members of peaceful, liberal democratic communities, we trust others as a matter of course. At the very least, we trust those around us to refrain from injuring us deliberately. Even more, we often trust others to follow shared rules (to smoke outside, to keep voices down in a restaurant, to refrain from speaking in a library) and, more positively, to help us if we have injured ourselves (for example, if we fall down, or if we are in a car accident, or to attempt to return a lost wallet or mobile phone). In these small ways, we trust those around us on a daily basis, even when we do not have the opportunity to test this trust.

In assessing the nature of trust, we can see that it is part attitude – we have a trusting attitude towards others – and part behaviour – we behave in a trusting way towards others. In trusting others, moreover, what we are doing is placing ourselves in a position of vulnerability (sometimes more and sometimes less deliberately) in relation to others (Baier 1994). In trusting someone – say, to help us once we've injured ourselves by slipping on some ice – we place ourselves in a position of vulnerability with respect to her good or ill will. We might say that a key element of being willing to trust others is the "disposition to believe that others are not ill-disposed toward the realization of one's interests" (Weinstock 2004, 112). If we claim to have a trusting attitude, but refuse to act on this attitude by placing our trust in others, we cannot claim to be genuinely trusting them – think of parents who claim they trust their children's driving abilities, but refuse to get in the car with them. Trust is characterized by a willingness to place oneself in a position of vulnerability with respect to others, and this willingness emerges in part from the belief that others do not bear us ill will (and may, indeed, bear us good will).

How does trust, understood in the way described above, matter to liberal democratic practices, especially in multicultural democracies? Scholars of trust typically make a distinction between social or interpersonal trust, that is, the trust that pertains among individuals as they go about their daily lives, and political trust, that is, the trust that characterizes the political arena. An emphasis on social trust is sometimes meant to signal the trust that exists among a rather larger group of people, say, towns or cities or even nations, whereas an emphasis on interpersonal trust is sometimes meant to signal the trust that exists among a rather smaller group of people, say, neighbours, or friends, or family. In both cases, however, the point is to separate the trust that pertains among individuals in general, from the more specifically political trust that defines (or does not define) the political sphere. Discussions of political trust often make an additional distinction, between horizontal trust – the trust that pertains among citizens in their capacity as political actors – and vertical trust – the trust that characterizes the relations between citizens and their elected (and sometimes appointed) political representatives. Here the point is to distinguish the more or less equal relations that characterize the political interactions among citizens from the apparently unequal relations that characterize the political relations between citizens and their representatives. In a formal sense, of course, citizens and their elected officials are equal – but designating the relationship as 'vertical' allows scholars to indicate the substantial power that is granted officials once elected or appointed by the agreed liberal democratic procedures. Additionally, it is sometimes suggested that one relevant form of trust in the political arena is the trust we have in liberal democratic *institutions*. But, as the term is used here, trust refers only to relations between people – following the sociologist Niklas Luhmann (1982), I will use the term 'confidence' rather than trust to refer to the ways in which individuals react to the institutions themselves. In other words, individuals may have trust in their political representatives, and confidence in the institutions in which their representatives operate.

Both social (or interpersonal) trust and political trust, in both its horizontal and vertical interpretations, are characterized by the features ascribed to trust more generally (Lenard 2008). It is of course true, as Soroka et al. (2004, 37) observe, that "trusting a government [i.e., the officials therein] entails a much greater leap of faith, since we rarely know government officials personally". Equally, both forms of trust play critical roles in sustaining a commitment to liberal democratic institutions and practices. The role that political trust plays in liberal democracies is more or less clear. In order to be an effective system of governance, a liberal democracy requires widespread voluntary compliance among those subject to the decisions made within its institutions. When we think of the reasons *why* we abide by the rules and regulations that govern our liberal democracy, it is of course true that we are often motivated by fear of the punishments associated with non-compliance. But, it is a mistake to suggest that the fear of punishment motivates *all* compliance with shared rules and regulations. A liberal democracy simply does not have the resources necessary to secure near-perfect compliance with its regulations; indeed, the more it must divert its resources towards enforcing compliance, the less it is able to provide the benefits typically connected to well-functioning democracies, such as generous welfare policies and material resources to facilitate political organization that may benefit ethnic minority interactions. In other words, the general compliance with rules and regulations that characterizes most well-functioning liberal democracies is sustained by widespread horizontal political trust among citizens, i.e., the trust that others are generally willing to comply with these rules. I can comply, therefore, and am not likely to find that others are free-riding on my willing compliance. Widespread horizontal trust secures the willing compliance of citizens with shared rules and regulations, then, and it is vertical political trust that enables citizens to put their trust in legislators, by electing them to positions of decision-making authority. When Locke (1980 [1690], Chapter 13) gave his well-known account of the authority invested in government representatives, he accurately described this relation as one of trust; citizens must trust those they elect to be concerned to make the best decisions possible on their behalf, and must have an effective mechanism by which to remove them if they have violated this trust.

As many scholars observe, it would be a mistake to suggest that only political trust is relevant in a democratic community. Social trust, as an essential component of social capital, is a vital foundation to any effective liberal democratic arrangement and multiethnic compact. The trust that is described as social, characterizes the vast majority of trusting relations we experience in our daily lives (Putnam 1993, 170). It is not dissimilar from horizontal political trust, in the sense that both characterize the relations among citizens in general. Whereas horizontal political trust is typically reserved for environments in which we think of each other specifically as political actors or fellow citizens, social trust refers to the non-political environments in which we interact with each other. As theorists of social capital have argued, at least since Robert Putnam's *Making Democracy Work*, social trust or social capital is deeply connected to citizens' willingness to participate in volunteer organizations of various kinds, and to engage in a cooperative manner with others in general, and this in turn generates a broader willingness to cooperate with fellow citizens in ways that serve liberal democracy well. Putnam (1993, 173) writes, "networks of civic engagement are an essential form of social capital: The denser such networks in a community, the more likely that its citizens will be able to cooperative for mutual benefit". The precise details of this argument – in particular whether participation in voluntary associations generates social trust or whether social trust motivates participation in voluntary associations – are of the subject of considerable and vigorous debate, and much beyond the scope of this chapter; the broad conclusion, however, that social trust is an essential ingredient of smoothly functioning liberal democracies is clear.[2]

Is There a 'Trust Problem' in the First Place?

If the analysis above is correct – that trust, in both its political and social forms, is essential to a smoothly functioning liberal democracy – then we have good reason to pay attention to levels of trust among multi-ethnic citizens in a liberal democratic community. We might be worried, for example, if we should see an ongoing decline in reported levels of trust among citizens – both if these reports show a decline in trust towards fellow citizens and if these reports show a decline in trust towards political representatives. There is considerable research that proclaims a decline in trust along both political and social dimensions at the national levels of most western liberal democratic nations, even as researchers debate the merits of the information provided by these kinds of large-scale surveys (Lenard 2005). To cite just one example, Evans (2006, 162–3) suggests that, at least in the United Kingdom, no such decline is in evidence.

There are a series of patterns or details that national-level surveys of trust mask, however, which are of more relevance here. One detail that is obscured by national-level surveys is the extent to which different segments of the population report startlingly distinct levels of trust – African Americans, for example, report considerably lower levels of trust than do White Americans (Patterson 1999). A similar distinction is found in research focused on first- and second-generation immigrants to Canada and the United States – first-generation immigrants report considerably higher levels of trust in fellow citizens and the national-level political system than do second-generation immigrants (Reitz and Banerjee 2007, 516). Another set of details that are masked by national-level survey research has to do with the extent to which *context* matters as individuals respond to survey questions. It is well-known that the general trust question – "do you believe that others can be trusted, or that in general, you cannot be too cautious with others?" – obscures *who* responders are thinking about in responding to the question. Individuals may report high levels of trust *in general*, even when probing reveals relatively lower levels of trust in specific groups of people (neighbours, citizens, police officers and so on). Of most relevance here is that national-level survey research obscures the extent to trust might well be *particularized* rather than *generalized*.

Describing trust as particularized is meant to highlight that it extends only to members of very specific, particular groups. If members of any given ethnic group only trust other members of the same ethnic group, then this trust is often described as particularized rather than generalized – "the particularized truster

---

2   Putnam himself observers the feedback loop between trust and cooperation: "Trust lubricates cooperation. The greater the level of trust within a community, the greater the likelihood of cooperation. And cooperation itself breeds trust" (Putnam 1993, 171).

has strong bonds within her community, primarily has faith in her own kind, and may reject the idea of a common culture" (Eisenberg 2004, 72). In multicultural, liberal democratic states, generalized trust is essential to the smooth functioning of shared democratic institutions. There is evidence that particularized trust is indeed a phenomenon with which we need to be concerned. For example, in a study of levels of trust in Canada, some scholars have recently found that "the larger is the visible minority's share [of the local population], the less trusting the majority is". The authors conclude, "ethnic context affects strategic considerations of trust" (Soroka et al. 2004, 40 and 51). Moreover, the majority (white) population retreats from generalized trust in the *increasing* presence of visible minorities. This kind of particularized trust is problematic since it will, over time, inhibit the large-scale voluntary compliance with shared rules and regulations on which liberal democracy depends upon. In other words, national-level survey data obscures the extent to which ethno-cultural diversity can, in some instances, hamper the generalized trust on which democracy relies.

It is worth noting that some scholars – Will Kymlicka and Keith Banting among them – express skepticism with respect to the suggestion that the stress in trust relations caused certain patterns of ethno-cultural diversity is a cause for real worry. For them, it is sufficient to observe the national-level patterns that, as I suggested above, fail to illustrate any kind of consistent trend between the presence of multicultural policies and decreased commitment to welfare state policies (Banting et al. 2006). Equally, a contributor to their most recent volume suggests that public opinion towards multicultural policies is relatively positive (Crepaz 2006; but see Saggar 2003 for an alternative interpretation). At present, they are inclined to discount small-scale research that has recently been conducted in an American environment, in which counties experiencing large influxes of immigrants vote, in plebiscites, to rescind welfare policies of various kinds (Banting and Kymlicka 2006, 22–30). The American racial and ethno-cultural environment is distinct – both because the status occupied by its African American population is unique, and because it is forced to deal with a great deal of illegal immigration. They suggest, therefore, that the political challenges these populations engender are sufficiently distinct that the evidence that emerges from this environment cannot be taken as definitive. I think they are right to reject a wholesale acceptance of conclusions that arise from any nation's unique context – yet, they are wrong to dismiss the suggestiveness of this research, which does illustrate that how individuals make decisions about their community environment depends significantly on *who* populates this community environment. Subsequent research may well emerge from other environments that indicate similar trends, and it is too early to dismiss the very real possibility that when given the opportunity, individuals will choose to retrench their own participation in local welfare state policies.

General Principles for Trust-Building in a Multi-Ethnic Environment

Any discussion of trust-building strategies in a multi-ethnic environment must begin with a caveat. The nature of trust – namely, that it is so contextually dependent – is such that any strategy aimed at building it (or sustaining it) can never be sure of success. Whatever conditions are impeding or stressing the willingness of individuals to extend trust to others may be alleviated in some way, but doing so simply cannot guarantee that trust will subsequently emerge. The insight that the emergence of trust cannot be guaranteed – even under the best of circumstances – can be in part credited to work done to investigate the 'contact hypothesis', i.e., the hypothesis that mere contact between hostile ethnic or cultural groups can breed trust between them. Scholars have well observed that mere contact is insufficient – the conditions under which this contact takes place matters as well (Forbes 1997). That said, even the best efforts to create an appropriate trust-building context can fail, and the possibility that trust will not emerge in spite of our best efforts must be borne in mind. A corollary of this observation is that trust-building strategies do not (necessarily) focus directly on trust – rather strategies are indirect, and focus on the conditions under which trust is most likely to emerge. The best that trust-builders can do is to aim to create the conditions under which trust is most likely to emerge, and then hope for the best. In some kinds of environments, moreover, doing so may be easier than in others.

Trust-building strategies must focus on the features of trust, as described above. Recall that trust is defined in part by an attitude or disposition and in part by behaviour. Recall, also, that to trust someone means to put oneself in a position of vulnerability with respect to the good or ill will of others. Successful trust-building strategies must focus on the vulnerability element of trusting others, by generating conditions under which the risk, i.e. the vulnerability, associated with trusting others is mitigated.[3] It is important here to address another relevant distinction, and this is the distinction between trust and trustworthiness. In general terms, in trusting others, we are (among other things) engaging in some form of evaluation of another's *trustworthiness*. We ask ourselves, can this person be trusted to carry out this action, or to behave with good will (or, at least, a lack of ill will) towards me and in general? In doing so, we gauge the likelihood – using whatever information we have available – that our trust will be rewarded, if extended. Anyone who trusts others without evaluating the trustworthiness of others is typically thought to be naïve; anyone who determines that no one is trustworthy is thought to be misanthropic.

In order to build trust, strategies may well choose to focus in one of two distinct directions. First, a trust-building strategy might attempt a focus on altering attitudes – i.e., to encourage a move from a disposition of distrust to a disposition

---

3   Since vulnerability is essential to trust (i.e., if we experience no vulnerability in our interactions with others, we are not trusting them), a *trust*-building strategy cannot be effective in building trust it if eliminates vulnerability entirely.

of trust. Efforts to emphasize what 'we' have in common are attempts to alter distrusting attitudes, as are attempts to provide accurate information about the conditions in which we are operating. The former – a focus on what 'we' have in common – attempts to harness the 'emotional' elements of trust, and the latter – a focus on providing accurate information – attempts to influence the 'cognitive' dimensions of trust. These are both attempts to reduce felt-vulnerability, by giving potential trusters the information they need in order to extend trust. Second, a trust-building strategy might focus on altering behaviours – i.e., to encourage individuals to move from behaving in ways that demonstrate distrust to ways that demonstrate trust *or* trustworthiness. This sort of strategy encourages individuals to behave *as if* they trust others, and *as if* they are trustworthy, even under conditions when they feel neither trusting nor trustworthy. In the ideal, these behaviours will be interpreted as evidence of trust or trustworthiness, and will be reciprocated in such a way that allows trust to emerge from 'as if' trust and trustworthiness. Behavioural strategies generally involve either a) removing whatever obstacles are preventing the emergence of trust, or b) generating institutions which serve to protect individuals who choose to trust others in situations of risk. Contracts are often described in this way – distrusting individuals are able to cooperate if the terms of their cooperation are specified in an agreed contract (so, it is the contract rather than trust that permits cooperation, from which trust might *ideally* emerge). The former strategy – removing obstacles – focuses on behaviours that indicate trustworthiness; the later strategy – generating protective institutions – focuses on behaviours that permit a limited form of trust to proceed.

Do Multicultural Policies Build Trust?

In order to evaluate whether multicultural policies as such can serve as trust-builders, we must first be clear about which policies are properly defined as multicultural. By and large, multicultural policies are those that target ethno-cultural groups who are largely the product of relatively recent immigration; we will see multiple examples in the Canadian case throughout this book.[4] There are exceptions, of course. In much of the literature, African Americans are among those groups who under the purview of 'multicultural policies', and most are not recent immigrants to the United States. I include them here – a decision that I realize is controversial – because some of the greatest challenges to trust in the United States have, as

---

4 I exclude, however, indigenous peoples and national minorities. Keith Banting and Will Kylicka suggest a connection between a nation's enthusiasm for multicultural policies and their history of accommodating indigenous peoples and national minorities. But, the worries that these groups – though, as they indicate, are much farther reaching – generate are distinct and, in my view, largely unrelated at least in the minds of the citizens of countries dealing with these issues.

their source, the ongoing marginalization of, and discrimination, against African Americans (see Allen 2004; Williams 1998).

Multicultural policies have a host of objectives. One objective of these policies is to accommodate the genuine grievances launched by members of ethno-cultural groups. Another objective is to encourage social and political integration of the sort that broadens the range of people we believe share our values and norms. Here, I will take multicultural policies to be those which allow for the following: 1) exemption from certain policies that put undue burden on certain cultural groups but not others, 2) material assistance that permits members of minority cultural groups to engage in activities that majority members can do without assistance, 3) self-government for certain minority groups, 4) some restrictions on the freedom of non-group members to protect the minority's culture, 5) formal recognition of a minority culture's legal system in adjudicating some disputes, 6) representation of minority cultural groups in the dominant political and legal systems, and 7) symbolic recognition of cultural groups intended to acknowledge their worth or contribution to the nature of the wider political community.[5] Although there is considerable variety among these policies, and what might legitimately be thought to be encompassed by any one of them, the general point is that these policies share a commitment to citizens that extends beyond the basic set of rights that are guaranteed, by virtue of citizenship, to all citizens of liberal democratic nations. In particular, they express a commitment to ensure the substantive rather than formal protection of basic rights. This contract is nicely operationalized throughout the chapters on this book: Herzog-Punzenberger and Rao's chapter on Austria, Yue's chapter on Germany or Fait's chapter on Italy, with Reiss' and Adsett's discussions on Canada or to a certain extent, Fleras, Nicolacopoulos and Vassilacopoulos' account of Australia. It is worth noting that many advocates of multicultural policies exclude anti-discrimination policies, the goal of which is the protection of civil and political liberties of all citizens – I include them here, insofar as they target ethno-cultural groups, again because they are deeply implicated in the trust relations in multicultural democracies.[6] If fairness is one concern of weak or moderate multiculturalism, as I'll suggest below, then it seems clear enough that

---

5   This taxonomy of multicultural policies is Jacob Levy's (2000). I defer to his justification, in Chapter Five of this book, of this way of categorising the policies. Readers will note that I've excluded one of Levy's categories, namely the acceptance of minority cultures' internal rules as a way to regulate minority members' behaviour. I think that this category of policies, alone among the policies described by Levy, does not serve to generate social and political integration, and it is social and political integration with which I am concerned here. This sort of integration is only one among many of Levy's concerns, however.

6   Keith Banting et al. (2006, 52) recent account is one prominent example of a categorization of multicultural policies that explicitly excludes anti-discrimination policies.

we need be concerned *in particular* with the implementation of anti-discrimination policies as they apply to ethno-cultural minority groups.

In offering an account of multicultural policies, some scholars distinguish between 'strong and weak' multiculturalism or between 'radical and moderate' multiculturalism. This categorization serves to distinguish between claims or petitions made by ethno-cultural groups that threaten the solidarity of the state from those that reflect a deeper concern with what Will Kymlicka has referred to as the fair terms of integration. As Moore (2001, 107) explains, weak (or moderate) multicultural policies are typically "claims to be treated fairly, to be included in the democratic debate and decision-making, to ensure that their history is part of the country's larger history". Moreover, weak or moderate multicultural policies are those that "do not seek to challenge the jurisdiction of the state in a range of areas, but only to ensure that their cultural practices are included in the larger society."

Strong or radical accounts of multiculturalism, however, are those that advocate enabling ethno-cultural groups to "maintain distinctive group identity and solidarity" by allowing them to claim rights "which reinforce their separateness from other people in the society" (Moore 2001, 107). They may well, therefore, prove to be "problematic from the standpoint of the state's function in ensuring public life". David Miller, for example, expresses this worry about radical forms of multiculturalism. Radical forms of multiculturalism suggest that ethno-cultural minorities should be permitted – and perhaps encouraged – to disassociate from the larger community, and that policies ought to be designed to permit this disassociation. As such, radical multiculturalism will pose a threat to the solidarity or trust that underpins a liberal democratic community.[7] Miller points to evidence that members of a host community tend to retreat from a commitment to multiculturalism (radical or weak) when immigrants are seen as unwilling to make an effort to adapt to the host country's public culture – in other words, when ethno-cultural minorities appeal to claims that are adequately described by the label 'radical', members of the host community show only a reluctant support for even weak multicultural policies (i.e., the policies that should *facilitate* rather than hamper integration (Miller 2006, 329–35)).

Some advocates – for example, Banting et al. (2006, 40) – express considerable skepticism towards the worry that Miller raises, and observe instead that "so far as we can tell, no country in the West has adopted radical multiculturalism". Indeed, this observation is true enough – no nation appears to have adopted a uniform policy of radical multiculturalism. Yet, this skeptical response inadequately deals with the worry in two ways. First, the skeptical response does not account for the frequency of demands for policies that are properly described as radical, even if no nation adopts a fully-fledged radical approach to dealing with its ethno-cultural diversity. There is evidence, and this is what Miller is concerned with, that ethno-

---

7   Shlomi Segall (2005) offers a compelling account of the relation between trust and solidarity, in which trust is one component of solidarity.

cultural demands for separation from the larger society does damage to the larger solidarity, even if it is not granted or adopted. Recent debates in the Canadian province of Ontario about whether to promote single-faith schools prompted just this worry, for example. Second, the skeptical response fails to acknowledge that even if a nation does not implement a full-scale radical multiculturalist policy, some nations have indeed adopted policies that encourage and enable a kind of separation that might fall under the rubric of radical multiculturalism, in ways that generate challenges to the trust that underpins a liberal democracy. For example, Sweden's decision to allow girls from ethnic minorities to marry at the age of 15, when 'native' Swedish girls are barred from marriage until they are 18, has been perceived to be a radical multiculturalist policy, which encourages separation from the wider community and, therefore, encourages distrust rather than to emerge between groups (Wikan 2004, 196). In other words, individual policies that are in some sense radical may undermine trust among communities, even when they are not part of a larger radical multiculturalist agenda.

Are multicultural policies ever able to build trust, then? And if so, what sorts of policies are best suited to this job? As is evident above, and as is demonstrated in the national contexts described in the following chapters, some multicultural policies *erode* trust. But, in some situations, they are able to build trust. Specifically, the argument here is this: multicultural policies serve to build trust insofar as they target – and aim to reduce – the vulnerability experienced by ethno-cultural minorities. It is sometimes observed that it is plight of immigrants to struggle against obstacles in their host countries – often immigrants will take poor paying or low-status jobs as a way to enter the economy of the host country, with the aim and intention of moving up the ladder, as it were. Immigrants often accept working and social conditions that are unacceptable and humiliating as simply part of what it means to be an immigrant in the first place. One author writes, "making them pariahs will not force immigrants to pick up and leave. They will continue to work hard in spite of the obstacles, which, though major, probably constitute better conditions than the ones they left behind" (Danticat 1999, x). And, it is of course true that immigrants must struggle just by virtue of having moved to a new nation, with new norms and values, with different mechanisms to achieve success and so on. As Scheffler (2007) observes, moreover, immigrants *expect* change, and generally harbour no resentment against the expectations that they adapt in the face of change – these adaptations to the new environment is part and parcel of what it means to immigrate.

But, what immigrants cannot be expected to suffer are injustices, injustices that often accompany, but are not inherent to, the experience of immigration. As a matter of empirics, immigrants can and do tolerate injustices of various kinds These injustices, by and large, have to do with the failure by members of the host community to treat immigrants fairly and equally, treatment to which they are entitled given their status as legal immigrants. Systemic discrimination against them, for example, prevents immigrants from fairly accessing employment opportunities. Ignorance and intolerance of their cultural practices, further, often prohibits the equal political and social participation of immigrants in the host community. The combination of systemic discrimination against immigrants, along with an intolerance of their cultural practices (many – if not most – of which are wholly compatible with liberal democratic values and norms), generates distrust in both directions. Members of the immigrant community subsist in many cases at the margins of society, as a result of the multifaceted discrimination (which in many, but not all, instances is formally illegal); members of the host community observe immigrants subsisting at the margin, failing to integrate, and come to distrust them, (often mistakenly) believing that what they are witnessing is an unwillingness to integrate. As Avigail Eisenberg rightfully observes, immigrants are often not to blame for their failure to integrate – it is often the discriminatory attitudes held by members of the host community that actively prevent their integration. Multicultural policies are often, therefore, best interpreted as attempts to proactively facilitate integration by tackling the discrimination that prevent it: they are often "specifically directed at addressing social problems such as racism and cultural alienation" (Eisenberg 2004, 71).

In doing so, multicultural policies target the vulnerability experienced by immigrants in the face of a hostile host community. The implementation of formal policies celebrating the achievements or contributions of immigrants, the active rather than passive attempts to forestall and rectify employment discrimination (a key part of which, at the moment, is generating efficient systems by which foreign credentials can be recognized), and so on, reduce the vulnerability felt by immigrants. They are thus given leeway to, at least, rely on a legal system that offers substantive rather than merely formal protection, and which therefore frees them to extend trust to the wider community. Their attempts to take advantage of the multicultural policies made available to them must be viewed in this way, that is, as gestures of trust.

How do Nation-Building and Multicultural Policies Fit into a Trust-Building Strategy?

Nation-building policies are often paired with multicultural policies as, in a sense, two sides of the same coin (see Kymlicka 2003). As Miller (2006, 338) suggests:

> we need to think hard about how integration polices [i.e., nation-building policies] can work *alongside* multicultural policies, so that citizens can respect one another's differences but still think of themselves as belonging to the same community with a responsibility to ensure equal rights for all.

Nation-building policies, I suggest, are as essential as are multicultural policies to an effective, comprehensive, trust-building strategy. Like multicultural policies, nation-building policies are various. They range from providing opportunities for immigrants to learn the official, national language, to providing citizenship education classes to new immigrants, to developing new school curricula that include the teaching of the contributions made by immigrants, and so forth. Policies that aim to introduce immigrants to the shared norms and values – the shared public culture – of the host nation are properly described as nation-building. To describe a state or a nation in terms of its shared public culture is to highlight that they are often defined as an 'ethos' – a set of shared norms and principles and values which define, as it were, how 'we' do things around here (Miller 1995).[8]

There are at least three key features of a shared public culture that are worth noting. First, the shared public culture is often defined by a set of shared values – in a liberal democratic community, these are often the typically liberal democratic values, including commitments to tolerance, freedom, equality and so on. There are many political philosophers who are skeptical of any attempt to define a shared public culture – and prefer to describe a state as defined only by a 'political culture', which itself is composed only of overlapping political values. But, an emphasis on political values alone fails to account for the vastly distinct ways in which liberal democratic values are legitimately interpreted, prioritized, and instantiated across democracies. A community's political culture is, in other words, defined not only by the existence of a set of values, which are largely standard across liberal democracies, but the ways in which these values are then actualized in practice. Second, a shared public culture is often defined by a set of shared norms, which have a less formal status than do the political values just described. That is, shared norms are not *legally* enforceable, but they do define the ways in which citizens interact with each other on a daily basis, as well as the ways in which they conceive of themselves as members of a shared community. The shared norms that define shared public cultures are wide-ranging, and can include the social practice of queuing patiently for the bus (as the Brits are often described as doing), as getting together for a 'turkey-meal' with one's family at 2pm to celebrate Thanksgiving (as the Americans have a reputation for doing), or as being rabidly committed to the nation's sports-teams (as the Australians are sometimes described). Third, a shared public culture must be *public*, in the sense that individual members of the community must have access to the environments – political, cultural, educational, and so on – where the public culture can be shaped. It is clear enough that newcomers will have difficulties accessing the public culture and, moreover, having an influence over its content. Yet, the way in which Canada's self-image as multicultural and tolerant has developed in response to its status as an immigrant-receiving nation is evidence that newcomers can and do have considerable influence over the shared public culture over time.

Remember that there are multicultural policies that can be described as weak, and so are consistent with the objectives of building a democratic community in which members are committed to its larger objectives, as well as those that can be described as strong or radical, and so are inconsistent with developing the

---

8   The shared public culture as Miller describes it has been subject to a range of criticisms. I defend the concept from some of these (Lenard 2007).

allegiance necessary to sustain larger-scale objections. So too can nation-building policies be consistent or inconsistent with developing an environment in which trust can emerge across groups in ways that sustain a commitment to the larger democratic community. In the literature, nation-building efforts that are sometimes described as assimilationist – those which have the aim of enforcing conformity with already established norms, and which therefore aim to erase or suppress the cultural and value differences that new immigrants may bring with them, have typically failed (in western, democratic communities) to build trust. They are, typically, a "one-sided process of adaptation" on the part of the minorities (Baringhorst 2003, 67). These kinds of policies send a message to immigrants that change is not welcome, that their contributions are not valuable, and that the immigration contract such as it is demands change on only one side, namely, the immigrants' side. Alternatively, nation-building policies that are described as integrationist are more directly focused on identifying which among the values and norms newcomers bring to the host country are compatible with the norms and values of the host country. Here, nation-building efforts that emphasize the two-way nature of integration – immigrants are asked to adapt in some ways (learn a new language, for example) and members of the host community agree to do the same (alter the school curriculum to recognize the contributions made by immigrants, or exempt immigrants from certain uniform regulations). Integrationist nation-building policies serve to build trust by sending the message that 'we' are all part of the larger nation-building project – there is a 'we' here, rather than an 'us' and a 'them'.

There is more, though, that we can say about the so-called 'integrationist' nation-building efforts and their impact on trust. In the main, by attempting to generate a real sense of the 'we' that underpins commitment to the larger democratic project, it is focusing on the *attitudinal* aspect of trust. Trust is a kind of disposition and nation-building policies that aim at developing solidarity – in effect, a psychological disposition – among a diverse group of people are precisely aiming to provide the conditions under which an attitude of trust can emerge. Recall that, above, the shared public culture was defined in terms of both formal political values and informal social norms. As many scholars observe, and sometimes lament, members of the host community often express the worry that their shared public culture is under threat in the face of newcomers who bring along distinctive norms and values: "immigrants are generally suspected of establishing parallel societies, of favouring segregation instead of an identification with the larger national society" (Baringhorst 2003, 70). This worry may or may not be warranted (indeed, it generally is not), but it is real, and attempts to generate nation-building policies are in large part attempts to assuage the perceived vulnerability of the host community's shared public culture. In imparting knowledge of the shared norms and values to newcomers, what is in fact being imparted is the basis on which trust is extended.

In other words, in (effectively) imparting knowledge of these values and norms to newcomers, the attempt is made to generate the conditions under which members of the host community can continue to extend trust on the same basis as they had done in the past. Trust emerges in part out of a kind of predictability – we trust others when we feel that we can predict how they will behave in certain kinds of environments – as well as a kind of comfort – we feel that we 'know' others sufficiently to extend them our trust. Integrationist nation-building policies have, as their objective, the generation of a capacity for predictability (in part, by teaching newcomers how others expect them to behave, as part of teaching them how 'we' are expected to behave), as well as the generation of a kind of comfort with the norms that define the community that the newcomers have joined. They do so by teaching the content of the shared public culture to newcomers, and by altering the shared public culture in response to newcomers' contributions. Further, in being willing to consider the possibility that any individual norm or value may be challenging for newcomers to adopt, and so to alter it (or grant exemptions), the signal is sent that immigrants too can extend trust on the basis of there being a real sense of 'we', to which they can contribute.

Conclusion

This chapter has aimed to illustrate that multicultural policies and nation-building policies are two elements of the trust-building strategy that is essential to a multicultural democratic community. The chapter began with the observation that multicultural policies have been accused, of late, of stressing the trust relations that underpin the welfare policies that are the pride of many liberal democratic communities. I pointed to evidence, in response, that the welfare state does not appear to be at risk in nations that have implemented multicultural policies. Yet, the chapter continued, we are not at liberty to leave aside the worry generated by ethno-cultural diversity and its connection to trust – if trust is essential to democracy, as I argued that it is, and if ethno-cultural diversity *in some conditions* can stress trust relations, we need to continue to pay attention to this diversity even if the welfare state is not directly at risk. These conditions are those in which there is a history of marginalization (as in the case of the African American population, who exhibit considerably lower levels of trust than do white Americans) or when there exists rapid changes in community composition (as exists in many communities faced with rapid immigration, where particularized rather than generalized trust tends to emerge).

Trust has many dimensions, and therefore offers many different routes by which it might be built or strengthened. Trust has an attitudinal element as well as a behavioural element, both of which are connected to the vulnerability that is inherent to any extension of trust. Multicultural policies aim to mitigate the vulnerability naturally felt by immigrants in a new social and political environment, especially one in which the host community struggles in some senses against the full and easy integration of newcomers. Nation-building polices aim to mitigate the vulnerability felt by the host community as it invites in immigrants whose norms and values are very different from their own. At the same time, the willing implementation of multicultural policies is a behaviour that is meant to demonstrate that the host community is itself trustworthy. Equally, the willing participation of newcomers in nation-building policies intended to encourage their adaptation in some respects is meant to demonstrate that they, too, are trustworthy. Both immigrants – via their participation in nation-building policies – and the host community – via the implementation of multicultural policies – aim to display behaviours that reassure others in such a way that an attitude of trust will, ideally, emerge. It is under these conditions that a multicultural democratic community can thrive.

References

Allen, D. 2004. *Talking to Strangers: Anxieties of Citizenship since Brown v. Board of Education*. Chicago: University of Chicago Press.

Baier, A. 1994. *Moral Prejudices*. Cambridge, MA: Harvard University Press.

Banting, K. and W. Kymlicka. 2006. Introduction: Multiculturalism and the Welfare State: Setting the Context. In *Multiculturalism and the Welfare State: Recognition and Redistribution in Contemporary Democracies*, eds K. Banting and W. Kymlicka, 1–45. Oxford: Oxford University Press.

Banting, K., R. Johnston, W. Kymlicka, and S. Soroka. 2006. Do Multiculturalism Policies Erode the Welfare State? An Empirical Analysis. In *Multiculturalism and the Welfare State: Recognition and Redistribution in Contemporary Democracies*, eds K. Banting and W. Kymlicka, 49–91. Oxford: Oxford University Press.

Baringhorst, S. 2003. Ethnicity, Religion, Culture: Collective Identities and Citizenship. In *The Challenge of Diversity: European Social Democracy Facing Migration, Integration and Multiculturalism*, eds R. Cuperus, K. A. Duffek and J. Kandel, 59–76. Munich: StudienVerlag.

Crepaz, M. 2006. If You Are My Brother, I May Give You a Dime! Public Opinion on Multiculturalism, Trust and the Welfare State. In *Multiculturalism and the Welfare State: Recognition and Redistribution in Contemporary Democracies*, eds K. Banting and W. Kymlicka, 92–120. Oxford: Oxford University Press.

Danticat, E. 1999. Forward. In *A Community of Equals*, eds J. Cohen and J. Rogers, ix-xii. Boston: Beacon Press.

Eisenberg, A. 2004. Equality, Trust and Multiculturalism. In *Social Capital and Social Diversity*, eds R. Johnston and F. Kay, 67–92. Vancouver: University of British Columbia Press.

Evans, G. 2006. Is Multiculturalism Eroding Support for Welfare Provision? The British Case. In *Multiculturalism and the Welfare State: Recognition and Redistribution in Contemporary Democracies*, eds. K. Banting and W. Kymlicka, 152–76. Oxford: Oxford University Press.

Forbes, H.D. 1997. *Ethnic Conflict: Commerce, Culture, and the Contact Hypothesis.* New Haven, CT: Yale University Press.

Kymlicka, W. 2003. Immigration, Citizenship and Multiculturalism: Exploring the Links. *The Political Quarterly*, 74(1): 195–208.

Lenard, P.T. 2005. Decline of Trust, Decline of Democracy? *Critical Review of International Social and Political Philosophy* 8(3): 363–78.

Lenard, P.T. 2007. Shared Public Culture: A Reliable Source of Trust. *Contemporary Political Theory*, 6: 385–404.

Lenard, P.T. 2008. Trust your Compatriots, but Count your Change: The Roles of Trust, Mistrust, and Distrust in Democracy. *Political Studies*, 56(2): 312–32.

Levy, J. 2000. *The Multiculturalism of Fear.* Oxford: Oxford University Press.

Locke, J. 1980 [1690]). *Second Treatise of Government*, ed. C. B. Macpherson Cambridge: Hackett Publishing Company, Inc.

Luhmann, N. 1982. *Trust and Power.* New Jersey: John Wiley & Sons Inc.

Miller, D. 1995. *On Nationality.* Oxford: Oxford University Press.

Miller, D. 2004. Social Justice in Multicultural Societies. In *Cultural Diversity versus Economic Solidarity*, ed. P. Van Parijs, 13–31. Brussels: De Boeck Université.

Miller, D. 2006. Multiculturalism and the Welfare State: Theoretical Reflections. In *Multiculturalism and the Welfare State: Recognition and Redistribution in Contemporary Democracies*, eds K. Banting and W. Kymlicka, 323–38. Oxford: Oxford University Press.

Moore, M. 2001. *The Ethics of Nationalism.* Oxford: Oxford University Press.

Patterson, O. 1999. Liberty against the Democratic State: On the Historical and Contemporary Sources of American Distrust. In *Democracy and Trust*, ed. M. Warren, 151–207. Cambridge: Cambridge University Press.

Putnam, R. 1993. *Making Democracy Work.* New Jersey: Princeton University Press.

Reitz, J.G. and R. Banerjee. 2007. Racial Inequality, Social Cohesion and Policy Issues in Canada. In *Belonging? Diversity, Recognition and Shared Citizenship in Canada*, eds K. Banting, T. Courchene and F.L. Seidle, 489–546. Quebec: The Institute for Research on Public Policy.

Saggar, S. 2003. Immigration and the Politics of Public Opinion. *Political Quarterly*, 74(1): 178–94.

Scheffler, S. 2007. Immigration and the Significance of Culture. *Philosophy and Public Affairs*, 35(2): 93–125.

Segall, S. 2005. Political Participation as an Engine of Social Solidarity. *Political Studies*, 53(2): 362–78.

Soroka, S., R. Johnston and K. Banting. 2004. Ethnicity, Trust and the Welfare State. In *Cultural Diversity versus Economic Solidarity*, ed. P. Van Parijs, 33–57. Brussels: De Boeck Université.

Weinstock, D. 2004. The Problem of Civic Education in Multicultural Societies. In *The Politics of Belonging: Nationalism, Liberalism and Pluralism*, ed. A. Dieckhoff, 107–24. Lanham, MD : Lexington Books.

Wikan, U. 2004. Deadly Distrust: Honor Killings and Swedish Multiculturalism. In *Distrust*, ed. R. Hardin, 192–204. New York: Russell Sage Foundation.

Williams, M. 1998. *Voice, Trust and Memory.* New Jersey: Princeton University Press.

Chapter 3
More than a Marketing Strategy: Multiculturalism and Meaningful Life

Andrew M. Robinson

The last decade hasn't been kind to multiculturalism. It has been losing ground in states where it once flourished like Canada, the Netherlands, and the United Kingdom. Critics have suggested that it is little more than a marketing strategy, describing it as *Selling Illusions* (Bisoondath 1994) or *Selling Diversity* (Abu-Laban and Gabriel 2002*)*. Advocates have even raised the possibility that Canada's motives for promoting multiculturalism may be 'self-interested', trying to make Canada appear "as an attractive place to visit, study, do business, or even settle permanently" (Kymlicka 2004, 831). While it must be conceded that such concerns are not without substance, this chapter argues that multiculturalism *should* and *can* be more than a marketing strategy.

While the previous chapter placed a strong emphasis on the role of trust in multi-ethnic nations, this chapter begins by elucidating key elements of a theory of human interests and agency, which I call the foundations of meaningful life. This theory is shown to inform a practical and principled approach to cultural accommodations that explains why and when cultural retention constitutes a tangible benefit, how cultural retention might be promoted without unduly restricting individual freedom, and why such cultural retention need not threaten social cohesion. This theoretical approach is then applied to three examples of multicultural politics: the general development of the Canadian federal policy since 1971, plus two recent developments in the province of Ontario. These demonstrate that multicultural policy delivered the tangible benefits advocated here, that it does less so today, but that it could do so again.

A Theory of Multiculturalism: The Foundations of Meaningful Life

I begin by describing a theory, the 'foundations of meaningful life', that addresses the status of multiculturalism in liberal-democratic states (Robinson 2007). The basic insight of this theory is that, properly understood, the values of personal autonomy and identification with community work together to realize an even more basic value – meaningful life. After describing key aspects of this theory, I explain how it informs three key inferences about cultural retention: 1) that it is a tangible benefit; and that it can be accommodated without 2) unduly restricting personal autonomy or 3) jeopardizing social cohesion.

The Foundations of Meaningful Life

What is meant by a *meaningful life*? As conceived here, it is characterized by the pursuit of subjectively significant purposes, the value of which is drawn from some context of value secured beyond the self. Two aspects of this definition require emphasis. First, it is anti-perfectionist – the purposes that can make a life meaningful must be subjectively determined by the individual; meaningful purposes cannot be externally imposed. Second, the context or contexts of value from which such purposes are drawn must have an objective existence outside of the self.

Three further concepts are required to explain where contexts of value originate and how people connect with them: situation, self-identity, and governing assumptions. As discussed in the introductory chapter, a person's *situation* is the totality of his or her unchosen attributes ranging from physical characteristics (primordial traits) to membership in groups, communities, and traditions (ascribed traits) (Archard 1992, 158). At birth each of us is *thrown*, to use Heidegger's term, into a life characterized by membership in communities that we experience as "always already having been" (see Young 1990, 46). *Self-identity* emerges out of situation when a person identifies with some of his unchosen attributes and not others. Those which he *is* are part of his self-identity; those which he merely *has* are not (Sandel 1982, 20). *Governing assumptions* stand in an intermediate position between, and serve to connect, purposes that give significance and meaning to a person's life and the communities with which he or she identifies. Substantively, they are that subset of values and principles (as well one's understandings of the relationship between them) that a person treats as authoritative when making important decisions about her life. They inform, to use Charles Taylor's (1994, 33–4) phrase, "who we are, 'where we're coming from' ... [that act as] the background against which our tastes and desires and opinions and aspirations make sense". They must originate outside of the self because, as Michael Sandel (1982, 165) writes, "[i]f my fundamental values and ends are to enable me, as surely they must, to evaluate and regulate my immediate wants and desires, these values and ends must have a sanction independent of the mere fact that I happen to hold them with a certain intensity."

What of these 'contexts of value'? This phrase refers to the way that values and principles can be embedded in communities and, more specifically, in the traditions that unite and define communities. Bhikhu Parekh (2000, 145) provides a useful illustration of such embedding: "Respect for human life, for example, does not remain an abstract moral principle but gets embodied in such things as the customs and rituals surrounding how we dispose of the dead, what we wear and how we conduct ourselves at funerals, how we treat strangers, help the old and the poor, and celebrate the birth of a child." People connect with such contexts of value when their governing assumptions and significant purposes are informed by the traditions embodied in the communities. While nations or 'societal cultures' (Kymlicka 1995) may act as contexts of value, other value-bearing communities, such as religious, immigrant/ethnic, and traditional communities, can as well.

While identifications with contexts of value inform purposes, they will rarely determine them. People who live in modern plural societies will develop different purposes depending on the idiosyncratic ways they understand the relationships between the often conflicting communities with which they identify. Further, even people who identify with fairly homogenous and complementary communities can develop very different purposes from the same identifications.

Shifting focus from community and identifications to identity and autonomy requires us to introduce two highly interrelated, yet distinguishable, aspects of human agency. *Normal agency*, which accounts for the bulk of human deliberation, proceeds *from* a person's governing assumptions. In normal agency one takes one's governing assumptions as given, transforms connections with contexts of value into significant purposes and pursues them. In *meta-agency*, conversely, one's governing assumptions *are* the subject of deliberation. Meta-agency is typically initiated when circumstances conspire to threaten the meaningfulness of a person's life by revealing shortcomings in his or her governing assumptions that are experienced as *dissonance*. For instance, a person may be unable to construct governing assumptions from her situation; her purposes may fail too often when put into practice; or previously unrecognized inconsistencies within her governing assumptions may become evident. Such dissonance presents a problem and an opportunity. It is a problem to the extent that it threatens the meaningfulness of a person's life and may lead to anomie. It is an opportunity to the extent that by successfully resolving it, a person can refine her governing assumptions and thus increase her reasons for having confidence in them. Resolution is reached, if it is reached, when the source of dissonance is addressed and meaning is recovered. This will typically involve transforming one's governing assumptions (and thus self-identity) – by prioritizing, reinterpreting, compartmentalizing, rejecting, or adopting identifications to increase internal consistency or consonance with objective reality – or by acting on external circumstances, where possible, to remove the source of dissonance. Meta-agency can, of course, fail; just as societies collapse and traditions peter out, some people who experience dissonance never fully recover a sense of meaning in their lives.

This conception of agency has implications for identity. It suggests a conception of self-identity that can be both fluid and fragile: *fluid* to the extent that people may exercise meta-agency to transform the identifications that constitute their self-identities; *fragile* to the extent that meta-agency may fail, leaving connections to important contexts of value severed without replacing them with identifications that could motivate new significant purposes. This *fluid-yet-fragile* conception of self-identity informs our conception of personal autonomy and, ultimately, our justification of accommodations for cultural communities designed to facilitate cultural retention.

I call the conception of personal autonomy associated with the foundations of meaningful life *situated autonomy*. It shares many important features with other conceptions of personal autonomy and in general, with liberal conceptions of freedom as discussed in the Adsett chapter. For instance, since meaningful life involves the pursuit of subjectively meaningful purposes, situated autonomy requires, with some exceptions, respect for negative liberty – freedom from coercive interference with the pursuit of one's purposes. Situated autonomy can also justify state support for positive freedom – the actual capacity, in terms of resources and opportunities, to pursue one's purposes. This reflects concern for equalizing opportunities to lead meaningful lives, not just access to some 'neutral' bundle of resources.

Two further requirements of situated autonomy follow from the idea of personal autonomy as 'self-governance'. First, for the self to *govern*, autonomous agents must regulate their lower-order preferences or purposes by invoking higher-order values and principles (for us, governing assumptions). Thus, situated autonomy requires the processes of normal agency through which people form and pursue their purposes to not be subjected to undue external influences, like hypnotic suggestion, manipulation, coercive persuasion, and subliminal influence (Dworkin 1988, 18). These are influences that, "were the agent to be made aware of their presence and influence, she would be moved to revise her desire set" (Christman 1987, 291). The second requirement is that the governing *self* (i.e., the agent's governing assumptions) must be properly *his or her own*. Here we must distinguish two cases in which people develop governing assumptions: one, when adults exercise meta-agency; the other, when children are socialized to form governing assumptions. The case of adults is straightforward – respect for meaningful life requires that they not be subjected to undue external of influences. The case of children is more complicated. While, as a general rule, coercion and manipulation are inconsistent with autonomy, the formation of the secure identifications upon which situated autonomy depends may require their exercise to steer children away from some influences and towards others. However, not all forms of socialization are consistent with respect for meaningful life. This is addressed below.

Cultural Retention As a Tangible Benefit

The justification of accommodations to help retain the cultural communities with which individuals identify emerges in the relationship between situated autonomy and self-identity. Since situated autonomy requires the exercise of normal agency, which in turn presupposes governing assumptions that find their origin in identifications with contexts of value embodied in communities, situated autonomy requires access to such communities.[1] Even if we accept this claim, we must ask whether the fact that a person requires access to *a* community can justify

---

1   Thus, autonomy requires community not because community provides a context of choice (Kymlicka 1995), but because it sustains contexts of value.

protection of some *particular* community? (Kymlicka 1995, 84) The answer is yes and no. Yes, where respect for meaningful life requires it; no, where it does not. Respect for meaningful life can justify accommodations for communities where three conditions are met: the community connects its members with a context of value that supports their capacity for situated autonomy and, thus, meaningful life; members are threatened with the involuntary loss of access to the community; and members would be unable to make alternative identifications with the communities presently available to them. The last two points require elaboration.

To understand why the threatened loss of a community must be *involuntary*, consider the relationship between individuals and the communities with which they identify and how this relationship can affect processes of change and continuity in traditions and in individual's self-identities. The relationship between individuals and their traditions is reciprocal—while individual members are shaped in part by communal traditions, traditions are shaped in part by the interpretations they are given by individual members. From the perspective of traditions, this relationship suggests that traditions evolve and change through individual member's struggles to sustain meaning. Each individual's exercise of meta-agency has the potential to transform a tradition for present and future members. Viewed in this way, the exercise of personal autonomy through meta-agency is not a threat to traditions; rather, it is essential to their vitality and continuity.

From the perspective of self-identity, the relationship between continuity and change takes the form of a narrative. Much as the continuity of a tradition persists, though some of its characteristics change, a person with self-identity 'a' is the same person as a person at a later time with self-identity 'b' if these identities can be linked by a narrative that explains, without self-deception, this change as a sequence of additions to, deletions from, and reinterpretations of, the identifications that constituted the earlier self-identity. No such narrative could link the individual to someone other than the individual's prior self or to some future person who might inhabit the individual's body were s/he suffer a loss of identity, due, say, to some form of brain damage. Further, while none of a person's identifications are so fundamental that they could never be replaced, at any particular stage in the process at least one identification must be taken as 'given' and thus retained from one point in time to the next. Most importantly, the reverse is also true: the content of a person's identifications may limit the range of new identifications that he or she can meaningfully adopt at a given point in time.

It is in this idea that a person's present governing assumptions could leave him or her unable to make new identifications (at least over the short-term) that we find the basis of the justification of communal accommodations. The reason is that to meaningfully make a new identification, a person must be able to make sense of it in terms of the values he or she accesses through her present identifications. To do otherwise would require an arbitrary choice that would conflict with the narrative account of continuity and change in self-identity. This idea is illustrated nicely by Harry Frankfurt's concept of 'volitional necessity.' It suggests that to treat an identification as authoritative (in his terms, to "care about it") a person must avoid contradicting the identification in his actions. As Frankfurt (1988, 86) writes, a person "who is subject to volitional necessity finds that he *must* act as he does. People are generally quite far from considering that volitional necessity renders them helpless bystanders to their own behaviour. Indeed many may even tend to regard it as actually enhancing their autonomy and their strength of will". Just like Martin Luther's, "Here I stand: *I can do no other*", Frankfurt continues, "An encounter with necessity of this sort, characteristically affects a person ... by somehow making it apparent to him that every apparent alternative to [his present] course is unthinkable". To be clear, my claim is neither that any particular identification is so constitutive that it could never be replaced nor that one's present identifications determine the identifications one might make in the future. Rather, I make the more modest claim that one's present identifications can determine which identifications one *can't make* at a particular point in time, at least not without jeopardizing the meaningfulness of his or her life. Meaningfulness is jeopardized, for instance, where the individual finds it impossible to pursue any projects associated with his or her identifications within the new context or to attach any significance to the projects that are available.

I must also stress that this account of self-identity only raises concerns about the *involuntarily* loss of identifications. The voluntary loss of an identification – by choosing to replace or reject it through meta-agency – is not problematic precisely because people normally reject and replace identifications for reasons that are meaningful to them. Where the loss is involuntary, however, the ability to sustain meaning by replacing identifications cannot be assured. When the loss is involuntary and there are no alternative communities with which a person may meaningfully identify, respect for meaningful life can justify accommodations designed to preserve the identification – either by preserving the community itself or by facilitating elements of cultural retention among affected individuals.

As concerns such accommodations, we can distinguish between a *remedial case* in which all three conditions justifying cultural accommodations have clearly been met and a *preventative case* where community members are concerned that the conditions will be met if no proactive measures are taken. Since the preventative case will necessarily depend upon counterfactual and speculative evidence, respect for meaningful life suggests the extension of a fair degree of deference to the opinions of those making such claims. While the extent of such deference should be determined on a case-by-case basis, a good general rule is that the degree of justification should be proportionate to the extent of the burdens it would impose on the ability of nonmembers to pursue their own significant purposes. In particular, where claimants establish a *prima facie* case for accommodations that would impose no significant burdens on others, their requests should usually be respected. Thus, for example, other things being equal, the request of an Orthodox Jewish community to create an eruv by stringing fishing line on poles around an urban neighbourhood (Trillen 1994) should require a lower degree of justification than, say, a request for public funding of private religious schools.

To this point we have seen that policies designed to accommodate cultural retention can be justified and that, where successful, they provide tangible benefits to their recipients by enhancing their capacity to lead meaningful and autonomous lives.

Principled in Tensions: Cultural Accommodations, Autonomy and Social Cohesion

By conceiving the relationship between autonomy and identification as complex and complementary, the foundations of meaningful life informs normative principles to guide policy governing the design of cultural accommodations and the socialization of children. I introduce each set of principles by first identifying the value conflicts that they address and then describing the principles and illustrating how they can deliver tangible benefits without overly-restricting personal autonomy or undermining social cohesion.

The main conflicts associated with the design of cultural accommodations concern how extensive they should be. The goal is to create measures extensive enough to preserve a valuable community without undermining personal autonomy or social cohesion. Personal autonomy may be threatened, for instance, by accommodations that are too extensive – as a general rule, the more extensive the accommodation, the greater the temptation for communal factions to exclude people whose situated autonomy depends upon having access to it and the greater the harm to anyone who is involuntarily included in the community. Similarly, social cohesion may be threatened by accommodations so extensive that the burdens they impose generate resentment among nonmembers.

I propose the four principles to address these conflicts. First, while the exact nature of appropriate accommodations will vary with circumstances, in the ideal case, they will only address a community's *minimal bases*. This is achieved when accommodations are no more extensive than necessary to sustain the community as a context of value. For example, the minimal bases of the indigenous communities of Australia or Canada might be a separate land base where its language, culture, and traditional means of governance can be practiced and reproduced. By limiting protection to such minimal bases, space is sustained within which the community's traditions can be carried on without predetermining which particular interpretations or purposes will be favoured over the long run. Second, since accommodations are only warranted when and for so long as they are justified by respect for meaningful life, accommodations must be *impermanent*. Impermanence may be incorporated into accommodations in a variety of ways, such as requiring periodic expressions of support for the accommodation by community members, or, more implicitly, by designing accommodations such that they cease to exist if members no longer avail themselves of them. A third principle, *freedom to exit the community*, acts as an impermanence principle for individuals. This reflects the potential fluidity of self-identity by requiring that people be free to leave communities with which they no longer identify. The fourth principle requires *explicit definition of the rights and obligations of membership*. Respect for meaningful life requires that obligations be clearly connected to the preservation of the community as a context of value. It also requires transparent membership rules that ensure, at a minimum, that everyone knows what obligations they are accepting by belonging to the community and so that all who are willing to undertake the obligations can enjoy the right to participate in the community.

Together, these principles are intended to create competing tensions that will encourage community leaders and individual members to strike a balance between autonomy and identification that favours equal respect for meaningful life. For instance, freedom of exit and the impermanence principle place pressure on community leaders to resist attaching obligations to membership that are so excessive or meaningless to members that they choose to dissociate themselves from the community. Transparent membership codes offer to promote autonomy in a number of ways: by protecting members from factional opponents who might arbitrarily exclude them for reasons unrelated to communal survival; by discouraging free riders and thus reducing burdens on non-members; and by ensuring that those who do not identify with the community are not subject to its obligations. The limitation of accommodations to minimal bases promises to reduce burdens on nonmembers that can be corrosive of social cohesion. And finally, the limitation of obligations to those clearly related to a community's minimal bases should provide maximal room for individuals to exercise situated autonomy and to sustain multiple identifications.

There are two main conflicts associated with the socialization of children. One is between children's interest in developing the secure identifications with communities that situated autonomy requires and their interest in retaining their capacity for situated autonomy. Respect for meaningful life suggests that while children's interest in developing secure identifications may justify the use of coercion and manipulation in processes of socialization that would never be acceptable if applied to adults, the legitimate scope of this is not unlimited. In particular, the socialization children receive must respect their capacity for meaningful life by being *sincere*, in that it is non-exploitive and veracious (i.e., it reflects the actual beliefs of the socializers), and by respecting children's *capacity to exercise meta-agency* in the future by ensuring that their socialization is capable of being renounced and that socializers are forthright about the existence of alternative ways of life.[2]

The second conflict is between ensuring that children develop secure identifications and sustaining the cohesiveness of the wider political community

---

2   I would like to thank the anonymous reviewer for raising the following questions: "Can minority groups (or dominant groups) be fully forthright about the existence of alternative ways of life without introducing significant existential doubts in the minds of young adherents? Would following this principle not ultimately imperil the child's cultural identity and, by implication, the long-term viability of the community?" I share these concerns and have addressed them elsewhere (Robinson 2007, Chapter 4, esp. 78–80).

that provides the cultural accommodations. Social cohesion may be threatened where communities are permitted to socialize children in ways that prevent them from developing identifications with their fellow citizens and the wider community. This can be addressed by authorizing the state to require that the socialization of children not imperil the state's functioning and stability. In particular, the state may require communities to socialize their children to identify with the wider community as a context of value, to accept the principle of equal respect for meaningful lives of all citizens, and to develop capacities necessary to function in a multicultural democracy, such as the ability to negotiate and to reach mutual understandings. As these commitments apply to all citizens, they can form the basis of a thin shared identity that can sustain social cohesion under conditions of cultural diversity.

These principles promise to create beneficial tensions for both minority and dominant communities. On the one hand, minority community leaders must balance any desires they might have to demand more freedom to socialize their children against the concern that if the accommodations are perceived to threaten their children's personal autonomy or the state's social cohesion, they may lose support for the accommodations altogether. On the other hand, members of the dominant community must balance their desire to prevent minority communities from developing in ways that might threaten social cohesion against their own interests in maintaining a state that shows equal concern for meaningful life.[3] It would be a hollow victory indeed to reign in an isolationist minority at the cost of undermining the very principle that justified accommodations for one's own valued communities.

Together, the tensions created by these principles represent, I believe, the most compelling balance between cultural retention, personal autonomy, and the social cohesion of the wider community that acts as guarantor of both. Once space for the exercise of autonomy has been maximized by these principles, however, individuals must choose either to constrain their choices out of respect for communal survival or to exit the community to maximize their personal freedom. Similarly, communities must adjust the ways they socialize their children to avoid undermining support for *and from* the wider political community that sustains all cultural communities in the first place. Another key advantage of these tensions is that they force communal leaders and members alike to confront the fact that their *real choice* is often not between their ideal conception of their community and other 'flawed' conceptions, but between having access to cultural communities

---

3   The anonymous reviewer helpfully raised the issue of power in negotiations between dominant and minority communities and questioned the dominant community's commitment to the principle of "equal concern for meaningful life." This raises issues too large to be dealt with adequately here. I will say two things, however. First, no normative argument of this nature is likely to persuade a majority or a minority that isn't concerned about being just. Second, I have addressed this issue more fully elsewhere (Robinson 2007).

that meets most, if not all, of their needs, and losing access to those communities altogether.

A Few Illustrative Examples

I will now consider three examples of 'multicultural politics' concerning the Canadian federal and Ontario provincial governments. By multicultural politics I mean political activities involving either formal government policies designed to address the concerns of non-British/French/Aboriginal Canadians or political claims that are, at least in part, inspired or legitimized by the existence of such policy. As policy that addresses citizens who arrived in Canada as individual and familial immigrants (and their descendents), multicultural policy was never intended to deliver the kind of accommodations that the foundations of meaningful life might justify for national or indigenous minorities (e.g., self-government on traditional homelands). Rather, it has always been at most about providing certain benefits or exemptions designed to help such Canadians resist primary integration into the private sphere of the dominant community (e.g., family life, religion, sports), while facilitating secondary integration into mainstream economic, political, legal and educational institutions (Kallen 2003, 140–41). In terms of our theoretical discussion, where multicultural policy promotes the retention of cultural communities and traditions that embody irreplaceable contexts of value, it provides tangible benefits that can be explained and justified by the foundations of meaningful life. In the discussion that follows, I seek to establish three broad points: that federal multicultural policy, as it began in 1971, was capable of delivering such benefits; that multicultural policy has shifted away from this; and that the shift is not irreversible.

Canadian Federal Multiculturalism Policy

The broad pattern of developments in the Canadian federal multiculturalism policy illustrates my claims that multicultural policy was fairly consistent with the implications of the foundations of meaningful life in the past but has since shifted away from this.

The original consistency is reflected in the policy principles pronounced by Canadian Prime Minister Pierre Elliott Trudeau in 1971. Unlike the final three principles that were concerned with facilitating secondary integration, we are interested in the first principle that addressed cultural retention. It pledged that the government would "support all of Canada's cultures and will seek to assist, resources permitting, the development of those cultural groups that have demonstrated a desire and effort to continue to develop, a capacity to grow and contribute to Canada, as well as a clear need for assistance" (Trudeau 1971). This is consistent with many of the principles set out above. Support for cultural retention was to be voluntary ('a demonstrated desire'), impermanent (only provided to those who continue to make an 'effort'), and minimal and justified (only provided where there is a 'clear need,' 'resources permitting'). These qualities were also reflected in early Canadian multicultural programs. Support to help adults retain identifications with their ethno-linguistic heritage through, for instance, ethnic clubs and festivals only lasts so long as individuals voluntarily join, can afford to participate, and feel they are getting something of value out of the experience. Similarly, assistance to help adults socialize their children to participate in, and to share the values of, their communities was delivered through Saturday schools and heritage language programs, which left students free to participate in public education systems and thus posed minimal threats to social cohesion.

The shift away from an approach that emphasized cultural retention and toward programs with a more exclusive emphasis on secondary integration began in the 1980s and was solidified in the 1990s (Fleras and Elliott 2002, Jedwab 2003). This is reflected in the *Canadian Multiculturalism Act*, 1988 which included race and racism as concerns of multicultural policy and extended the program's focus to include systemic discrimination. As Fleras and Elliott (2002, 68) note, federal multicultural policy now aims to encourage members of ethnic minorities to participate more actively as Canadian citizens by focusing "on what we have in common as rights-bearing individuals and equality-seeking individuals, rather than on what divides us". Interestingly this is also noted in the Nicolacopoulos and Vassilacopoulos' and Fleras' chapters in respect to Australia. This shift is also reflected in changes to federal funding guidelines (Jedwab 2003, 338) that, at least in my assessment, tend to discourage funding for purposes related to cultural retention. Thus, by 2001 the Multiculturalism Directorate reported that while multicultural policy once concerned enabling "groups to preserve and celebrate their cultural identities ... [it] now focuses more on assisting marginalized groups to build their capacity to better influence [mainstream] social, cultural, economic and political institutions ... " (Canada 2001, Part 1).

Even from this brief review, it should be clear that while multicultural policy today may not deliver the kind of tangible benefits associated with the foundations of meaningful life, the fact that it has done so in the past suggests that it could do so again. While it is undoubtedly true that antiracism policies are necessary to help non-European immigrants integrate into Canadian society and, thus, to pursue the purposes that motivated them to leave their homelands, it is also true, as the developments discussed in the next section indicate, that many immigrants also hope to retain, to live according to, and to pass on to their children, some of the identifications they brought with them from their homelands. There is no practical reason, so far as I can see, that policies that facilitate this by promoting cultural retention cannot be pursued alongside policies that combat racism and discrimination. In fact, to the extent that both types of policy help enable individuals to pursue their significant purposes, both are consistent with the foundations of meaningful life.

Recent Developments in Ontario

Whatever the state of official federal policy, a certain ideal of multiculturalism has taken on a life of its own in Canada. Federal policy has both legitimized claims-making by multicultural Canadians and informed an ethic that many citizens have taken seriously in provincial and local governments, private workplaces, schools, and other institutions. In this section I discuss two recent controversies in Ontario that illustrate the ongoing resistance to cultural retention policies that could deliver the tangible benefits suggested by the foundations of meaningful life.[4]

The first controversy concerned a Muslim group in Ontario, the Islamic Institute on Civil Justice (IICJ), which in October 2003 publicly expressed the desire to establish arbitration panels that would use Islamic religious law (Sharia) under Ontario's then-Arbitration Act. The Arbitration Act allowed parties to sign an agreement authorizing a third person to adjudicate their disputes concerning some matters of family and inheritance law (including division of property upon dissolution of marriage, spousal support and matters concerning children such as custody, access, support, and moral and religious education) according to an agreed upon set of principles or legal system, including religious law (Bakht 2004, 3–5). While the Arbitration Act was not a multicultural policy in inspiration (Kymlicka 2007, 82 n. 32), it had been accessed by couples wishing to adjudicate disputes according to Jewish and Christian principles. The IICJ's proposal and the seriousness with which it was taken reflected the influence of the multicultural ethic. After much public debate, the Act was amended in November 2005 to prohibit the use of any religious law.

From our theoretical perspective, the Act appeared capable of providing accommodations that could deliver tangible benefits by facilitating the pursuit of meaningful lives. It could do so by enabling people to adjudicate their private disputes according to principles consonant with the contexts of value with which they identified and about which they felt the pull of volitional necessity. As Marion Boyd (2004b, 1–2) noted in her report to the provincial government: "arbitrated decisions may be more acceptable to the parties, and more reflective of some elements of the parties' shared values"; arbitration could be conducted in the party's own language; and it could enable groups to "maintain their cultural identity, by allowing them to continue to control their definitions of family and community". Further, the Act was consistent with our principle that protection must be focused on a community's minimal bases since it only applied to those who voluntarily availed themselves of it and it was up to the parties themselves, not some communal elite, to decide which legal system (in this case, which school of Sharia law) they wanted the adjudicator to apply.

This said, the IICJ's proposal was controversial, and not without good reason. While many critics disapproved of the patriarchal nature of the rules to which

---

4   The "reasonable accommodations" debate in Quebec suggests that this resistance is not limited to Ontario (see Seguin. 2007).

women might agree, this cannot be our primary concern (subject of course to the various provisos noted above). Given our focus on meaningful life, and thus our willingness to respect situated autonomy by generally refusing to interfere with individuals' pursuit of their *subjectively* significant purposes, our concern is with the nature of such women's consent.[5] Thus, in what follows, I discuss three concerns about the quality of their consent with the aim of demonstrating that it was possible to design a policy that showed adequate respect for these women's autonomy without eliminating the accommodation altogether.

One concern was that women's formal consent may simply reflect their being in a position of unequal power with their husbands, either because they are being abused or are recent immigrants who have been sponsored by their husbands. While this concern is reasonable, it is neither peculiar to Muslims nor does addressing it require the denial of the accommodation. Since respect for meaningful life requires the state to prevent adults from being subjected to undue external influences in exercising their autonomy, a justifiable accommodation must include safeguards like, for example, Boyd's (2004b, 8) recommendation that arbitrators receive training to identify issues of power imbalance and domestic violence.

A second concern is that the ability of new immigrants to truly consent may be hampered by linguistic barriers or ignorance of their rights in Canada (Bakht 2004, 19–20). Here again, adequate safeguards appear possible. In this case, the state might treat recent immigrants as relevantly analogous to children in that both are new entrants to the political community. As such the state can legitimately require that the process by which they are integrated (as opposed to socialized) into the community protect their capacity for situated autonomy by ensuring that the information they receive about Canadian society is veracious and forthright about alternatives. For instance, Boyd (2004b, 6–7) suggests that before signing an agreement, both parties receive independent legal advice to ensure that they understand their general rights and obligations under Canadian law, the remedies under Ontario family and arbitration law that they will be waiving, and the consequences of such waiver.

Third, and more complex, is the possibility that women may sign these agreements because of communal pressure. The concern is that women and their children may be threatened with exclusion from the life and institutions of the ethno-cultural community if they refuse to sign (Boyd 2004a, 107). This is especially troubling because the source of the pressure is not raw coercion, as with spousal abuse, but the exercise by individuals, as individuals and as members of religious institutions, of their right to freely associate, or not associate, as they choose (Boyd 2004a, 89). This presents a genuine dilemma. On the one hand, it suggests refusal of the accommodation, since the community would only be in a position to exert such pressure because the state created the arbitration process

---

5   As Bakht (2004, 22, n. 119) suggests, simply seeking to protect women from themselves is to engage "in the very infantilizing of Muslim women that one accuses patriarchal culture of".

in the first place. On the other hand, though, this solution has its own costs; it would deny everyone the tangible benefits that they could otherwise derive from the accommodation.

If it happened that the arbitration agreements were used by the community in this way, and I am not suggesting that they would be, the foundations of meaningful life suggests that it would have been best to leave the arbitration act in place, implement safeguards of the type Boyd recommended, and allow the kinds of competing tensions identified above to play themselves out. The likely results would be far from perfect, but I believe that they are the best that can be hoped for under the circumstances. On the one hand, some women would find the resulting terrain quite navigable: those who saw the arbitration agreements as an expression of their religious commitments would be happy to participate; others, who believed the agreements were too high a price to pay for membership in the community, would exercise their freedom to exit the community. (Of course, if enough women were in the latter group, this would likely place pressure on community leaders to weaken the requirement as a condition of membership.) On the other hand, some women might feel overwhelmed by having to choose between their intellectual and emotional attachments to the institutions and individuals that constitute their communities and their desire to enjoy equal treatment with their husbands in matters of family and inheritance law in Ontario. Such situations can be traumatic, and no individual should be faced with them if they are avoidable. In this case, however, the alternative – prohibiting the agreements altogether – would simply impose a different kind of loss, in this case by proscribing the option of living in accordance with a significant religious commitment. The virtue of resolving this dilemma by retaining the arbitration agreements (with safeguards) is that the choice of whether to participate in the agreements would be left to individuals to exercise in ways that were meaningful to them, not precluded by the state.

The second controversy concerned the demand that the government of Ontario expand public funding to faith-based schools beyond the Catholic system. Due to a constitutional arrangement predating the creation of Canada in 1867, the province of Ontario fully funds Catholic schools from kindergarten to grade 12, but provides no funds to other religious schools. This perceived inequality has been the subject of a Supreme Court case (*Adler v. Ontario*), a communication to the United Nations Human Rights Committee (HRC) (*Waldman*), and most recently, it was made an issue by the opposition Progressive Conservative Party (PC) in the 2007 provincial election. Polling conducted during the election and the sound defeat of the PCs indicated that this proposal was not popular with Ontarians (Thomson 2007, A6).

From our theoretical perspective, public funding of religious schools can act as an accommodation to assist communities in socializing their young to develop the secure identifications that situated autonomy requires. Given the principle of equal respect for meaningful life, other things being equal, the only just outcome would be to fund all religious schools or none at all. This, it should be noted, put considerable pressure on supporters of funding for Catholic schools who opposed it for other religious schools not to push too hard for fear that they might achieve the 'hollow victory' of undermining public support for public funding of *all* forms of religious education.

A key issue in this respect was indicated by the government's defense of its policy before the HRC. Ontario argued that other things were not equal; to promote tolerance and equal respect in Ontario's highly diverse society, the government said it was justified in encouraging citizens to send their children to public schools (by not funding the education they might otherwise choose) (*Waldman*, 4.3.4). In our terms, this was a case of the state asserting its legitimate interest in ensuring that citizens are socialized in ways that will not imperil its functioning and stability. In this case, however, Ontario's stance would be more convincing were it true that not funding non-Catholic faith-based schools is the only way to achieve its goals.

As the PC's proposal indicated, options do exist that can respect the government's legitimate interests while providing substantial accommodations to communities' interested in taking greater control of their children's socialization. The PC's proposal was to extend funding to faith-based schools, but only to those that agreed to join the public education system, teach the provincial curriculum and employ provincially-certified teachers (Thomson 2007, A6). From the community's perspective, this would have helped them enjoy separate environments within which to socialize their children, including formal instruction in their faith (and perhaps, heritage languages) and a school environment in which their faith was normalized, for example in the selection of celebrations and holidays. From the state's perspective, the terms of funding would allow them to ensure that children received education that respected their capacity to exercise meta-agency and that would promote the state's functioning and stability.

While I think the PC's proposal was on the right track, I'm not convinced that common curriculum and teacher education can necessarily overcome the drawbacks to social cohesion and stability that would likely arise from creating denominational educational silos from Kindergarten to Grade 12. (This said, I must admit that the current Public/Catholic silos do not appear to be producing students who are markedly intolerant or incapable of exercising personal autonomy).[6] Although a political non-starter for the foreseeable future, a more satisfactory balance between children's interests in developing secure identifications and the state's interest in social cohesion and stability would fund denominational education up to a certain grade (say between 4 and 6) at which point all students would be socialized together in public schools. This would provide children with the opportunity to develop secure identifications with their cultural communities while still socializing them to function as citizens in the wider community.

---

6   Dr Hasmath has helpfully pointed out that this may be due in part to the fact that, at least in major centres in Ontario, recent immigration of Catholics from Latin America and some Asian countries like the Philippines and Korea has resulted in Catholic school systems that, like public schools, are multiracial.

Whatever one may think of the particular balances suggested here to address these recent controversies in Ontario, the key point is that in both cases alternatives to the present policies, which would provide more tangible benefits in terms of cultural retention while respecting concerns for personal autonomy and social cohesion, are available but are being resisted by the Ontario public and its government.

Conclusion

This chapter has presented, in the theory of the foundations of meaningful life, an ideal conception of policy principles for a multiculturalism that would provide tangible benefits in the form of cultural retention without sacrificing concern for personal autonomy or social cohesion. Application of this theory to three illustrative cases demonstrated that such a multicultural policy is possible, but that it is not generally being realized in Canada today. Thus, I conclude that while, at least in terms of the promise of cultural retention, multiculturalism may not be much more than a marketing strategy today, it has been in the past, it could be in the present, and it should be in the future.

Finally, as the cases indicate, it is unlikely that any theory that addresses demands for cultural accommodations within liberal democracies will be able to maximize respect for all valuable interests and objectives all of the time. There will often be situations and circumstances that can only be resolved through compromise and the balancing of interests. This being the case, the foundations of meaningful life has three key virtues that recommend it as an approach to reaching such compromises: it recognizes the importance of identity and identifications to human well being; it suggests principles for balancing the individual's interests in cultural retention and personal autonomy and the state's interests in democratic governance and social cohesion; and, perhaps most importantly, where hard choices have to be made, it advocates leaving them as much as is possible to the individual him- or herself to negotiate in ways that he or she finds most meaningful.

References

Abu-Laban, Y. and C. Gabriel. 2002. *Selling Diversity: Immigration, Multiculturalism, Employment Equity, and Globalization*. Peterborough: Broadview Press.

Adler v. Ontario, [1996] 3 S.C.R. 609.

Bakht, N. 2004. Family Arbitration Using Sharia Law: Examining Ontario's Arbitration Act and its Impact on Women. *Muslim World Journal of Human Rights* 1. Available at: Berkeley Electronic Press http://www.bepress.com/mwjhr.

Bissoondath, N. 1994. *Selling Illusions: the Cult of Multiculturalism in Canada.* Toronto. Penguin.

Boyd. M. 2004a. *Dispute Resolution in Family Law: Protecting Choice, Promoting Inclusion.* Toronto, Ministry of the Attorney General. Available at: http://www.attorneygeneral.jus.gov.on.ca/english/about/pubs/boyd/.

Boyd, M. 2004b. Executive Summary. In *Dispute Resolution in Family Law: Protecting Choice, Promoting Inclusion.* Toronto, Ministry of the Attorney General. Available at: http://www.attorneygeneral.jus.gov.on.ca/english/about/pubs/boyd/.

Canada. 2001. Department of Heritage. *12th Annual Report on the Operation of the Canadian Multiculturalism Act, 1999–2000.* February. Available at: http://www.pch.gc.ca/progs/multi/reports/ann99–2000/contents_e.cfm.

Christman, J. 1987. Autonomy: A Defense of the Split-Level Self. *Southern Journal of Philosophy* 25: 281–94.

Dworkin, G. 1988. *The Theory and Practice of Autonomy.* Cambridge: Cambridge University Press.

Fleras, A. and J.L. Elliott. 2002. *Engaging Diversity: Multiculturalism in Canada* 2nd ed. Toronto: Nelson.

Frankfurt, H.G. 1988. The Importance of What We Care About. In *The Importance of What We Care About*, 80–94. Cambridge, U.K.: Cambridge University Press.

Jedwab, J. 2003. To Preserve and Enhance: Canadian Multiculturalism Before and After the Charter. In *The Canadian Charter of Rights and Freedoms: Reflections on the Charter After Twenty Years*, eds J.E. Magnet, G-A. Beaudoin, G. Gall, C. Manfredi, 309–44. Markham, Ontario: Butterworths.

Kallen, E. 2003. *Ethnicity and Rights in Canada* 3rd ed. Toronto: Oxford University Press.

Kymlicka, W. 1995. *Multicultural Citizenship* Oxford: Oxford University Press.

Kymlicka, W. 2004. Marketing Canadian Pluralism in the International Arena. *International Journal* 59(4): 829–52.

Kymlicka, W. 2007. Ethnocultural Diversity in a Liberal State: Making Sense of the Canadian Model(s). In *Belonging: Diversity, Recognition and Shared Citizenship in Canada*, eds K. Banting, T.J. Courchene, and F. Leslie Seidle, 39–86. Montreal: Institute for Research on Public Policy.

Parekh, B. 2000. *Rethinking Multiculturalism: Cultural Diversity and Political Theory.* Cambridge, Mass.: Harvard University Press.

Robinson, A. 2007. *Multiculturalism and the Foundations of Meaningful Life: Reconciling Autonomy, Identity and Community.* Vancouver: UBC Press.

Sandel, M.J. 1982. *Liberalism and the Limits of Justice.* Cambridge: Cambridge University Press.

Seguin, R. 2006. 'Would International Adjudication Enhance Contextual Theories of Justice? Reflections on the UN Human Rights Committee, *Lovelace, Ballantyne*, and, *Waldman. Canadian Journal of Political Science* 39 (2): 271–91.

Seguin, R. 2007. Quebec Strikes Commission to Resolve Minorities Debate. *Globe and Mail*. February 9, A4.

Taylor, C. 1992. The Politics of Recognition. In *Multiculturalism*, ed. A. Gutmann, 25–74. Princeton, NJ: Princeton University Press.

Thomson, A. 2007. Liberal Lead over Tories Dips in Ontario: Poll; Majority of Voters Oppose PC Plan to Fund Faith-based Schools. *National Post*. September 10, A6.

Trillen, C. 1994. Drawing the Line. *The New Yorker*. December 12, 50–62.

Trudeau, P. 1971. Statement to the House of Commons on Multiculturalism. House of Commons. *Official Report of Debates*, 3rd sess., 28th Parliament, October 8, 1971, 8545–46.

Waldman v. Canada. United Nations Human Rights Committee. Communication No. 694/1996, U.N. Doc. CCPR/C/67/D/694/1996 (1999).

Young, I.M. 1990. *Justice and the Politics of Difference*. Princeton, NJ: Princeton University Press.

Chapter 4

The Notion of Multiculturalism in Canada and France: A Question of Different Understandings of Liberty, Equality and Community

Margaret Adsett

Multiculturalism was adopted as the official policy of Canada in 1971.[1] It found a place in the *Canadian Charter of Rights and Freedoms* of 1982 as Section 27: "This Charter shall be interpreted in a manner consistent with the preservation and enhancement of the multicultural heritage of Canadians". Some maintain this section officially recognizes multiculturalism as a Canadian value. In 1988, the *Canadian Multiculturalism Act* came into effect, giving Canada's multiculturalism policy the force of law, and for a while, departmental status in the federal government. General public support for this policy has grown since then, from 63 percent in 1989 to 74 percent in 2002, though it decreased in the early 1990s, at least for a while (Dasko 2004). More recently, 67 percent of Canadians agreed that Canadian society should encourage mixing various cultures to form a new national community, and 69 percent disagreed that society should discourage minorities from forming communities and urge them to abandon their cultural practices.[2]

It has often been suggested that the Canadian federal government implemented multiculturalism policy as a strategy to cool the flames of Quebec nationalism or to make official English-French bilingualism more palatable to the West, especially to Ukrainians and others of non-French and non-British ancestries. It can also be said that multiculturalism has served as a great marketing strategy to attract

---

1   Please note that the opinions and ideas expressed in this chapter are those of the author and should not be construed to reflect those of the Department of Canadian Heritage or the Government of Canada.

2   These data were collected by Leger Marketing on behalf of the Association for Canadian Studies in October 2007 as part of Immigration and Minority Issues and are based on a representative sample of 1,500 Canadians 18 years of age or older. Also note that francophone Quebecers of Canada's only officially unilingual French speaking province often provide less favourable responses to questions related to the desirability of multiculturalism, depending on whether the question illicits ideas of the place of diversity in their province or the place of their own culture and language in the rest of Canada.

and retain immigrants to Canada, such as the Caribbean population, discussed in the next chapter. However, few have considered that multiculturalism might have been used as a deliberate strategy to increase the market value of diversity in Canadian society. Indeed, a former prime minister of Canada and the architect of the famed multiculturalism policy, Pierre Trudeau, detested Anglo-conformity. As he remarked on October 9, 1971 at the Ukrainian-Canadian Congress: "[u]niformity is neither desirable nor possible in a country the size of Canada ... A society which eulogizes the average citizen is one which breeds mediocrity", and "what the world should be seeking, and what we in Canada must continue to cherish, are not concepts of uniformity but human values".[3] The idea that diversity is of value to society can be found in the works of John Stuart Mill, a nineteenth century liberal philosopher from Britain, in particular in his *On Liberty* of 1869.[4] It should come as no surprise that Pierre Trudeau was an admirer of John Stuart Mill (see Radwanski 1978). Liberty, or more particularly the primacy of individual freedom, was one of the most important themes of both thinkers and John Stuart Mill was perhaps the first in his time to make arguments for the value of diversity that extended very obviously to the cultural realm. It is surprising that so little recognition has been given to the link between this philosophical tradition and Canadian multiculturalism.[5]

In France, multiculturalism as an approach to integration or even as a declaration about the nature of society does not exist. In fact, the mere mention of the word causes the French to cringe with visions of '*communautarisme*', societal fragmentation and American ghettos. A 2006 study by Sylvain Brouard and Vincent Tiberj reinforces the notion that multiculturalism lacks currency in France: only 8 percent of the French electorate can be considered 'multiculturals' who support diversity in both the public and private spheres, 28 percent are republican who support diversity in just the private sphere, and 59 percent are 'assimilationists' who believe immigrants should abandon their differences completely and be just like the French.[6] Also, when asked in the same study whether promoting cultural differences between the French or insisting on what the French have in common was

3   As cited in *Essential Trudeau*, ed. Ron Graham, Toronto: McClelland and Stewart 1998.

4   The online version of *On Liberty* used in this paper is at http://www.bartleby.com. heir posted version is from London: Longman, Roberts & Green 1869.

5   For the purposes of this Canada-France comparison, multiculturalism can be defined as the promotion, recognition and acceptance of diversity and its expression in both the public and private spheres of society. Of course, multiculturalism arguably means much more than this in the Canadian context.

6   A fourth category labeled 'worried or insecure protesters' (*protestataires anxieux*), was more difficult to define and comprised four percent of the sample. Interestingly, the percentage distribution across the four groups changed rather substantially after the fall 2005 riots outside Paris. Before the riots, the percentages were 36 percent for the *républicains*, 46 percent for the *assimilationnists*, ten percent for the *multiculturels* and eight percent for the *protestataires anxieux*.

more important, 62 percent indicated that the latter was more important.[7] France's constitution neither makes reference to the value of diversity, nor provides for its recognition. In fact, the French claim their constitution prohibits the recognition of diversity by virtue of Article 1 (4 October 1958), which states "France shall be an indivisible, secular [*laïque*], democratic and social Republic".[8] However, it is not immediately obvious to a non-French reader how what is stated in Article 1 would prohibit the recognition of diversity. A deeper understanding of France's political culture and philosophical tradition is required. For example, the idea that France is indivisible is not about succession but rather, about France's understanding of the political community, the people as a collectively, as well as solidarity, and goes hand in hand with the French conception of equality. I submit that the present day understanding of several fundamental concepts in French political culture, such as liberty, equality and community, can be found in Jean-Jacques Rousseau's *The Social Contract, Or Principles of Political Right* of 1762. There is probably no other single philosopher who has influenced French thought in these regards more than Jean Jacques Rousseau. Further, an understanding of these fundamental concepts leads to a better understanding of France's approach to diversity today.[9]

Why does one country embrace, even encourage diversity, especially in the public sphere, while another rejects it.[10] Following the Robinson chapter, one may be inclined to argue this involves various foundational conceptions of a meaningful life. Suffice it to say, questions of this nature can clearly not be answered without looking at the political cultures and philosophical traditions in which they are embedded. In this chapter I shall use the works of Rousseau and John Stuart Mill as heuristic devices to demonstrate a different understanding in the two political cultures of the meaning of liberty, equality and community, and that these differences in understanding of these concepts leads to two very different approaches to the

---

7 The study by Sylvain Brouard and Vincent Tiberj of CEVIPOF (Centre de recherches politiques de Sciences Po in Paris) is called '*Le Baromètre Politique Français (2006–2007), Troisième vague – Hiver 2006. Les Tensions autour de l'immigration dans l'opinion : crispation et polarisation*'.

8 All translations of the French constitution have been taken from the website of the *Présidence de la République de France*. These are not always the best translations but are adequate. They are available on the web at: http://www.elysee.fr/elysee/anglais/the_institutions/founding_texts/the_1958_constitution/the_1958_constitution.20245.html; Also, the French word *laïque* has been retained because while "secular" is the best English translation of the word, it does not adequately describe the French concept. The meaning will become clearer as one proceeds through this work.

9 The translation of *The Social Contract* used in this paper was undertaken by G.D.H. Cole http://www.constitution.org/jjr/socon.htm.

10 What constitutes the public sphere in concept, let al.one as a matter of fact, varies from one country to another. In this work, 'public sphere' refers to the state and its institutions, so as to be comparable with the French usage. However, one has to consider, that compared to Canada, the long arm of the French state makes for a much larger public sphere than what exists in Canada.

management of diversity. It will be argued that multiculturalism in Canada is an outcome of British liberal philosophy, of the ideas of John Stuart Mill in particular, and it is unlikely that multiculturalism could have been successfully marketed in Canada without the understanding of the ideas of liberty, equality and community, that most Canadians share. It is similarly argued that the French understanding of these concepts, rooted in the philosophical works of Rousseau, renders a French marketing strategy of multiculturalism difficult, if not impossible, to conceive.

Liberty

John Stuart Mill's primary concern in *On Liberty* was the encroachment of the liberal state on the freedom of individuals to live their lives as they saw fit. He was equally concerned about the tyranny of public opinion on diversity, whether it be diversity of opinion, beliefs or ways of living. His problematic was how to maximize personal freedom. His maxim of a meaningful life was that individuals should be free to live their lives as they wish, to do as they want, as long as they do not cause harm to others. To Mill's way of thinking, as to Trudeau's, individuality and diversity are to be valued and cultivated as social goods that guard against mediocrity, promote innovation and progress, and ensure good democratic government. This is the philosophy behind Trudeau's remarks in the *House of Commons* on 8 October 1971 when Canada's policy of multiculturalism was introduced:

> A policy of multiculturalism within a bilingual framework commends itself as the most suitable means of assuring the cultural freedom of Canadians ... out of this can grow respect for that of others and a willingness to share ideas, attitudes and assumptions ... In conclusion, I wish to emphasize the view of the government that a policy of multiculturalism ... is basically the conscious support of individual freedom of choice. We are all free to be ourselves. But this cannot be left to chance. It must be fostered and pursued actively. If freedom of choice is in danger for some ethnic groups, it is in danger for all. It is the policy of this government to eliminate any such danger and to 'safeguard' this freedom (Government of Canada 1971, 8545).

John Stuart Mill's understanding of freedom is referred to in literature as negative liberty, in the spirit of Isaiah Berlin's path breaking essay, *Two Types of Liberty*.[11] It can also be referred to as a libertarian or liberal (as in liberalism) conception of freedom. Negative liberty is the freedom one has to act, think or behave, without state interference. This understanding is reflected in Section 1 of the *Canadian*

---

11   Freedom and liberty are used synonymously in this chapter. While a distinction could be made between the two in English, it would not be of much use since only one word exists in French to denote the two concepts.

Charter of Rights and Freedoms wherein it states that the *Charter* 'guarantees the rights and freedoms set out in it, subject only to such reasonable limits prescribed by law as can be demonstrably justified in a free and democratic society'. In other words, the state must prove that the requested limitation is an important and pressing enough social problem to override a constitutionally protected freedom or right and that the restriction it proposes is reasonable for the problem at hand, and demonstrably justifiable. To John Stuart Mill's way of thinking, the state is the enemy of freedom. An example where the Canadian state has been successful in restricting a constitutional freedom would be in the creation of a category of crime called 'hate' in Canadian law, which limits freedom of speech/expression.

Trudeau's ideas about cultural freedom, expressed in Canada's multicultural policy, would also fall within the definition of negative freedom, as long as the state's efforts to safeguard them do not constitute interference. One such mechanism for safeguarding cultural and religious freedom in Canada is the concept of reasonable accommodation, which has arisen in Canadian law as a natural corollary to the right to equality. Reasonable accommodation "attempts to break from the trend of promulgating the norms of the majority as the dominating values in Canadian society" (Barnett 2006, 6). John Stuart Mill would have been pleased because one of his concerns in *On Liberty* was the tyranny of the majority. The Canadian courts have ruled that Sikh students have the right to carry a *kirpan* in public schools despite school policies that ban knives from school premises, Sikhs also have the right to wear turbans as part of the Royal Canadian Mounted Police uniform and students in public schools have the right to wear the headscarf or any other type of religious head covering, provided there is no issue of safety involved (see Barnett 2006 for other examples).

The French, following in the footsteps of Rousseau, have what Berlin (1958) refers to as a positive conception of liberty. This understanding of liberty, alien to Canadian political culture, is also referred to as the Republican conception. Basically, positive liberty, especially the Republican or Rousseauean conception, refers to the ability to participate in the decision-making of the nation as citizens, in the formation of the general will. The general will, in turn is the common interest (which is not simply the sum of private wills), what the people collectively will for the common good, which, in the end, is the law. This latter idea is echoed in Article 6 of the *Declaration of the Rights of Man and of the Citizen* of 1789, "Law is the expression of the general will".[12]

Freedom for Rousseau is also obeying the laws that individuals have collectively made, as he states, "[w]e might, over and above all this, add, to what man acquires in the civil state, moral liberty, which alone makes him truly master of himself; for the mere impulse of appetite is slavery, while obedience to a law which we prescribe to ourselves is liberty" (Rousseau 1762, I, viii). Further: "[w]hoever refuses to obey the general will shall be compelled to do so by the entire body; this

---

12   The Declaration of the Rights of Man and of the Citizen of 1789 will hereafter be referred to as simply 'the Declaration'.

means nothing less than that he will be forced to be free; for this is the condition which, by giving each citizen to his country, secures him against all dependence" (Rousseau 1762, I, vii). Giving each to his country refers to Rousseau's idea of what happens when man moves from the state of nature through a real or imagined social contract to civilized society. What is important to understand is that for Rousseau, it is through belonging to the Republic, and through interaction with fellow citizens that man transforms himself, self-actualises; and one of the greatest threats to freedom for Rousseau is personal dependence. The state is therefore an instrument of liberation and independence. It is not only France's conception of freedom but also France's welfare state that is rooted in these Rousseauean ideas.

While the explicit grounds in the *Canadian Charter* for limiting liberty are whether the state can justify it in a free and democratic society, in the French context, the explicit grounds for limiting certain rights and freedoms, religious expression in particular, is public order.[13] As Article 10 of the *Declaration* states, "[n]o one shall be disquieted on account of his opinions, including his religious views, provided their manifestation does not disturb the public order established by law". However, it would appear that what is meant by public order is not only security but also the moral order and this can be gleaned from the discussions, court rulings and ultimately, the ban on wearing the Islamic head scarf in public schools in France (see Stasi 2003 and *Haut Conseil à l'Intégration* 2000, 58). In this case, the moral order established by law in need of protection can be defined as *laïcité*. One of the central laws establishing *laïcité* in France is the *Law of 1905 Concerning the Separation of Churches and the State*; along with Article 10 of the *Declaration*, cited above; the preamble of the French constitution of 1946, to be discussed shortly; and Article 1 of the constitution of 4 October 1958 cited in the introduction to this chapter[14] (see Baubérot 2007 for a more thorough discussion of the legal basis and understanding of *laïcité* in France). Among other things, these legal instruments establish the obligation of the state to be neutral with regard to religion; to start with, this means that the state can not recognize any religion in the public sphere, and it will be blind to religion in the private sphere, provided any given religious practise is in keeping with the laws of the land and the principle of tolerance. However, it is through various court

---

13   What is meant here is that public order is not explicitly mentioned in the Canadian Charter as grounds for limiting freedoms. However, public order, along with safety, health, public morals or the fundamental rights and freedoms of others are limiting factors considered by Canadian courts in cases having to do with religious freedoms (as outlined in the Supreme Court decision of *R. v. Big M Drug Mart Ltd.*). Also, public order does not have the same prominence in Canadian law when it comes to religious expression, as it does in French law (see Barnett 2006).

14   Article 1 of the French Constitution (5 October 1958), which is discussed again in more detail in the section of this work entitled '*Community*', stipulates that France shall be a *laïque* Republic. However, this Article does not define what it might mean for the state to be *laïque*. That understanding comes from interpretations on the part of the Courts.

rulings that the meaning of state neutrality has been established and the definition of state neutrality that has emerged over the years requires that the state and its institutions not only act neutrally, but also appear to be neutral in concrete terms (see Stasi 2003 for a list of some of these court rulings). It is this strict definition that has lead to the banishment of the headscarf (and other religious signs) from the state, its institutions and its employees; and more recently, from students in public schools.[15] This leads one to suspect that the state's actions in these regards, particularly with regard to the new law that bans headscarves and other religious signs from state schools, should be understood in the context of Rousseau's state guarding the general will, the interests which all citizens share in common. Support for this notion can be found in *The Secular Principle* by Jean Baubérot, France's foremost expert on the history and sociology of *laïcité* in France, wherein he states: " … the French notion of secularity appears as a means of grounding the social bond in values recognized as universal … The essential point is that secularity is to be understood as a particular way of embodying shared values" (Baubérot 2007, 1). Indeed, according to Charlot (2000), the idea of *laïcité* in its historic form, has its origins in the definition of the general will advanced by Rousseau.

One might be tempted to think that *laïcité* takes precedence over religious freedom in France upon learning that employees of the state are, in effect, strongly discouraged from wearing headscarves or other forms of religious dress to work, especially given that the Preamble of the French constitution (27 October 1946) states "[n]o person may suffer prejudice in his work or employment by virtue of his origin, opinions or beliefs".[16] However, as the Stasi Report states many times throughout, *laïcité* is what makes religious freedom possible. It is the absence of religion in the public sphere that allows for religious freedom in the private sphere (Baubérot 2005). This makes sense upon recognizing that the French state has elected to have a public sphere (the state and its institutions) devoid of religion or religious expression rather than impose a state religion; and clearly the French Republic's history of struggle with the Catholic Church and its successful efforts to overthrow its privileged status and influence would explain the French Republic's

---

15   See the *Report of the Commission of Reflection on the Application of Laïcité in the Republic (La commission de réflexion sur l'application du principe de laïcité dans la République)*, known as the Stasi Report, which was submitted to the President of the Republic on 11 December 2003, for an understanding of why the Commission recommended a law banning the wearing the headscarf and other religious signs by students in state schools in France. The ban became law on 15 March 2004 with the passage of the Law on the Secularity and Conspicuous Religious Behaviours and Symbols in Schools.

16   Section 2.2.1 (Neutrality of the State) of the Stasi Report discusses "the duty of strict neutrality" on the part of state officials and the public service – reinforcing the decisions of the Conseil d'Etat (from the 1950s). The section writes: "All manifestations of religious beliefs in the public service are forbidden and the wearing of religious symbols as well, even if the officers are not in contact with the public."

choice about religion in this regard.[17] However, one can turn to Rousseau for an explanation as well. Rousseau objected to the idea of religion within the state and its institutions because he believed it divided the community, enslaved man and distracted man from this world and the business of the state, i.e. good citizenship. Rousseau was after all, trying to find the type of political community or association that would protect the individual, secure rights and freedoms, and yet, allow individuals the freedom accorded in a state of nature, i.e. before a social contract brought him into a Republic. What Rousseau proposed instead of a state religion or instead of religion within the state, was a civil religion: "[t]here is therefore a purely civil profession of faith of which the Sovereign should fix the articles, not exactly as religious dogmas, but as social sentiments without which a man cannot be a good citizen or a faithful subject" (Rousseau 1762, IV, viii). What Rousseau is essentially proposing here is what the French Republic came to produce, and that is, the *Declaration of the Rights of Man and of the Citizen* of 1789. One can also see the roots of French *laïcité* in Rousseau's thoughts on this subject:

> The subjects then owe the sovereign an account of their opinions only to such an extent as they matter to the community … the dogmas of that religion concern the state and its members only so far as they have reference to morality and to the duties, which he who professes them is bound to do to others. Each man may have, over and above, what opinions he pleases, without it being the Sovereign's business to take cognisance of them; for, as the sovereign has no authority in the other world, whatever the lot of its subjects may be in the life to come, that is not its business, provided they are good citizens in this life (Rousseau 1762, IV, viii).

Canada has never experienced the degree of social and political turmoil created by religion that France has; conflicts between church and state were relatively resolved in Europe by the time Canada came into being. This helps explain why there is no constitutional provision in Canada that officially separates church and state. The church has traditionally played a large role in the public sphere in Canada (as it has in France). In fact, as pointed out in the Robinson chapter, in jurisdictions such as the Province of Ontario, the state funds both a public school system and a separate Catholic school system. God is even mentioned in the Preamble of Canada's 'modern' Charter. Canada is founded on principles that recognize the supremacy of God and the rule of law; though it remains to be seen whether this inclusion for the benefit of the Catholic electorate will ever amount to anything more than symbolism. The Bible still has a presence in Canadian courts and even in the federal public service as part of any oath of allegiance, though often alternatives can be used, such as the Koran. In fact, "public schools are the only

---

17   France, like Canada, does have state holidays related to major Christain observances. Interestingly, the Stasi Report of 2003 recommends that state holidays be designated for the major observances of other religions.

place in which it has been clearly determined by the courts and through legislation that religion can not be present in any institutionalised form" (Barnett 2006, 6). This does not include the religious dress of students, should they so choose, as a number of court rulings and the principle of reasonable accommodation have made clear. While the French have a very strict understanding of state neutrality with respect to religion, in Canada, state neutrality is merely an indirect obligation stemming from the guarantees of religious freedoms and freedom of conscience set out in the *Canadian Charter.* This allows for a Canadian approach to religion that promotes multiculturalism "by celebrating the expression of various religions while recognizing the supremacy of none" (Barnett 2006, 5) or, by recognizing all, as opposed to the French approach of recognizing none. The weak sense of state neutrality and the fuzziness between religion and the state in Canada has allowed this secular society more freedom of religious expression in the public sphere than in France.

The type of liberty that Rousseau refers to (positive) pertains to the public sphere, or to man as citizen. It would be misleading to not point out that French political culture also has an understanding of the negative conception of liberty, and this is what confuses many outsiders. As proof of the negative conception, Article 4 of France's *Declaration* states: "[l]iberty consists in the freedom to do everything that injures no one else; hence the exercise of the natural rights of each man has no limits except those which assure to the other members of the society the enjoyment of the same rights. These bounds may be determined only by Law". This sounds very much like John Stuart Mills' conception of freedom. Article 5 of France's *Declaration* is perhaps even closer to John Stuart Mill's conception when it states "[t]he Law has the right to forbid only those actions that are injurious to society. Nothing that is not forbidden by Law may be hindered, and no one may be compelled to do what the Law does not ordain". This is the conception of liberty that governs the private sphere in France, and as a number of French authors have pointed out, there has been a growth in France in the negative idea of liberty, in part as a result of the spread of consumerism and the expansion of the market. As Leterre relates, "[w]hat we are talking about here is a transformation of *la civitas* to an immense political market where one no longer mobilizes for the purposes of engagement in the public domain, but rather for the purposes of an immense 'each for himself/herself'" (Leterre 1997, 10; author's translation). There is obvious potential in France for tension or conflict over different conceptions of the meaningful or good life, and between the negative and positive conceptions of liberty, one anti-state, the other pro-state, translating into potential tension between France's dual tradition of liberalism and republicanism. The Stasi Report offers a good example of this tension in the context of freedom of religious expression and the state school system.

In short, in France, there are two understandings of liberty, one positive and the other negative, but the positive conception predominates in the public sphere. The positive conception relates to the ability to participate in the decision making of the nation, in the formation of the general will. It is through this participation that citizens self-actualize. In that, individual freedom, especially as it relates to religion, is theoretically relegated to the private sphere, and the boundary between the public and private spheres is sharp. This is how France guarantees religious freedom. Canada has primarily a negative conception of freedom, that is, individual freedom to do what one wants, as long as it does no harm to others. Especially since the implementation of the *Canadian Charter of Rights and Freedoms* and the *Canadian Multiculturalism Act*, the expression of diversity is allowed if not also promoted by the state, and the boundary between the public and private spheres is somewhat blurred, particularly where religion is concerned. This is in part because of a weaker or different conception of state neutrality in Canada and a fuzzy divide between church and state. As the next section demonstrates, these differences in the understanding of liberty (and secularity) are inextricably tied to different understandings of the community, which again have implications for the treatment of diversity, religious expression in particular, in the public sphere.

Community

True to John Stuart Mill, the public good in Canadian political culture is achieved through individuals freely choosing their own path in life and developing themselves and their individuality to the fullest, without state or community interference: "[i]t is not by wearing down into uniformity all that is individual in themselves, but by cultivating it and calling it forth, within the limits imposed by the rights and interests of others [that] human beings become a noble and beautiful object of contemplation ... by the same process [human beings] become rich, diversified, and animating, furnishing more abundant aliment to high thoughts and elevating feelings, and strengthening the tie which binds every individual to the race, by making the race infinitely better worth belonging to' (Mill 1869, III, v). The state's role is to foster an environment where this can occur and to interfere only when the rights or well being of others are hampered. It follows that the common good in Canadian political culture is the aggregate of individual interests and the community is the sum of the individuals that compose it.

In traditional French political culture, the conception of community, reflected in the writings of Rousseau, renders the individual's existence somewhat tenuous. As Sabine (1937) explains, for Rousseau: "[h]uman beings must be made citizens before they can be made men, but in order that they may be citizens, governments must give liberty under the law, must provide for material welfare and must create a system of public education by which children are 'accustomed to regard their individuality only in its relation to the body of the state'" (Sabine 1937, 58). This understanding of the community is reflected in Article 1 of the French constitution (4 October 1958) wherein it states that France shall be a social Republic. In French political culture, as in the writings of Rousseau, individuals are social beings who learn to conceive of their individuality in relation to the community and who are "forced to transcend the self" to universalise themselves (see Froese 2001). It is through this process of transcendence that one arrives at the common good, the community, the universal republican, a point Dominique Schnapper has made on several occasions (e.g. Schnapper 2000 and 2002) to explain the Republican model of integration or citizenship. In fact, the idea of universality is rooted in Rousseau's very meaning of the word Republic (see Rousseau 1762, II, vi). Thus, French political culture, the common good and the community can all be seen as being beyond the sum of the individual interests and beyond the sum of the individuals who compose it.

Article 1 of the 1958 French constitution also states that France shall be an indivisible Republic. This notion goes hand-in-hand with notions of transcendence and universality: "[e]ach of us places his person and all his power in common under the supreme direction of the general will; and as one we receive each member as an indivisible part of the whole" (Rousseau 1762, I, vi). Sovereignty, like Rousseau's general will, is similarly indivisible: "[s]overeignty, for the same reason as makes it inalienable, is indivisible; for will either is, or is not, general; it is the will either of the body of the people, or only of a part of it. In the first case, the will, when declared, is an act of Sovereignty and constitutes law: in the second, it is merely a particular will, or act of magistracy — at the most a decree" (Rousseau 1762, II, ii). The link between Rousseau's neutral state, unable to recognize the diversity of its members, and his indivisible community, is probably nowhere more explicit than when he states "the Sovereign recognizes only the body of the nation, and draws no distinctions between those of whom it is made up" (Rousseau 1762, II, iv). Rousseau's ideas about partial associations or partial societies are also closely connected to his idea about the indivisible community; for Rousseau, partial associations or partial societies pose a serious threat to freedom because they divide the body politic and therefore impede the formation of the general will. Ethnic communities within the state are viewed as a type of partial society in French political culture.

The corollary of an indivisible body politic is majority rule; and here is another point at which John Stuart Mill and Rousseau as well as Canada and France depart. For John Stuart Mill, majority rule brings with it the potential for a tyranny of the majority. Granted Rousseau is able to escape this problem in theory with his quasi-metaphysical concept of the general will, i.e. one is obeying the laws that he/she made as a 'universal republican' in support of the general will. However this tyranny is not as easy to escape at the level of *praxis*. True to John Stuart Mill's idea that government should guard against the tyranny of the majority, the Canadian state has been founded on one of the two options that John Stuart Mill proposed to avoid this type of tyranny; that is federalism (John Stuart Mill's other option was a proportionate representation of minorities). In Canadian political culture, as for John Stuart Mill, the political community cannot be regarded as an undifferentiated whole because it is believed that true democracy would not be best served in this way. In French political culture, as for Rousseau, the body politic must be indivisible if it is to be Republican, if there is to be a general will, if there is to be positive freedom, and to the extent negative freedom depends on positive freedom, if there is to be any freedom at all. The implications for the acceptance and recognition of diversity in the public sphere, of these two different political cultures, are obvious.

Given the foregoing, one has to surmise that the French have what could be termed a strong conception of community. It is not simply something that arises out of individuals expressing their individuality free from constraints by the state, but rather, something that exists independent of, if not also prior to, the individual, i.e. human beings must be made citizens before they can be made men. However, the relationship between individuality and the conception of the political community in France is fragile as far as liberty is concerned. Too much individuality and not enough conformity would jeopardize liberty in that citizens would no longer be able to universalise themselves, which is to say, to generate the general will out of the common interest. Too much individuality would require too much of Rousseau's "forcing people to be free". This is what Neidleman (2001, 37) means when he asserts that "Rousseauean democracy cannot be libertarian" because if people were to live as they pleased, "they would imperil the conditions for self-government" and "without a sense of shared purpose, people inevitably slip into relationships of dependence that undermine freedom". For these types of reasons, the Republic tends towards cultural homogenisation. As Dieckhoff explains, "citizenship is, in theory, a principle to overcome concrete 'marker'. Yet, its full realization requires, in the framework of classic republicanism, a strong cultural homogenisation of the public space. In fact, starting from the moment where true liberty consists of active participation in political deliberations, the mutual understanding between citizens must be maximal and demands therefore the formation of a uniform cultural foundation" (Dieckhoff 2000, 163; author's translation). In fact, "self-government, which requires a community of citizens able to make decisions about what is best for the Republic, that are at the same time in the best interests of each individual making those decisions, is more important in France than the greatest personal liberty possible since in France, democracy does not have as its objective to ensure in the absolute, the greatest personal liberty possible. Its ultimate goal is to form a community of citizens, essentially in the political sense of the term" (Crozet *et al.* 2000, 342; author's translation). These ideas are echoed in the Stasi Report, in the section on 'defending' public services, in particular, the schools, where the main discussion is about the Muslim head scarf; in this section, the report states that after having heard the position of various people, the Commission estimates that "it is no longer a question of liberty of conscience, but of public order" (see Stasi 2003, 58). Schnapper (2002) reveals that there is an historical context to the primacy of the political community in France when she relates that France discovered democracy first, and then liberty, while the English discovered liberty first, and then democracy.

Thus the French conception of the community places constraints on the ability of the state to recognize diversity in the public sphere, particularly religious diversity, and therefore, to exercise individual liberty in the public sphere. In fact, the recognition of religious diversity would jeopardize the community and liberty, as these concepts are understood in France; and it would go against *laïcité* as a fundamental value of the Republic. In fact, from a variety of angles, the political philosophy behind the French Republic seems to be premised on a need for cultural homogenisation; *laïcité* is neither the sole issue nor the sole explanation. In the Canadian context, the recognition of diversity goes hand in hand with Canadian concepts of liberty and community; diversity is a social good that ensures good government through keeping discussion open about what is good and what is right, and its recognition and accommodation in the public sphere protects against the tyranny of the majority. Though the Canadian understanding of the political community has the potential to produce what the French often refer to as a *de facto* fragmented and weak community, it allows for a maximum of possibilities of what the community can be through allowing, to the maximum, the development and expression of the individuality and diversity of its members. Furthermore, the potential for fragmentation inherent in the Canadian conception (*communautarisme* in French parlance) relates not to the Canadian orientation towards diversity per se, but rather to the Canadian conception of the community in general, i.e. a community that consists of the sum of the individuals who compose it, which is the basis of the philosophy of individualism. France, with its strong concept of the community, does not allow for as much exploration into what the community could be, especially where the expression of diversity in the public sphere is concerned, religious diversity in particular, and risks implosion should it fail to indoctrinate a sufficient number of its members into sharing that common conception of the community. I would suggest that it was in the interest of reinforcing this shared conception of the community that the 15 March 2004 law on secularity was premised.[18]

Equality

The last essential piece of the puzzle to understanding differences between the French and Canadian approaches to diversity or why multiculturalism is acceptable to one, but not the other is differing concepts of equality. Article 1 of the 1958 French constitution makes reference to equality; it states that France "shall ensure the equality of all citizens before the law without distinction of origin, race or religion". Article 1 of the *Declaration* similarly states "[m]en are born and remain free and equal in rights. Social distinctions may be based only on considerations of the common good". Section 15 (1) of the Canadian *Charter* would appear to be proclaiming a similar idea: "[e]very individual is equal before and under the law and has the right to the equal protection and equal benefit of the law without discrimination and, in particular, without discrimination based on race, national or ethnic origin, colour, religion, sex, age or mental or physical disability". However, equality in the French context refers to a strict and formal notion of equality found in classical liberal thought – it is the idea of equal treatment regardless of

18   See footnote 15.

circumstances. It is an abstract conception that does not take into account socio-economic inequalities as discussed in Reiss' or Hasmath's chapter. In application, the French concept is rigid – all must be treated the same. This long-standing understanding of equality in France can in part be explained by the enduring influence of the French Revolution; the revolution sought to overthrow all forms of privilege (see Neidleman 2001). Also, without this abstract conception of equality, the indivisible and undifferentiated character of the French community would not be theoretically possible; after all, concrete inequalities do exist in France, just as they do in Canada. In this regard, the French often associate equality with the idea of *universalism*; equality is a universal principle that must be applied to all citizens equally. This equal application ensures a community with equal rights, again, at least in theory. These ideas can be seen in the following passage from Rousseau: "[f]rom whatever side we approach our principle, we reach the same conclusion, that the social compact sets up among citizens an equality of such a kind, that they all bind themselves to observe the same conditions and therefore should enjoy the same rights" (Rousseau 1762, II, iv).

The French conception of equality is also closely associated with *laïcité;* as Baubérot points out, *laïcité* "ensures complete equality of citizens in matters of belief and freedom of conscience" (Baubérot 2007, 1). In fact, according to the *Haut Conseil à l'Intégration's* 2000 report concerning *Islam in France*, the exclusion of religious expression on the part of Muslim employees in the public service is justified on the basis of the relationship between *laïcité* and *égalité*, in other words, the obligation of each public official to be neutral with regard to his or her beliefs is justified by the necessity of ensuring equality of treatment of all users of the public service (*Haut Conseil à l'intégration* 2000, 57). These ideas are also expressed in the Stasi Report, and interestingly, one of the reasons for the Stasi Commission's recommendation to implement a law banning the wearing of the headscarf and other religious signs in state schools, was the concern for sexual equality.[19]

The Canadian concept of equality was once quite similar to the classical liberal conception. However, it began to change in the late 1970s when it became obvious that the model of labour market access, promotion and competition was based on the biological and social realities of men and that this model disadvantaged women in the work force. Contradictions inherent in the classical conception also emerged through the civil rights movement in the United States and also influenced Canadian thought. In other words, contradictions between the classical idea of equality and just and fair treatment surfaced at this time. By the time the *Canadian*

---

19   Another reason behind this recommendation was the belief that a law banning headscarves in state schools would remove the pressure that some Muslim public school children wearing the headscarf exerted on other Muslim public school children who chose not to wear it. Such pressure was clearly already against French law, but difficult to ascertain, as well as contrary to the French manner of ensuring freedom of religious conscience in the public sphere (see Weil 2004).

Charter of Rights and Freedoms was being crafted, a new idea of equality had solidified in Canada. Equity emerged as a concept embodying the idea that in order to treat some people or groups fairly (e.g. women and people of colour, the latter of which came to be designated as visible minorities) it sometimes means treating them differently rather than the same. The idea of equality of outcomes or condition emerged. Substantive equality soon gained social and legal currency, necessitating a taking into account of differences between social groups in the law, policies and activities in order to avoid prejudicial effects on individual members of those groups. Article 15 (2) of the Canadian Charter provided some legitimacy to this line of thinking when it rendered affirmative action (employment equity) programs legal: "[s]ubsection 1 does not preclude any law, program or activity that has as its object the amelioration of conditions of disadvantaged individuals or groups including those that are disadvantaged because of race, national or ethnic origin, colour, religion, sex, age or mental or physical disability". However, this newfound idea of equality has, in many respects, merely replaced one idea of procedural equality with another. While employment equity programs had the promise of leading to something more, it has yet to be demonstrated that they actually help 'disadvantaged' *individuals* from the groups enumerated in Section 15. In the Canadian legal context, the disadvantaged are individuals or groups who encounter or are assumed to encounter discrimination because of their difference (disadvantage due to social class is not considered). It would seem that employment equity programs might provide 'advantage' to middle class individuals who have the educational qualifications for the labour market to begin with (and educational attainment is and always has been highly correlated with social class). To the extent this is true, employment equity programs could be reinforcing existing class based inequalities between ethno-racial groups in Canada. It is also difficult to know whether Canada's reconceptualization of equality has had an impact on the nature of its cultural mosaic, in part because of Canada's emphasis on discrimination in dealing with diversity issues to the exclusion of questions of social class.[20]

---

20   Since Canada institutionalized its newly found ideas about equality, there have been very obvious improvements in the socio-economic status of francophones and in the labour market equality of women in Canada. Part of the difficulty in answering the question with respect to 'non-Charter' ethno-racial groups (non-Aboriginal, non-British and non-French) is the continuous change in the nature of immigration flows to Canada in terms of ethno-racial composition, social class and education levels; this makes comparisons of the 'performance' of various ethno-racial groups, especially across cross-sectional generational data, difficult to determine. Another reason is the emphasis in Canadian research on labour market discrimination, using the earnings of various diversity groups, controlling for education, age, knowledge of English/French and other relevant variables (which, as a side point, produce less than satisfactory conclusions because of inadequate measures of actual labour market experience and language capabilities) rather than equality of social or socio-economic status (which can be guaged by social distance data; and a decriptive analysis of the earnings, income and educational attainment of various ethno-racial groups).

Current Canadian ideas about equality as they relate to diversity are alien to French political culture and in direct opposition to the French conception of equality. However, the idea of equality in outcome or condition, *albeit*, without explicit recognition of individual characteristics related to race, religion, culture and the likes, is not foreign to French thought and gained new life in the 1996 annual report of *le Conseil d'État* under the label of *'discrimination justifiée'*. On a territorial basis, such as in priority education zones and sensitive urban zones, problems of equal opportunity related to race, religion or culture are dealt with as social class issues (see De Rudder and Poiret 1999 and Schnapper 2000). As Schnapper (2000) explains, "the republican universal is today strongly corrected by the policies of the welfare state, in the largest sense of the word. It brings a necessary correction to the perverse effects of the republican universal. But the values that the latter implies; namely, the equal dignity of all individuals and the equality of their civil, legal and political rights beyond their diversities and inequalities, can remain only an organizing principle of collective life in democratic societies" (Schnapper 2000, 21; author's translation). In other words, France has its ways of dealing with inequality. Indeed, France might have more concern for inequality than Canada. The difference is that the French state, required to be blind to religion and to a lesser extent national origins and the likes in order to ensure equal treatment for all, deals with problems of inequality through social class. Canada, in focusing on problems of inequality related to diversity, especially race, i.e. visible minorities, including Aboriginal peoples, tends to be blind to the social class origins of the 'diversity' issues it seeks to solve.

Conclusion

French concepts of liberty, equality and above all, community that evolved out of the French Revolution and that are clearly articulated in the works of Jean Jacques Rousseau, have shaped a particular French approach to diversity. The French approach is not conducive to the acceptance of diversity in the public sphere because liberty (defined as the freedom to be an active member of the political community and hinged on the ability to see oneself reflected in the general will), equality (in the context of a community of indivisible and equal citizens) and the community itself would be jeopardized. With the core of French identity resting on these particular notions, France cannot simply graft Canadian multiculturalism onto its approach to diversity. Canadian ideas of liberty, equality and community, reflecting to a great extent the ideas of John Stuart Mill, have shaped a different approach to diversity, involving respect for, recognition of, and promotion of difference in the public sphere. Both countries' approaches to diversity are a reflection of their respective political values, modes of political thought and

If the question is phrased in terms of the latter, the persistence of social and socioeconomic inequality for some groups in Canadian society is abundantly clear.

political traditions that are deeper than the topic of diversity. In this regard, the words of John Stuart Mill are fitting: "[t]he practical question, where to place the limit – how to make the fitting adjustment between individual independence and social control … No two ages, and scarcely any two countries have decided it alike; and the decision of one age or country is a wonder to another" (Mill 1869, I, iii). In Canada, multiculturalism has indeed been a great marketing strategy for the promotion of the value of diversity and has facilitated the acceptance of diversity in the public sphere and large-scale immigration to Canada. However, it was John Stuart Mill who did the marketing job long ago. In the case of France, there is no market for the idea of multiculturalism; *laïcité* has to be reinforced, the religious neutrality of the public sphere guarded, and expressions of diversity in the public sphere accepted only in small doses in order for the Rousseauean Republic to function without undue stress. The trade-off for the emphasis on sameness is an emphasis on equality of condition and on equality of civil, legal and political rights, beyond diversity, which the French Republic strives to achieve for all its citizens through a very generous '*état-providence*'.

References

Barnett, L. 2006. *Freedom of Religion and Religious Symbols in the Public Sphere.* Law and Government Division. Library of Parliament. Canada. Available at: http://www.parl.gc.ca/information/library/PRBpubs/prb0441–e.htm.

Baubérot, J. 2005. *La Crise de la Laïcité en France.* (*The Crisis of Secularity in France*). A presentation given at the Conference on The Principle of Secularity in France, Centre for Interdisciplinary Research on Citizenship and Minorities, the University of Ottawa, April 26, Ottawa, Canada.

Baubérot, J. 2007. *The Secular Principle.* Available at: http://www.ambafrance-uk.org/Secular-principle-PM-s-Office.html.

Berlin, I. 1958. *Two Types of Liberty.* Oxford: Oxford University Press.

Charlot, B. 2000. Violence à l'École: La Dimension 'Ethnique' du Problème. *L'Universel Républicain à l'Épreuve: Discrimination, Ethnicisation, Segregation.* (Violence at the School: The 'Ethnic' Dimension of the Problem in the Republican Universal Revisited: The Republican Universal to the Test: Discrimination, Ethnicization, Segregation). *VEI Enjeux* 121 (Juin): 178–89.

Crozet, Y., D. Bolliet, F. Fauvre and J. Fleury. 2000. *Les Grandes Questions de la Société Française.* (The Big Questions in French Society). Paris: Nathan.

Dasko, D. 2004. Public Attitudes Towards Multiculturalism and Bilingualism in Canada. *Canadian and French Perspectives on Diversity.* Strategic Policy and Management Branch. Department of Canadian Heritage. Ottawa, Canada. Available at: http://www.canadianheritage.gc.ca/pc-ch/pubs/diversity2003/dasko_e.cfm.

De Rudder, V. and C. Poiret. 1999. Affirmative Action et 'Discrimination Justifiée.' (Affirmative Action and 'Justified Discrimination'). In *Immigration et Intégration: l'État des Savoirs.* (Immigration and Integration: The State of Knowledge), ed. P. Dewitte, 397–406. Paris: Éditions La Découverte et Syros.

Dieckhoff A. 2000. *La Nation dans tous ses États: les Identités Nationales en Mouvement.* (*The Nation in all its States: National Identities in Movement*). Paris: Flammarion.

Froese, K. 2001. Beyond Liberalism: The Moral Community of Rousseau's Social Contract. *Canadian Journal of Political Science* 34(3): 579–600.

Government of Canada. 1971. *House of Commons Debates*, October 8, 8545–848. Mimeographed copy available at http://www.ethnocultural.ca/Text-4pages.html.

Haut Conseil à l'Intégration. 2000. *L'Islam dans la République.* (*Islam in the Republic*). November. Available at: http://www.ladocumentationfrancaise.fr/rapports-publics/014000017/index.shtml.

Leterre, T. 1997. La Naissance et les Transformations de l'Idée de Citoyenneté. (The Birth and Transformations in the Idea of Citizenship). *Cahiers français* 281(May-June). Paris: La Documentation Française.

Mill, J.S. 1859. *On Liberty.* Available at: http://www/bartleby.com/.

Neidleman, J.A. 2001. *The General Will Is Citizenship: Inquiries into French Political Thought.* NewYork: Rowan and Littlefield Publishers Inc.

Radwanski, G. 1978. *Trudeau.* Toronto: Macmillan.

Rousseau, J.J. 1762. *The Social Contract, Or Principles of Political Right.* Trans. G.D.H. Cole. Available at: http://www.constitution.org/jjr/socon.htm.

Sabine, G. 1937. *A History of Political Theory.* New York: Henry Holt and Company.

Schnapper, D. 2000. L'Universel Républicain Revisité. *L'Universel Républicain à l'Épreuve: Discrimination, Ethnicisation, Ségrégation* (The Republican Universal Revisited in the Republican Universal to the Test: Discrimination, Ethnicization, Segregation). *VEI Enjeux* 121 (June): 10–22. Available at: http://www.communautarisme.net/docs/universel-republicain-revisite.pdf.

Schnapper, D. 2002. *La Démocratie Providentielle: Essai sur l'Égalité Contemporaine.* (Democratic Welfare: An Essay on Contemporary Equality). Paris: Editions Gallimard.

Stasi. 2003. Rapport au Président de la République: Commission de Réflexion sur l'Application du Principe de Laïcité dans la République. (Report to the President of the Republic: The Commission of Reflection on the Application of the Principle of Secularity in the Republic). Submitted December 11. Available at: http://www.ladocumentationfrancaise.fr.

Weil, P. 2004. *A Nation in Diversity: France, Muslims and the Headscarf.* March 25. Available at: www.opendemocracy.com.

Chapter 5

Immigration, Race and the Crisis of National Identity in Canada

Suzanna Reiss

In 1967, the Canadian government threw a tremendous birthday party to commemorate the centennial of its confederation. Across the country exhibitions, tours, festivals, and the crowning event, the World Exposition, provided the opportunity to celebrate and define Canada's identity on an international stage. A government pamphlet released by the Centennial Commission insisted that "there is no Canadian type" and extolled the putative social cohesion underpinning Canada's diversity:

> Canada belongs to the twentieth century. It's a country of the future, a country
> where people of widely differing backgrounds and heritages have learned to live
> with each other, sharing only their common sense of diversity and their sense of
> the adventure of the land. (Centennial Commission 1967, 4)

This evaluation, picturesque in its optimism that Canada's diverse peoples had, in 1967, already "learned to live with each other" was challenged the same year when, due to changes in Canadian immigration policy, Canada began to experience an influx of immigrants from the former colonized countries of the British Commonwealth. The Centennial Commissions' optimistic gloss, however, can partially be attributed to the celebratory nature of the centennial and the pamphlet's immediate objective: to advertise, define and celebrate Canada's birthday. The centennial celebration was the symbolic culmination of a decade-long public effort of self-conscious, re-definition from Commonwealth to Canadian, from the Great White North divided by Franco and Anglo conflict to a multicultural country celebrating its unity in diversity. This Canadian nationalist renaissance grew in tandem with the worldwide success of national, anti-colonial movements that were transforming Canadian relations with the Caribbean, the radical implications of which emergent policies like multiculturalism sought to contain.

Hyperbole was par for the course, and in Toronto, Ontario fast becoming Canada's most multicultural city, headlines blared "Ontario Plans to Outdo World" with the largest performance at the World Exposition. The province paraded a 1,200 strong troupe, consisting of "singers, dancers, musicians and gymnasts" who represented "nearly all the ethnic groups in Ontario." Newspapers celebrated the show as "full of feeling", a celebration "to honor the people of so many backgrounds" who were taking the opportunity to show they were "proud of their province." While Ontario's delegation performed at the World Expo in Montreal, steel band musicians flown in for the Trinidad and Tobago pavilion, traveled in reverse migration by bus to Toronto. There, without rest and in the pouring rain, they performed before a crowd of eight thousand people who shouted "More! More!" as they "swung in the rain" (*Toronto Daily Star* 1967c and d).[1] In Toronto, August 1967, whose Caribbean population was becoming one of the largest visible minority populations in Canada, the crowds came out for carnival.

One year earlier, in preparation for the Centennial commemoration, the federal government encouraged "ethnic groups to come up with ideas to show how their cultures were contributing to the new Canada." A group of West Indian professionals formed the Caribbean Cultural Committee (CCC) and together decided a carnival would "best capture the spirit of the Caribbean" for the Canadian celebrations. Embracing the Canadian government's emphasis on diversity, they claimed a special role for the Caribbean which they saw as "perhaps the original testing ground for this concept of multiculturalism" given its blend of European, African, Asian and North American populations. Carnival, definitively multicultural, was thus especially appropriate to this new Canadian context. The name Caribana itself signified this fusion, "capturing the notions of Canada, the Caribbean, bacchanal and merrymaking."(Foster 1995, 19–22). And so, in Ontario, carnival came to the city of Toronto as the West Indian community's contribution to the national celebrations. Caribana, after two days, was labeled the "the event of the year." Attracting more than 50,000 people to Toronto's islands, extending festivities "by popular demand!" to include an additional weekend, and inspiring Toronto's Mayor William Dennison's suggestion that it become an annual affair, Caribana made an auspicious official debut (*Toronto Daily Star* 1967c, e and g). This paper historically situates expressions of nationalism and multiculturalism being performed at Caribana, as a window onto the larger, post-colonial negotiation of Canadian-West Indian relations in the context of ongoing domestic challenges to white Canadian hegemony.

Caribana '67 proved enormously successful, drawing vast crowds to the week-long festivities. From its first moments a vast and colorful parade featuring "West Indian costumes, steel bands, Calypso singing and pretty girls," attracted "merrymakers" who flocked to see the "authentic West Indian party." "Delightful chaos!" cried the *Globe and Mail*, a national newspaper, while the local *Toronto Star* marveled at an island-style, tropical atmosphere brought right home to Canada: "Calypso music drifted over the cool, green water and a warm breeze carried the sound of steel band and singing off into the summer night. A floating party in the Caribbean? Would you believe Toronto Harbour?" The week was filled with music, ferry cruises, balls, a beauty contest, and steel bands played at an open air

---

1   This research draws upon newspaper coverage from 1967 through 1980 including *The Toronto Daily Star*, *The Toronto Telegram*, *The Globe and Mail*, *West Indian News Observer*, its successor *Contrast*, *The Financial Post* and *Uhuru*.

market of Caribbean cuisine transforming Toronto's Center Island. "The colors rioted and swam and swarmed around the bandstands and any glumness stayed on the mainland," while "razzle-dazzle costumes flown in from Trinidad and carnival bands delighted startled Torontonians" (*Toronto Daily Star* 1967f).

Torontonians indulged in the fantasy and exotic colors of this "authentic West Indian" spectacle and confronted the transformative spirit behind the carnivalesque with a national dialogue emphasizing a static and non-threatening version of West Indian culture. In the relatively conservative *Toronto Telegram*, descriptions of Caribana emphasized color over content in a typical rendering of one scene: "Blue and Gold flags, women and men in beaded trousers, Islanders in top hats, tails and shorts, bands swinging in red, white and black silk shirts, shimmering neon dresses, floppy straw hats, feather headdresses, T-shirts with slogans." Nebulous slogans, blue, gold, red, white and black paraded before reader's eyes and perhaps, conveyed a sense of the saturnalia, but trivialized the political messages conveyed by the national colors of Barbados and Trinidad-Tobago. No mainstream newspaper mentioned Caribana was timed to coincide with the Independence Day celebrations of Trinidad and Tobago, and Jamaica. Yet, this synchronicity was more than arbitrary. Late twentieth century Carnival, with its origins in the usurpation of French Lenten celebrations by African slaves in the Caribbean, was, at a fundamental level, a symbol of freedom and contested control. "The gigantic party is a celebration of life, of culture, of freedom and, in part, of the [British] emancipation of black slaves in 1834" (*Equinox* 1987, 60). With the success of anti-colonial struggles in the 1960s, the concurrence of these Independence Day celebrations necessarily infused Caribana, for some, with a political conscience. Yet, the colorful, the foreign and the exotic in popular conversation folded numerous expressions of extra-Canadian nationalism into an apolitical, strictly "cultural" realm.

Caribana, for most, was undoubtedly a time to jump up and enjoy friends, music and the general revelry. However, Caribana was also an opportunity for political performance by Canadian and local government officials, and by the revelers alike. Promoting a positive image of national and international relations between Canada and the West Indies, Mayor William Dennison gave a Caribana "welcoming speech" in which he took the opportunity to make "amends" with the West Indian community by correcting his mispronunciation of Guyana which a few weeks earlier had "cost him unfavorable publicity" when greeting the Guyanese Prime Minister (*The Telegram* 1967). Other members of Toronto's political community also made appearances at Caribana. For one, Parks Commissioner Tommy Thompson was in attendance. It was reported that the commissioner "donned a Caribbean-style straw hat and did a solo dance before a cheering crowd ... After his dance, Thompson helped choose the Caribana beauty queen ... and to further cheers, danced with her." This entertainment-based diplomacy – indicative of the direction and meaning of a nascent Canadian "multiculturalism" – unfolded in the midst of competing expressions of nationalism evident among the diverse crowd. Thus, while steel bands played the national anthem "O Canada," entertaining the "happy throng," elsewhere a young "enthusiast ... leaped on stage to swing the flag of Trinidad high over his head in wild exuberance" (*The Toronto Daily Star* 1967c).

Colonies, Nations, Empires

Canadian and Caribbean nationalism extended beyond spontaneous eruptions from the Caribana crowd. They were reflections of ongoing struggles over sovereignty within Canada, within the Caribbean and in relations between the two; factors profoundly influencing the federal government's embrace of multiculturalism. In the context of British imperial decline, the rise of nationalist anti-colonial movements and Cold War imperial rivalries, Canada attempted to self-consciously transform itself from a British Commonwealth country to a Canadian nation in a hemisphere dominated by the growing global power and influence of the United States. Thus, the 1960s in Canada was a decade of intense involvement of government representatives, academics, journalists, foreign policy advisors and others to redefine the national identity. The "identity crisis" was a mainstream preoccupation, as one contemporary put it, "concern over finding herself [Canada] has become so much a part of today's Canadian folklore that it cannot easily be dismissed" (Leach 1967, 312). The Royal Commission on Bilingualism and Biculturalism's preliminary 1965 report on national discord declared: "Canada, without being conscious of the fact, is passing through the greatest [identity] crisis in its history" (Canada 1965, 13). While the Commission's original mandate was to address tensions between the English and French, ethnic groups that belonged to neither of the two "founding" cultures successfully pressured for their inclusion in the proceedings which ultimately led to a national policy of multiculturalism. While government commissions held hearings to determine how best to chart the future of the Canadian identity, the transformation from empire to nation was achieved symbolically with the 1965 adoption of the Maple Leaf flag, a new official Canadian flag to replace the British Union Jack.

Such symbolic gestures were accompanied by practical revisions in foreign policy and immigration law designed to usher in the new age. Canada, with its own colonial history, in many ways bridged the gap between the colonizer and colonized. Canada's identity crisis and heightened nationalism in the 1960s emerged out of ambivalence towards its own Commonwealth status and ongoing tensions between the English and French, the two "founding" nationalities in Canada. However, as a white and European colony (which itself colonized the indigenous populations) Canada – the "First World" role it assumed in relation to global capitalist expansion, immigration, tourism and development aid – was aligned with those of the great imperial powers; the United Kingdom and the United States. Therefore, Canadian sovereignty, demonstrations of independence from both British and American spheres of influence, found its most concentrated expression in an effort to usurp Britain's financial and political role in the former

Commonwealth Caribbean. Examining this evolving Canadian-West Indian relationship helps contextualize the emergence of multiculturalism policy and the competing political messages which infused Caribana's sonic and visual landscape.

Canada's interaction with the Caribbean long predated the dramatic transformations of the 1960s. While Canadian influence had been subject to British imperial strictures, there had been periodic efforts (from the 1890s to the 1920s) on the part of commercial interests to bring the West Indies into a political union with Canada. A group of Canadian financiers marketed the venture to white Canadians with national expansionist rhetoric bolstered by visions of acquiring a "Canadian back yard in the sun": Canada's territory should soon extend to "a great South as well as a great West," so that "Legislators ... from the smiling fields of Ontario and the ancient cities of the St. Lawrence ... shall sit in parliament with their fellow British-Canadians from the lands of perpetual summer" (Winks 1968, 16–19). However, these efforts were thwarted by both white racial fears on the Canadian continent, and, more significantly, by British imperial prerogative which refused to countenance any interference in the region which might raise tariff rates and weaken control over its colonies (Wigley 1988, 222–31).

Canada's Caribbean presence was shaped both by its historic relations with the UK and by the growth of US economic and political influence in the Caribbean. During World War Two, Canada became more involved in the region, bolstering British Imperial power there. The Canadian government sent "peacekeeping" troops to the Bahamas to protect the British Colonial Governor in the wake of rioting by black workers against British troops. The workers were protesting their low wages in relation to those being paid by Americans for military base construction (the troops remained from 1942–6). A Canadian military presence was also established regionally, including troops sent to British Guyana from 1942 to 1945 at the request of the Canadian owned mining company Alcan (Murray 1988, 280 and 289; Preston 1971, 314). US-British rivalry did not prevent collaboration between Canadian and American interests. Alcan was a subsidiary of an American mining company which extracted bauxite from the Caribbean in a joint venture between US and Canadian capital. Limited by British imperial structures, there was nevertheless extensive Canadian economic involvement in the Caribbean, often in conjunction with American commercial ventures. Private Canadian interests had, since the turn of the century, exported raw materials including petroleum, bauxite, oxide, aluminum, asphalt, cocoa, arrowroot, molasses and spices, while establishing an extensive banking and trading infrastructure in the Caribbean. By 1959, along with numerous other Canadian banks and commercial interests, the West Indies were home to some seventy-five branches of the Royal Bank of Canada (Quamina 1996, 82–3).

Under the British Imperial umbrella, from World War Two until the 1960s, Canada promoted its international role as the "honest broker, the fair minded middle power which could interpret French culture to English and English to French, Britain to the US and America to Britain, [and] the 'white Dominions' to the Colored Commonwealth'," while pursuing its own economic interests (Winks 1968, 7). By the 1960s, British decline and American growth prompted changes in Canadian foreign policy, fueled primarily by anxiety over American hegemony in the hemisphere. As candidly expressed by the Nobel Peace Prize winner, Canadian Prime Minister Lester Pearson in 1966:

> Today, a greater portion of Canada's resources and industrial production come under foreign – largely American – control than is the case with any other industrial country in the world … Our anxiety in these matters is perfectly natural. It is also increasing. (Leach 1967, 308–9)

These fears guided changes in foreign policy; the more passive strategy of "liberal internationalism" was replaced by a new policy of "Canadian Nationalism" which eschewed mediator status and worked to secure Canada's own economic influence (Mahler 1993, 79–81).

From the late 1950s onwards, unprecedented levels of Canadian investment were channeled into the Caribbean tourist industry; Air Canada added the Caribbean to its flight routes and Canadian interests monopolized the construction of Holiday Inns in the Bahamas, Antigua, St. Kitts, St. Lucia, Grenada, Barbados and Trinidad (Tennyson 1988, 18). Between 1951 and 1957, the number of Canadian tourists traveling to the region doubled and continued to rise through the end of the next decade. Canadian bankers guided economic restructuring of the newly independent states of Jamaica (1962), Trinidad and Tobago (1962), Guyana (1966), Barbados (1961 internal governance, full independence 1966) and the Bahamas (1964 internal governance, full independence 1973) (Tennyson 1988, 17). In 1964, 1966 and 1971 a series of Canadian development plans sought to stabilize faltering Caribbean economies in order to secure this "vacation area for sun-seeking Canadians." Along with tourists and aid came Canadian commodity exports which increased by 39.4 per cent (Preston 1971, 322–5; Winks 1968, 40–43). Historian Richard Leach's 1967 essay on "Contemporary Canada" articulated the ideological vision behind these initiatives: "The Caribbean member states of the Commonwealth have been of particular concern to Canada. She has begun to feel a special responsibility for them as Britain has found it necessary to abdicate her former imperial role" (Leach 1967, 311).

This "special responsibility" was being transformed into policy as Canada began to work more closely with a number of Caribbean heads of state. The "high water mark" of this relationship, according to a Canadian Member of Parliament, was a 1966 conference convened by the Canadian government with all West Indian Prime Ministers invited to attend. While officially hailed as "a new mile-stone" in Canadian-West Indian relations, the position of these leaders did not go unchallenged (Canada 1971, 43–4). Much as Canadian nationalism inspired the pursuit of international development aid policies – and wariness towards the accompanying influx of Caribbean immigrants – a number of Caribbean nationalist movements challenged Canadian intrusions on their own national sovereignty. In Trinidad, a group of university intellectuals known as the New World Group (NWG) characterized Canadian development aid as elitist "post-colonial development strategies." The National Joint Action Committee (NJAC) – representing a coalition of students, workers, urban unemployed and middle class Trinidadian nationalists espousing a Black Power agenda – adopted a more activist approach. In 1969, on the heels of the formally established "special relationship," protesting Canadian "imperialism and racism," NJAC "barred the Canadian governor general from entering the University of the West Indies' [Trinidadian-based] Saint Augustine Campus" (Bennett 1989, 130–32).

Responding to ongoing West Indian accusations of Canadian neo-colonialism, Canadian political scientists defended these development policies as investments in education, transportation and water. They argued Canada was being confused with the US and fervently cautioned against "the radical view that Canada is no different from other imperialist aid givers" (Berry 1977; Paragg 1988, 341). Nevertheless, there was a clear hegemonic quality to the relationship given the requirement that development aid (mostly loans) have "an 80 per cent Canadian content" (reduced in 1971 to 66 67 per cent). In other words, the loans had to be spent in Canada or on Canadian projects (Preston 1971, 310–12) Furthermore, the majority of investment promoted Canadian tourist and manufacturing interests in the region; transportation (mostly airport construction), water development (including hotel plumbing networks), and with the establishment in 1969 of the Caribbean Development Bank, on natural resources. Educational funding constituted 13 per cent of the total, three quarters of which went towards the construction of technical and agricultural colleges – including hotel training schools – in the Caribbean while only one quarter went towards funding post-secondary education in Canada (Paragg 1988, 328–30; Tennyson 1988, 19).

Among the most visible consequences of these development policies, by the 1970s tourism had supplanted natural resources as the leading earner of foreign exchange in the Caribbean, and Canada was the largest tourist influence in the region (until usurped in 1979 by the United States) (Paragg 1988, 334; Mahler 1993, 79–81). In addition, as was typical of post-industrial corporate decentralization across North America, some Canadian factories relocated production to the West Indies, exploiting the weaker, first-world-dependent economies of the region, by availing themselves of cheaper labor and production costs (Tennyson 1988, 17–18). By the early 1970s the traditional ties of investment and trade which had characterized Canadian-West Indian relations within the Commonwealth for half a century were usurped by attention to tourism and "development assistance." Consequently, the occasion of the Mayor of Toronto's "slip" with regards to the pronunciation of Guyana – and its subsequent correction at Caribana – was emblematic of the recent shift in Canadian foreign policy towards actively marketing a new and improved "special relationship" with the governments of former British colonies in the Caribbean.

Immigration and Colonial Conquests

> Barbados is looking like a strange place to me these days … First thing,
> everybody who isn't old, or who have a few dollars, pulling out for Britain or
> for the States. And now that Britain don't want we coloured people in Britain,
> and since the States never wanted we … well the only place left back is Canada.
> Canada is so popular nowadays in Barbados … Out of every ten white people
> you see walking 'bout in shorts in Bridgetown, exposing their funny looking
> legs and toots, well eight or nine is Canadians. They taking over the place …
> They all over all the beach and hotels like ants. All that freedom that we used to
> know is stopped now. The hotels coming from all up in Canada and they putting
> up fence and wire round the hotels and a common person can't pass there no
> more. (Clarke 1973, 135–7)

In Austin Clarke's novel *Storm of Fortune*, the character Bernice reads this letter
from her boyfriend in Barbados whom she supports along with her own family
with remittances acquired as a domestic worker in Canada. Immigration to Canada
is presented as both the only economic opportunity for Caribbean people and as
simultaneously having been made possible by Canadian tourist appropriation of
the Caribbean. The marketing of a "special relationship" between the Canadian
government and newly independent Caribbean states meant that as Canadian
companies and white travelers rushed to exploit the Caribbean market, the
government was pressured to open up its immigration policies.

Reflecting the general state of transformation which gripped Canada in the
1960s, Canadian immigration policies were revised three times during the decade.
Until these changes, Canadian immigration policy was governed by a philosophy
introduced at the turn of the century with regards to potential black candidates.
As summed up in 1912 by W.D. Scott, the superintendent of immigration under
whose tenure the Immigration Act of 1910 was introduced:

> There are certain countries … and certain races of people considered as suited
> to this country and this condition, but Africans no matter where they come from
> are not among the races sought, and hence Africans no matter what country they
> come from are in common with other uninvited races, not admitted to Canada.
> (Schultz 1988, 258–61)

However, responding to pressure exerted by West Indian governments, motivated
by a desire to fill a pressing need for both skilled and unskilled labor, and seizing
an opportunity for positive Canadian publicity with regards to race in the wake of
recent restrictions in British immigration law, Canada revised its immigration policy
in 1962. The new legislation stated that "race, color, national origin or the country
from which he comes" could no longer be used as selection criteria for screening
potential immigrants, although much was still left to the discretion of individual
immigration officers. However not until 1967, following resolutions agreed upon

at the "Special Relationship" conference of 1966, was the immigration policy revised to lower Caribbean entry requirements to match those already offered to Europeans (Winks 1971, 43–4). The same year Canadian immigration offices were opened in Jamaica and Trinidad, and even later for Haiti, Guyana and Barbados, ameliorating an absence which had "seriously handicapped potential immigrants" (Walker 1984, 12). Subsequently, West Indian immigration to Canada increased dramatically, peaking between 1973 and 1978 when ten per cent of all landed immigrants were from the Caribbean (Henry 1994, 27). Between 1967 and 1990, 66.1 per cent of all Caribbean immigrants to Canada settled in Ontario, with the majority of them – a significant factor for the growth and significance of Caribana – settling in Metropolitan Toronto (Richmond 1989, 5).

Prior to these changes the only available immigration route from the West Indies to Canada was under the far more limited auspices of the 1955 West Indian Domestic Immigration scheme negotiated between the Canadian and West Indian governments. Caribbean women were admitted to Canada if they agreed to work as a domestic servant for at least one year after which they became eligible for landed immigrant status. Establishing a tradition continued by immigration policies in the 1960s, these women were recruited and then admitted to Canada "for specific, and usually lower-level occupations," incommensurate with their education and experience (Innis 1974, 140). Motivated by dire economic circumstances in the Caribbean, from 1955 to 1965, 2,690 women chose this indentured servitude. The exploitative nature of these policies and the implicit assumptions regarding Caribbean women's appropriate occupational roles is amplified by the fact that the majority of these women were trained in skilled occupations (Walker 1984, 10–11). This tradition of labor exploitation and racially restrictive occupational opportunities continued; a survey conducted by Employment and Immigration Canada revealed that between 1969 and 1976, after six months in Canada, Caribbean men earned 60 per cent less than all other recent immigrants (Richmond 1989, 5).

Hemispheric Racial Orders

> I can trace my German ancestry back to Lunenburg, Nova Scotia in the mid 1800s; I can trace my English ancestry back to Halifax, Nova Scotia in the early 1800s; I can trace my French ancestry back to the late 1700s just west of Weymouth, Nova Scotia; I can trace my negro ancestry back to the mid 1700s in Nova Scotia. Oh, yes, I can also trace my Canadian ancestry, of which I am proud, (as I am of all my ancestors), back to that unknown date when the Canadian Indian alone populated this country ... Yet, I am not white, nor do I appear white. Even on this date, because I did not choose to give money to a panhandler, I was advised by this same unfortunate person that I should go back to where I come from, and leave Canada to the Canadians. – Toronto Resident, W. Jackson (*Toronto Star* 1974).

As the presence of visible minorities in Toronto escalated with the influx of West Indians, the marketing of cultural diversity was paired with representations which inaccurately located race as originating exclusively outside the Canadian nation. During the year of Canadian centennial celebrations, protests and uprisings reverberated throughout the hemisphere. Race riots in Detroit, Newark and other American cities made headlines across Canada. "Ravaged" by racial discord, the US became Canada's unruly, uncontrollable neighbor. While Caribana was lauded as an "authentic West Indian party," the same report concluded by deliberately contrasting the event with racial tensions south of the border: "if everyone got along like we are tonight there would be no race riots" (*The Toronto Daily Star* 1967b). In contrast to the US, an immigrant "West Indian party" proved Canada provided the best black North American experience. This contributed to what Rinaldo Walcott has described as the "hyper-visibility of Caribbean blackness mak[ing] 'indigenous black Canadians' invisible" (Walcott 1997, 39). This collapsing of race into immigrant cultural difference enabled official Canada to ignore populations with less festive implications: black Canadians whose presence derived from a more intimate history of Canadian slavery. This community of African descent had helped establish the city of Toronto. Caribana celebrations ironically coincided with a civic holiday honoring Ontario's first lieutenant-governor, a leader of British Loyalists who fled the American Revolution, with their African slaves.

Racial tensions and questions of cultural diversity came to be discussed within the framework of a benevolent Canadian immigration policy. In 1967, the *Toronto Telegram* characterized Caribana as a "West Indian Thank You." In this context, labeling the event "West Indian" enabled white Canada to avoid the contemporary significance of Caribana as a 'black' event – a designation far more common among the organizers and celebrants alike. Seeing it as an opportunity for black diasporic empowerment, one visiting reveler described it as: "the best way I can relate to the black community. We could use the funds from Caribana to help our people or our cause." *Contrast*, the most popular Afro-Carribean publication in Toronto, embraced this vision: "Caribana," it observed, "serves as a powerful cultural force in the black community as a means of warding off alienation in this society which is basically European oriented" (*Contrast* 1970a–c, 1971a–e). This "black" imaginary was animated by the US civil rights struggle and the success of anti-colonial movements worldwide. In this context, a multicultural discourse obscured Caribana's political implications. Moreover increased "racial" diversity within Canada's "cultural" diversity meant discussions of multiculturalism depicted racism as the consequence of immigration policy, rather than one of its historically defining principles. One suggestive letter, published August 3, 1967 in *The Toronto Daily Star*, reveals how readily multiculturalism obscured racial intolerance:

> Since 1967 changes in immigration policy, multiculturalism has, in my opinion, become a dirty word. It is being used for an excuse to accommodate the demands of the new breed of immigrant who, under the guise of making a cultural

contribution to this country, is in effect, destroying the homogeneous spirit we enjoyed for many years ... [this] can only result in the disease known as racism. We didn't create it, it was imported. (1967a)

Skeptical of the politics of multiculturalism, this reader responded to the increased former British colonial, largely West Indian, presence in Toronto by suggesting it was immigration policy itself generating racism as "the new breed of immigrant" intruded on Canadian homogeneity.

Challenging this overt hostility, another contributor, a Ms. Watton of Toronto, interestingly responded: "If we are so bigoted and selfish that we cannot share our great country with others less fortunate than ourselves, well then, I believe we have already lost our souls" (*Toronto Star* 1967). While inscribing Canada's neo-colonial discourse of benevolence, Ms. Watton reinforced the position of her white "opponent" as they both addressed race and bigotry as immigrant issues imported from elsewhere. Without acknowledging racism within Canadian society, popular discourse easily collapsed race into a discussion of immigration, and by extension, "multiculturalism" was oddly construed as a (contested) accommodation of the threatening and foreign.

Politics of Culture

In response to such tensions, official "multiculturalism" promoted a domestic 'tourist' imaginary which divorced culture from politics in an effort to contain the potentially radical nature of masses of black and brown people celebrating in the streets. Emphasizing exotic cultural performance over politics, public discussions of Caribana, veiled very real tensions and conflicts surrounding Canadian racism and foreign policy. A striking example of this deteriorating relationship occurred in 1969 when a group of Caribbean students staged a protest over racial discrimination at Sir George William University in Montreal. Protestors' thirteen day occupation of a campus computer facility culminated in a much publicized stand off with police. In March 1970 six Trinidadian students went on trial before a jury of 11 white men and were fined $33,500 for "conspiring to illegally occupy the computer centre and the faculty lounge." Justice Kenneth MacKay invoked their foreignness to explain why he was not sending them to jail (although they were to remain in jail until their fine was paid): "You have already cost the Canadian taxpayers enough. I will not burden them with the cost of having to support you in Canadian prisons" (*Contrast* 1971d).

Dr Eric Williams, Prime Minister of Trinidad and Tobago, offered to pay the fines immediately, nevertheless, this incident dovetailed with ongoing grievances over Canadian economic policies in the Caribbean, and Canadian-owned businesses were soon targeted by urban uprisings in Port of Spain. The NJAC leadership protested that "racism and foreign capital were related to systemic problems confronting Trinidad" including "unemployment, racism and material dispossession." In the face of these protests and demands for greater local economic control, Williams announced a takeover of the Bank of Montreal in Port of Spain. Nevertheless, the NJAC protests escalated into a massive Black Power demonstration that by April 1970 had "paralyzed Trinidad and Tobago." A state of emergency was declared on April 21st, and subsequently the revolt was effectively neutralized. The government in Trinidad cracked down on Black Power leaders in the country and banned other activists in the Caribbean, Canada and the United States from entering. Despite these efforts, and much to the "wrath of the Caribbean governments," Canada "as an answer to the wave of anti-Canadian feeling in the Caribbean," unilaterally abrogated aspects of the 1966 trade agreements (Bennett 1989, 134–38).

The hemispheric protest movements fuelled heated conflict in Canada, belied by deceptively calm headlines such as *The Toronto Star's* "Caribana '70 Struts Its Stuff." Diverging from mainstream reticence, the black community was deeply divided over Caribana and its relationship to black struggles at home and abroad. The most vocal public critics of Caribana at that time were the editors of *Uhuru*, a Montreal-based "Black Community News Service." Boldly challenging the organizers of Caribana, the editors declared that "Uhuru thinks that to carry on Caribana in its present form – an *apolitical* mass gathering – is, in 1970, no less than criminal." The editors premised their denunciation on "a few facts", one of which was that "to masquerade, dance, sing, and spend so much time and money, is to leave the impressions that blacks have no problem in Canada. This is the exact image that the Canadian government has been trying hopelessly to sell to the West Indies and other parts of the world to her own advantage." Attacking Canada's efforts to "sell" a positive image of multicultural diversity *Uhuru* aligned itself with the Black Power Movement and anti-imperial struggles, and suggested this marketing endeavor was linked to economic and political exploitation. The editors' emphasized Caribana's complicity in undermining liberation struggles in the Caribbean by "showing the world their satisfaction with their condition" and providing a forum for "the advertisement of Canadian investors" (*Uhuru* 1970).

Weighing in on this debate about the relationship between politics and culture, the mouthpiece for the CCC's "community objectives" since 1968, *Contrast* rapidly jumped to Caribana's defense. A 1970 *Contrast* article outlined the vast economic contributions made by blacks in Canada in defensive reassurance to participants that "they will not just be masqueraders ... they are an integral part of Canada, a people who matter. Really matter" (1970b). Embracing an emergent discourse of multiculturalism that emphasized entertainment and displays of cultural heritage, carnival was a time for "people to put aside their differences, forget their cares, throw caution to the wind ... More important, however, Caribana also affords non-West Indians a chance to take part in a festival that is *truly* West Indian." The following year, after *Contrast* investigated the CCC's financial problems, the publishers had a falling out with the Caribana committee, the University of Toronto's Black Students Union (BSU) used *Contrast* as a forum for condemning Caribana. The union explained that its opposition was arrived at after "questioning the role of Caribana in our future development as a community in the heart of racist Canada" (1971b). The BSU condemned "the happy go lucky imagery of Caribana and hope[d] that progressive Black people [would] continue to struggle against white racists and their black cohorts."

While white Canada gave scant public attention to these debates which raged in the black-Canadian community, and remained largely silent on the ongoing foreign policy crisis in Trinidad, the mechanisms of the Canadian state were mobilized to diffuse the situation and included the "police surveillance of Black organizations by both municipal and federal forces." The Royal Canadian Mounted Police brought in a former FBI agent who "provided them with inside information about the political activities of Black and Caribbean organizations." And, in 1971, citizen protest groups successfully challenged racist propaganda used "in Toronto for training in police work" that linked the US Black Power Movement to an international communist conspiracy aimed at overthrowing the government (Stasiulus 1989, 66). However, black mobilizations often had more specific grievances as one member of Canadian parliament delicately assessed the situation: "Canadians take the view that all tourism that is directed to the Caribbean countries by Canadians is valuable. It can be touchy when Canadians live in very luxurious hotels … often to the benefit of the Canadian hotel owners and the Canadian tourists, without too much benefit going to the countries themselves" (Canada 1971, 43–5). A multicultural tourist imaginary (both at home and abroad) increasingly masked the economic and political discontent that galvanized social movements of the day. In a revealing moment at the 1972 Commonwealth Conference in Ottawa, a Canadian participant commenting on the recent success of Labour parties in Australia and New Zealand, remarked: "if Canada is not careful at this conference, it could easily find itself outflanked on the liberal-left, no longer the white country closest to the colored countries" (*Toronto Star* 1973a). Canada's self-image was based on relative comparisons with other white countries as opposed to being directed towards a substantive examination of its own relations with the "colored countries", or indeed, with indigenous "colored" populations living within its own borders.

Market Multiculturalism

Despite the willingness of Caribbean Cultural Committee organizers to promote Caribana within a Canadian multicultural framework, from the year immediately following the centennial celebrations Caribana – complementing the West Indian experience in Canada – began a perpetual struggle for economic viability and acceptance. In 1968 Mayor William Dennison's promises of annual support went unfulfilled as the Toronto city council refused to grant Caribana any subsidies. Moreover, when organizers linked support for Caribana with raising funds for the creation of a West Indian Community Center in Toronto they apparently threatened to disrupt an official preference for cultural spectacle over community-based organizing. Caribana was considered "NOT the cultural project it was last year," triggering a city's Parks Commission fee of 15 per cent of its gross income (*West Indian News Observer* 1968a, b). The limit of white Canada's multiculturalism was abundantly clear.

This lack of government funding – paired with public profit – was not new. Caribana's debut had been funded almost exclusively by members of the Caribbean community; of a total $50,000 budget, only $1,000 was contributed by the Ontario Centennial Commission (*The Toronto Daily Star* 1967f). Subsequently, funding continued to come exclusively from donations by members of the black community (largely subsidized by the CCC board members themselves) until modest government subsidies followed once "Multiculturalism" became national policy in 1971. Despite the fact that Caribana was being lauded by the city of Toronto as its tourist event par excellence, public funding was incommensurate with the profits Caribana brought into the city. The CCC advertised Caribana's commercial potential as it unsuccessfully sought government funding "They could do a whole lot better. We bring a lot of business to this town" (*Toronto Star* 1973a). The Committee unsuccessfully canvassed the Metro Toronto business community for support – perhaps more striking when considered in contrast with their extensive investments in the Caribbean tourist industry.

Not only was funding insignificant in light of the total amount of money Caribana brought in to the city by 1971, but it was dramatically less support than the government was willing to give other festivals and organization. Just one week after Caribana's festivities came to an end, "Carnival Toronto" descended on the city. "We love Toronto ... We've got more going for us, than any place, anywhere. We are the beautiful people of every beautiful race." This overstated emphasis on racial diversity was a deliberate contrast with Caribana (read "black"), and was able to capitalize on Caribana's financial difficulties: "What's this, another carnival? Yes, but it's *different*. There are no tickets to buy, no booths to enter and you have to become totally involved to have fun ... Sounds like fun for the whole family!" (*The Toronto Star* 1971). Carnival Toronto's "difference" was the skin color of the organizers and those who were expected to attend, and this dramatically influenced the amount of interest and support it was given. "Carnival Toronto" was organized by a Greek immigrant and "successful restauranteur" who initiated the event because "Toronto is already known around the world and its time we joined the rest of the world's famous carnival cities" (*The Financial Post* 1971). Despite the number of tourists (40,000 in 1971) and the tens of thousands of Torontonians (mostly black) lining the parade routes, Caribana was apparently not up to the task, or at least not within the dominant community's preferred racial sphere. Embodying the unspoken limits of multiculturalism, this carnival was for white Toronto, as attested to by the predominantly white crowds attending the event.

White "Carnival Toronto" was "different" with "no tickets to buy" because "Carnival Toronto" was subsidized by a $25,000 grant from the city which was matched by an additional $25,000 from the province (and was backed by Metro

Council in a petition to the federal government to provide a similar donation), dwarfing the pitiful $6,500 total that Caribana had received. Government support was augmented by the Toronto business community, with 2,000 businessmen signing "a declaration supporting the idea of 'Carnival Toronto.'" The most powerful members of the economic and political community lined up behind this alternative carnival including public utilities and an array local retailers and international corporations, while Odeon Theatres (Canada) and Famous Players Canadian showed films of Carnival "as a means of stirring up interest in the idea" (Tennyson 1988, 18). The disparity between support received by Caribana and that which inundated Carnival Toronto exposed the limits of Toronto's multicultural rhetoric and the early pairing of multiculturalism with profit-oriented commercial interests. While Caribana out-lasted Carnival Toronto, it has, forty years later, yet to receive anything close the amount of support given Carnival Toronto at its debut.

Conclusion

By 1971 the relationship between Canada and the Caribbean had rapidly deteriorated, and in the midst of hemispheric – including domestic – struggles over economic and racial discrimination, the Royal Commission's recommendations informed Prime Minister Pierre Trudeau's implementation of a Canadian policy which declared that "Multiculturalism" be the grounds for constructing and understanding Canada's national identity. Trudeau told the House of Commons that Multiculturalism "commends itself to the government as the most suitable means of assuring the cultural freedom of Canadians. Such a policy should help break down discriminatory attitudes and cultural jealousies ... the government will assist members of all cultural groups to overcome cultural barriers to full participation in Canadian society" (Roberts and Clifton 1990, 137). The policy itself "encourage[d] the preservation, enhancement, sharing and evolving expression of multicultural heritage in Canada (Bissoondath 1993, 372). This policy of "preservation" readily assimilated existing conversations about Caribana which relegated West Indian-immigrant carnival to a static, exclusively cultural realm. The policy responded and tried to mute racial politics and solidarities that promoted Caribbean nationalism, Black Power and struggles for economic equality. The 1971 multicultural policy exclusively funded projects "concentrated on the cultural-retention concerns of communities," which in Caribana's case precluded raising funds for a community center (Gauld 1992, 10–11).[2]

---

2   This was the case until the Multiculturalism Act of 1988 which began to address systemic obstacles with attention to things, such as employment equity. However these changes have not replaced the cultural emphasis or significantly altered the parameters of debate.

This apolitical, cultural emphasis ensured that, according to a 1979 study on the disbursement of funding, "there was a heavy emphasis in the granting of funds under the multiculturalism programmes on projects concerned with visible cultural manifestations and a consistent refusal to grant assistance for projects concerned with material or political problems" (Stasiulus 1980, 34). Forged in the context of an emergent national Canadian identity, a dramatic influx of Caribbean peoples in the midst of imperial upheavals and North American jockeying for influence over the labor, natural resources and tourist potential of the Caribbean, multicultural policy sought to contain racial and anti-colonial struggle while expanding Canada's political and economic influence.

Multiculturalism, as Caribana, represented more than simply an internal policy initiative within the Canadian nation. Multiculturalism was deployed internationally by the Canadian government as an example of Canada's model performance with regards to race relations; a middle power broker and alternative to American and British imperial regimes. As one enthusiast later suggested, multiculturalism provided that "Canada is looked to as a model nation of tolerance and respect for minority groups" (Mazurek 1992, 22). However, the origins and history of Caribana attest to the erasures, misrepresentations and limitations obscured by the apparent inclusiveness of the term "multicultural." In Lenard's terms (Chapter Two), creating a false pretense of inter-ethnic social trust by utilizing the term. As the Caribbean population continued to grow in Toronto, Caribana's popularity grew in tandem. By the 1990s some two million people – from across Canada, the Caribbean, England and the United States – came to carnival in downtown Toronto pouring more than $250 million dollars into the local economy (Foster 1996, 250). The 1996 Toronto government task force lauded Caribana as an event which "benefits the Municipality of Metro Toronto, the Province of Ontario, Canada and its residents," and which was indicative of a government and "community which nurtures, supports and promotes its multicultural, multiracial diversity within Canada and abroad" (Toronto 1996, xv). Despite Caribana's success, its international prominence, and its appropriation by Canadian government spin-masters, Caribana continued to struggle, as cultural critic Dionne Brand observed, in "racial[ly] hostile territory every year for viability and acceptance" (Brand 1994, 179). The CCC struggled beneath inadequate funding, increased police surveillance and negative publicity. The US usurped Canada's primacy in the ex-Commonwealth Caribbean, and the black population in Toronto continued to struggle against discrimination in immigration, housing and employment. Culture does not exist apart from politics and economics, which is why the marketing of multiculturalism was a crucial aspect of trying to contain some of the more radical implications of Canadian diversity.

References

Bennett, H.L. 1989. The Challenge of the Post-Colonial State: A Case Study of the February Revolution in Trinidad. In *The Modern Caribbean*, ed. F.W. Knight and C.A. Palmer, 129–46. Chapel Hill: The UNC Press.

Berry, G.R. 1977. The West Indies in Canadian External Relations: Present Trends and Future Prospects. *Canadian Public Policy* 3(1): 55–62.

Bissoondath, N. 1993. A Question of Belonging: Multiculturalism and Citizenship. In *Belonging: The Meaning and Future of Canadian Citizenship*, ed. W. Kaplan, 368–87. Montréal, Quebec: McGill-Queen's University Press.

Brand, Dionne. 1994. *Bread Out of Stone: Recollections, Sex, Recognitions, Race, Dreaming, Politics*. Toronto, Coach House Press.

Canada. 1965. *A Preliminary Report of the Royal Commission on Bilingualism and Biculturalism*. Ottawa: Queen's Printer.

Canada and J. Arthur Lower. 1971. *Selections from Hansard: House of Commons Debates, 28th Parliament, 3rd Session, October 8, 1971 – June 30, 1971*. Canada: McLelland and Stewart Ltd.

Centennial Commission. 1967. *The Hundredth Year: The Centennial of Canadian Confederation 1867–1967*. Ottawa: Centennial Commission.

Clarke, Austin. 1973. *Storm of Fortune*. Toronto: Little, Brown and Company.

Contrast. 1970a. Editorial, *Contrast*, August 1–15.

Contrast. 1970b. Where Blacks are Worth Millions. August 1–15.

Contrast. 1970c. Why Caribana is a Must. August 1–15.

Contrast. 1971a. 1970 Review. January 6, 8–9.

Contrast. 1971b. Black Student Union on Caribana. August 1.

Contrast. 1971c. Man about Town. August 1.

Contrast. 1971d. Time to Redeem Pledges, August 16.

Contrast. 1971e. Is it Self-Indulgent Nostalgia or Gainful Exoticism? September 1.

Equinox. 1987. Playin' Mmas: Caribana's Largest Annual Street Party, Transforms Toronto the Good into Toronto the Fun. 6(2) March/April: 58–67.

Foster, C. 1995. *Caribana: The Greatest Celebration*. Toronto: Ballantine Books.

Foster, C. 1996. *A Place Called Heaven: The Meaning of Being Black in Canada*. Toronto: HarperCollins Publishers, Ltd.

Gauld, G. 1992. Multiculturalism: The Real Thing? In *Twenty years of Multiculturalism: Successes and Failures*, ed. S. Hrynick, 9–16. Winnepeg, Manitoba: St. John's University Press.

Henry, F. 1994. *The Caribbean Diaspora in Toronto: Learning to Live with Racism*. Toronto: University of Toronto Press.

Innis, H.R. 1974. *Bilingualism and Biculturalism: An Abridged Version of the Royal Commission Report*. Canada: McClelland and Stewart Ltd. The Secretary of State Department and Information Canada.

Leach, R.H. (ed). 1967. *Contemporary Canada*. North Carolina: Duke University Press.

Mahler, G.S. 1993. Foreign Policy and Canada's Evolving Relations with the Caribbean Commonwealth Countries: Political and Economic Considerations. In *A Dynamic Partnership: Canada's Changing Role in the Americas*, eds. J. Haar and E.J. Dosman, 79–91. London: Transaction Publishers.

Mazurek, K. 1992. Defusing a Radical Social Policy: The Undermining of Multiculturalism. In *Twenty Years of Multiculturalism: Successes and Failures*, ed. S. Hryniuk, 17–28. Winnipeg: St. John's College Press.

Murray, D. 1988. Garrisoning the Caribbean: A Chapter in Canadian Military History. In *Canada and the Commonwealth Caribbean*, ed. B.D. Tennyson, 279–301. Maryland: University Press of America.

Paragg, R. 1988. Canadian aid in the Commonwealth Caribbean: Neo-Colonialism or Development?" In *Canada and the Commonwealth Caribbean*, ed. B.D. Tennyson, 323–45. Maryland: University Press of America.

Preston, R.A. 1971. Caribbean Defense and Security: A Study of the Implications of Canada's 'Special Relationship' with the Commonwealth West Indies. *South Atlantic Quarterly* 70(3): 317–31.

Quamina, O.T. 1996. *All Things Considered: Can We Live Together?* Toronto: Exile Editions.

Richmond, A.H. 1989. *Caribbean Immigrants: A Demo-Economic Analysis*. Ottawa: Minister of Supply and Services Canada.

Roberts, L.W. and R. Clifton. 1990. Multiculturalism in Canada: A Sociological Perspective. In *Race and Ethnic Relations in Canada*, ed. P.S. Li, 120–47. Toronto: Oxford University Press.

Schultz, J. 1988. White Man's Country: Canada and the West Indian Immigrant 1900–1965. In *Canada and the Commonwealth Caribbean*, ed. B.D. Tennyson, 257–277. Maryland: University Press of America.

Stasiulus, D.K. 1980. The Political Restructuring of Ethnic Community Action: A Reformulation. *Canadian Ethnic Studies*, xii, 3(80): 19–44.

Stasiulus, D.K. 1989. Minority Resistance in the Local State: Toronto in the 1970's and 1980's. *Ethnic and Racial Studies* 12(1): 63–83.

Tennyson, B.D. 1988. Introduction. In *Canada and the Commonwealth Caribbean*, ed. B.D. Tennyson, 11–23. Maryland: University Press of America.

The Globe and Mail. 1967. Caribana 67: Sun, sand, Steel Bands. August 7.

The Financial Post. 1971. Parades, Bands, Barbecues – if Carnival Toronto Gets $. July 3.

The Telegram. 1967. Parade Features West Indies. August 5.

The Telegram. 1967. Caribana '67 is a Swinger. August 8.

The Telegram. 1967. West Indian Thank You: Caribana '67 is a Swinger. August 8.

The Toronto Daily Star. 1967a. Ontario Plans to Outdo World with 1,200 Cast Expo Show. August 3.

The Toronto Daily Star. 1967b. After the Race War, a Blueprint for Peace. August 5.

The Toronto Daily Star. 1967c. Caribana Crowds Islands. August 8.

The Toronto Daily Star. 1967d. Ferry Cruises Harbor to Calypso Beat. August 9.

The Toronto Daily Star. 1967e. Caribana Show Will Go On. August 10.

The Toronto Daily Star. 1967f. The Island in Limbo – 8,000 Swing in the Rain. August 10.

The Toronto Daily Star. 1967g. Caribana Whoop-Up May Become Annual Affair. August 14.

The Toronto Star. 1970. Caribana Struts its Stuff. August 1.

The Toronto Star. 1971. Love of Life is your Ticket to Fun at Carnival Toronto. August 7.

The Toronto Star. 1973a. Caribana counting on good weather to solve financial problems. August 2.

The Toronto Star. 1973b. Interesting Insights into Commonwealth Picked up at Talks. August 3.

The Toronto Star. 1974. 'Canadian' Means Citizenship Not Racial Origin. August 7.

The Toronto Star. 1976. Confused Understanding of Racism. August 3.

Toronto. 1996. *The Report of the Caribbean Cultural Committee / Metropolitan Toronto Chairman's Task Force on Caribana January* 1996. "A Jewel Worth Polishing." Toronto: The Municipality of Metropolitan Toronto.

Uhuru. 1970. Editorial, August 3.

Walcott, R. 1997. *Black Like Who?: Writing Black Canada*. Toronto: Insomniac Press.

Walker, J. W. 1984. *The West Indians in Canada*. Ottawa: Canadian Historical Association.

West Indian News Observer. 1968a. Caribana '68. July.

West Indian News Observer. 1968b. Caribana in retrospect. August.

Wigley, P. G. 1988. Canada and imperialism: West Indian aspirations and the First World War. In *Canada and the Commonwealth Caribbean*, ed. B. D. Tennyson, 215–55. Maryland: University Press of America.

Winks, R. 1968. *Canadian – West Indian Union: A Forty-Year Minuet*. Toronto: The Athlone Press, University of London.

Winks, R. 1971. *The Blacks in Canada: A History*. New Haven: Yale University Press.

Chapter 6

The Identification, Settlement and Representation of Ethnic Minorities in Beijing

Reza Hasmath

While cities such as Toronto, Canada and Sydney, Australia have had a relatively recent history of ethnic diversity arising from post-World World Two immigration, the contrast with Beijing's long history dealing with ethnic minorities makes it a compelling comparison. This begs the question whether the contrasting histories can explain the differences in the development and behavioural patterns of their ethnic enclaves and economies, in the management of ethnic differences, and among on-the-ground ethnic group interactions? This chapter will examine the historical development of ethnic minority populations in Beijing, with a focus on ethnic minority identification, settlement and location patterns, and contemporary ethnic group interactions and representation.

Identification

In the People's Republic of China, the concept of ethnicity appears to be straightforward, definitive, and by some accounts rigid, especially in comparison to Canada, Australia or the United Kingdom. Although relative to East Asia, China is arguably at the forefront for providing specific minority rights enshrined in its Constitution, and is a leader, on paper, for providing allowances (e.g. exemptions, special rights and autonomy) for ethnic autonomy in parts of the nation, the system of categorizing minorities is ripe with difficulties. Ethnic minorities refer to the 105 million individuals officially identified as 'minority nationalities' (*shaoshu minzu*) by the Communist Party of China (CPC). When the CPC came into power in 1949 they commissioned studies to categorize ethnic groups within the boundaries of the People's Republic. Teams were sent into regions heavily populated with ethnic minorities to conduct research and field work, investigating minorities' social history, economic life, language and religion. Although 400-plus separate groups applied to be formally recognized, after detailed study by the CPC they found that there was a lot of overlapping, and a significant number of groups that claimed to be separate actually belonged to existing groups, albeit with different names. As a result, 39 ethnic groups were officially recognized in 1954; and by 1964,

another 15 were identified, with the Lhoba ethnic group added in 1965.[1] The Jino
were added in 1979, bringing the present-day count to 56 official ethnic groups,
inclusive of Han. All Chinese citizens were subsequently registered by nationality
status in household registration and personal identification – a practice that still
remains today.[2]

In determining what constituted an ethnic group, the CPC leaders, who
were inexperienced in administrative matters, followed a Soviet model which
politicized and institutionalized the identification and categorization of ethnic
minority groups as mentioned in the first chapter. Inspired by Joseph Stalin's
(1953) "four commons", the criteria are: 1) Distinct Language – While there are
virtually hundreds, perhaps thousands, of dialects spoken across China, a minority
language is not simply a dialect. It is a language with distinct grammatical and
phonological differences. Among the 55 official ethnic minority groups identified,
four of the world's largest language families are covered, including Sino-Tibetan
(e.g. Tibetan), Altai (e.g. Kazak, Uyghur, Mongolian, Manchu, Korean), Austro-
Asiatic (e.g. Miao), and Indo-European (e.g. Tajik, Russian). Twenty-one ethnic
minority groups have unique writing systems. (2) A recognized indigenous
homeland – a common territory – within the boundaries of China. For example,
the majority of the nation's 5.8 million Mongol ethnic population lives in the Inner
Mongolia Autonomous Region in Northern China. (3) A common economic life.
(4) And, a strong sense of identity and distinctive customs, ranging from dress,
religion, foods.

In practice, when local officials initially classified members of ethnic groups,
there was a widespread practice of using the language origin of place names to
determine whether individuals in a locality fit an ethnic minority category. For
example, Brown (2002) describes a scenario of a family who were suspected of
being Tujia due to their surname. Although the family lived in a village that was
too small to have formal historical records, they lived in an area with place names
that derived from the Tujia language. Officials concluded that since the place
names were Tujia and there was no evidence of individuals with their surname
in the area, the family must have been local (i.e. not Han migrants) and should
therefore be classified as Tujia.

---

1   By early 1965, there were 183 nationalities registered (based on the 1964 census),
among which the government recognized only 54 (see Minorities International 2007).

2   Note, there are alternate spellings for many minority groups in China. Most common
alternatives are Bonan (Bao'an); Bouyei (Bouyi or Buyi); Bulong (Blang); De'ang (Deang);
Drung (Dulong); Du (Tu); Gelao (Gelo); Hani (Ahka or Hakka – especially outside of
PRC); Hezhen (Hezhe); Jingpo (Kachin); Jino (Junuo); Kazak (Kazakh); Kirgiz (Kirghiz);
Korean (sometimes referred to as Chaoxian especially among the elder population); Lhoba
(Loba or Luoba); Menba (Moinba or Mongba); Miao (sometimes referred to as Hmung);
Mulam (Mulao); Naxi (Nakhi or Nahi); Oroqin (Orogen); Tatar (Tartar); Uyghur (Uygur or
Uigur); Uzbek (Ozbek); Wa (Va); Yugur (Yugu) and Xibo (Xibe or Sibe).

Even at a macro-level, the CPC's ethnic group classification is unusual as demonstrated in the Uyghur example. Although a collection of peoples known as Uyghur has existed in Xinjiang since the eighth century, this particular identity was lost from the fifteenth century onwards (see Gladney 1994a). The modern classification of Uyghur was resurrected by the CPC incorporating a non-homogeneous group of peoples (who are loosely Muslim Turkish) into an overarching ethnic nationality. With large scale Han resettlement into Xinjiang, almost half of Xinjiang's population is now Han. This has created juxtaposition between Han Chinese and Uyghurs, further perpetuating a perception of homogeneity of the Uyghur identity. In effect, as an anonymous anthropologist at the Central University for Nationalities summarizes it: "they are told what they are, and they get used to it".

A similar line of argument can also be made for the *dominant majority* Han, which has a national population of 1.137 billion persons (NBS 2005). Similar to the situation in Taiwan, the Han nationality groups together a wide array of culturally diverse populations, including eight vastly different linguistic groups (Mandarin, Gan, Hakka, Southern and Northern Min, Wu, Xiang, Yue). There is even great diversity within the linguistic sub-groups. Among the Yue language family for example, there is great difficulty for Cantonese and Taishan speakers to understand each other. Few commentators on China (and Taiwan as a matter of fact) seem to question the validity of a unified Han nationality and often they accept Han as representative of 'Chinese' in general. While the notion of the Han *ren* (person) has existed since the time of the Han dynasty (206 BC – 220 AD), the Han nationality is an entirely modern phenomenon, which arose with the shift from Chinese empire to modern nation-state. Gladney (1994a, 179) uses this analogy:

> While the concept of a Han person certainly existed, it probably referred to those subjects of the Han empire, just as "Roman" referred to those subjects of the Roman empire (roughly concurrent with the Han). This tells us little about their "ethnicity" and we would be hard-pressed to determine who was Roman today. The "Han" are still thought to be around, however.

This notion of a unified Han nationality – a Pan-Hanism – gained its modern popularity under Sun Yat-sen, the co-founder and leader of the Kuomintang (KMT) who were instrumental in overthrowing the last imperial empire of China, the Qing Dynasty (1644–1912); and as a party, were force to retreat to Taiwan in 1949 after being defeated by the Communists during the Chinese Civil War where the dominated political control of Taiwan in a single party system. Sun Yat-sen was influenced by the strong tones of Japanese nationalism during his long stay in the country and the writings of fellow KMT member, Dai Jitao, who frequently voiced his strong dissatisfaction of imperial rule (see Hon 1996). In order to initially mobilize the masses to overthrow Qing rule, Sun Yat-sen, Dai Jitao, and the KMT promoted an argument that over 390 million out of the 400 million population during this period were an indivisible unitary group, Han Chinese,[3] and thus, they should rally together to remove all "foreign occupiers" (see Attane and Courbage 2000, Zarrow 2004; Zhao 2004, Leibold 2006).[4] By employing the reconstituted understanding of Han, Sun Yat-sen sought to foster a nationalistic sentiment that would bring together a large Cantonese contingent, northern Mandarin speakers, and the economic power of Zhejiang and Shanghainese peoples, into one superimposed nationality (see Gladney 1994a).

Ironically, after imperial rule was removed, the KMT faced the daunting task of incorporating the heterogeneous peoples of the Qing empire into the new Chinese state (see Leibold 2006), who had a majority population in the strategically important, large territories of the nation's bordering areas.[5] The notion of the "Five Races of China" (*wuzu gonghe*): the Han, Manchu, Mongolian, Tibetan and Hui soon became an important and re-popularized concept promoting a penta-racial republic.[6] In effect, the KMT emphasized Hans and the four other nationalities belonged to a supra-ethnic, nation-state that had been in existence as this entity from time immemorial.[7]

Although the categorization of 55 ethnic minority groups by the CPC was a step forward from the KMT's denial of the existence of a wide variety of different ethnic groups in China, the process of official ethnic group recognition in present time has sparked further debate. For example, Chinese sociologist Fei Xiao Tong

---

3   Attane and Courbage (2000, 258) point out statistical yearbooks at the time provided a count of approximately 26 million ethnic minorities. Even then, this may be a significant undercount.

4   Radical Han Chinese nationalists such as Zou Rong and Liu Shipei went as far as to negate that China was a multi-ethnic empire (see Zarrow 2004). In response to Pan-Hanism during this period, Chinese historian Jiegang Gu argued that China before the Qin Dynasty (221–206 BC) was ruled by groups with different ethnic backgrounds. Gu continued to prove that a unified China was not only a relatively late development, but also the result of a long process of conquest by stronger ethnic tribes (Hon 1996, 322). In effect, Gu's efforts unmasked the political agenda behind the KMT attempt to promote a Pan-Hanism or policy of Hanhua (Hanification or Sinification).

5   Chiang Kai-shek, who became the leader of the KMT after Sun Yat-sen's death, even attempted to suggest that "since the 1911 Revolution, Manchus and Hans have fused into one entity that there is no trace of distinctiveness" (quoted in Zhao 2004, 172). However, KMT's policy of assimilation was never a complete success, especially in Northern China and the frontier regions.

6   The idea of the "Five Races of China" can be traced as far back as Emperor Qianlong, the fifth emperor of the Manchu, Qing Dynasty from 1735 to 1796. In order to legitimize his reign – claiming his rule was not linked to his Manchurian ethnicity – and justify territorial expansion into East Turkestan (later called Xinjiang or literally "New Frontier" in Manchu), Outer Mongolia (what is known as Mongolia today) and Tibet, he defined China within a wuzu gonghe context.

7   Ando (1974) suggests when Sun Yat-sen gave speeches to Han audiences he never used the term wuzu gonghe. However, when Manchus or Mongolians were present, the term was widely used.

(1981) points to the Chuanqing Blacks, who, although they had a close relationship with Hans, had unique features in language, location and economic life that would warrant minority recognition based on the four criteria. However, it was determined by CPC researchers that the Chuanqing Blacks were not a separate nationality, but rather descendants of Han garrison troops who intermarried with the local population during the Ming dynasty. In a contrasting example, in 1978, 30,000 Fujianese who no longer practice Islam, were recognized as members of the Hui (Islamic) nationality using historical records of foreign ancestry (see Gladney 1994a). They were able to prove descent from Muslim officials and traders who settled in the area between the ninth and fourteenth centuries. This practice would appear to create precedence for many groups to seek nationality recognition based on historical records of foreign ancestry. However, the CPC has not recognized a 'new' ethnic group in nearly thirty years. In fact, among the 350 plus groups who were not originally classified as a separate ethnic group, only fifteen groups are still officially being considered for nationality recognition. Today, the *wei shibie minzu*, literally the "undistinguished ethnic groups", total around 730,000 people (Minority Rights International 2007). Examples of these groups include the Gejia, Khmu, Kucong, Mang, Deng, Sherpas, Bajia, Yi and Youtai (Jewish). In other words, these individuals are regarded as ethnically different, but do not currently fit into the CPC's official ethnic minorities' framework.

It thus should come as little surprise that state imposed ethnic categories often contrast with on-the-ground ethnicity. Certain official ethnic groups are near extinction or borderline assimilated into Han, which begs the question whether a re-categorization or abolition of official ethnic minority groups is needed in the near future. For example, when discussing with Cui, an ethnic Xibo living in Beijing, about what it means to be an ethnic minority, she replies: "We don't eat dogs or horses. Otherwise we are the same as Han". Elaborating further, her explanation was her grandparents will wear traditional clothing during festivals, otherwise, their cultural and social lives are virtually identical as a Han. Few Xibos she knows can speak the traditional dialect fluently, a trend that will continue as the number of elders diminish. Cui, like many young ethnic minorities in Beijing, can barely speak their ethnic language or dialect, and certainly do not practice it everyday. While officially she is considered a member of an ethnic minority, her personal customs and way of life are indistinguishable from Han.

This situation has vivid resemblance to Moerman's (1965) study on ethnic relations in Thailand, where he pondered "Who are the Lue?" While attempting to describe who the Lue were in his research, in ways that were distinctive for other ethnic groups, he encountered numerous problems. While querying individual Lues on their typical characteristics they would mention cultural traits which were shared with other (often dominant) neighbouring groups. They lived in close interaction with other groups in the area; they had no exclusive livelihood, language or customs. Why was it appropriate to describe them as an ethnic group?

The purpose of officially classifying ethnic minority groups in China rather than adopting a self-identification method used in Canada, Australia and the

United Kingdom lies in the history of the CPC and the modern-day public benefits that are afforded to minorities. During the "Long March" of 1934–1935, Chinese Communist leaders became aware, first-hand, of the sheer ethnic diversity and cultures of China as they moved from the southwest to northwest of China. Gladney (1994a, 176) quoting Edgar Snow, describes the journey of the Marchers "harried on one side by the Japanese and the Kuomintang, and on the other by the 'fierce' barbarian tribesmen". Facing near defeat, the Communists made promises of special treatment, recognition and the establishment of autonomous regions to minorities – notably the Miao, Yi, Tibetans, Mongols and Hui – in exchange for their support.[8] It is thus from this modern legacy that ethnic nationality identification and ethnic minority policies have emerged.

It can also be suggested that a minority identification policy has allowed the new People's Republic to forge a nation-building project under the leadership of the dominant Han nationality. Projecting the image of Han superiority became useful for the Communists who incorporated it into Marxist ideology of progress. Recognized minority nationalities were categorized according to five major modes of production: primitive, slave, feudal, capitalist, and socialist. The Hans were ranked the highest on this scale, reinforcing the Han idea that minorities are backward and perpetuating the Communists' portrayal of Hans as the "vanguard" of the people's revolution. Ethnic minorities were thus encouraged to follow the Han example.

Prior to the founding of the People's Republic, it was out of political necessity by the Communists to secure the support of ethnic minorities to ensure their survival against the Republican Kuomintang and Japanese forces. However, with China no longer facing these threats, as the "benevolent patron of minorities" the CPC slowly turned its attention to "modernizing" and improving the livelihoods of "brother nationalities" akin to the standard of more developed Han areas (Zhao 2004, 194). While many of the development efforts were slowed by the Cultural Revolution, significant changes began to appear for minorities after 1978 with the adoption of China's modernization scheme.

With the onset of China's market reforms and modernization scheme, the CPC instituted systematic and procedural "special rights" and preferential treatment for ethnic minorities, reaffirmed in various national (e.g. 1999 National Minorities Policy) and local (e.g. Beijing Minority Rights Protection Policies) public policies.[9] The "one-child" policy typifies such a preferential treatment.

8　There are currently six autonomous regions which have political autonomy in theory – among them Inner Mongolia, Tibet and Xinjiang. Moreover, autonomous cities, prefectures and municipalities where minority nationalities are territorially concentrated are still present. The Constitution stipulates that the leaders of an autonomous area must be members of the area's main ethnic nationality. According to the People's Daily (2000) there are 2.824 million ethnic minority government officials, or 6.9 percent of the national total.

9　Potentially, the CPC were worried to have a former USSR situation emerge, where ethnic minority regions vehemently supported independence. The preferential treatment

Since 1982, and reinforced by the Population and Family Planning Law in 2002, China's population policy seeks to control the size of the population, calling for late marriages and fewer births. In effect, it strongly encourages couples to have only one child. Special exemptions in the population policy have been afforded to ethnic minorities, whereby couples from ethnic minorities are usually exempt or have a higher quota for children.[10] For example, in Beijing ethnic minorities can have two children. Other special exemptions vary by province, autonomous region or even municipalities. They include paying lower taxes; lower required scores for entry into university; easier access to public office; greater freedoms (relative to Han) for religious practices; and funding to express their cultural difference through the arts and sports. Due to these advantages and preferential treatments afforded to ethnic minorities in China, the status of an ethnic citizen cannot be altered at his/her discretion.[11]

Settlement

Notwithstanding the contemporary hyper-politicization of ethnic minority identification and categorization, the history of Beijing is littered with diverse ethnic groups interacting with one another as a result of high internal and external ethnic migration caused, in large part, by a quest for improved economic prosperity and the aftermath of conflicts. For instance, the Hui people who settled in Beijing were descendants of Muslim traders and officials who began to arrive in China during the middle of the seventh century. In fact, the term Hui itself derived from the Mandarin word "Huihui", which was used in the Yuan Dynasty (1276–1368) to refer to a diverse group of Central and Western Asian, Persian and Arab Muslim merchants residing in the nation. In particular, the Persian and Arab Hui descendants came via sea routes, who found trade profitable enough to justify a permanent presence. As a result, large Muslim communities were forged in coastal cities, first in the

---

and special rights can be seen as an initiative to appease the major ethnic populations.

10   Since ethnic minorities are exempt from the one-child policy, Ma (2004, 662) suggests this is one of the main reasons why many farmers tried to change their nationality status from Han to a minority group. As a matter of fact, from 1982 to 1990, several minority groups have doubled their population size mainly by re-registration, e.g. the Manchu population increased from 4.3 million to 9.8 million, and Tujia increased from 2.8 million to 5.7 million during this 8 year period.

11   Save in the situation where a child is born by mixed parents due to inter-ethnic marriage. Here the ethnic status will be determined by the parents before the child reaches 18 years of age. However, when the child reaches 18, s/he can choose which parent's ethnic status to adopt. After the age of 20 no alteration can be made. In practice, the large majority adopts the ethnicity of their father. Also, in cases where the CPC was mistaken in nationality status recognition, an individual can apply for "correction" of their status. In practice, most individual apply to correct their status due to nationality recognition "errors" during the Cultural Revolution.

south, in Yangzhou, Guangdong and Fujian, and then slowly migrating to the north, culminating in a permanent population established in Beijing by the tenth century. They were later joined by Muslim soldiers from Central and Western Asia who were members of Genghis Khan's army and moved eastward as the Mongol, Kublai Khan, established the Yuan Dynasty with Beijing as its capital (see Lipman 1997, Wang et al. 2002). Through the passage of time many Huis intermarried with local Chinese, which led to a rapid numerical growth of their population and increased their assimilation into Chinese mainstream society (see Israeli 1982). This pattern of intermarriage and assimilation will be repeated time and again throughout Beijing's history with different ethnic minority groups.[12]

Beijing has also prospered in spite of repeated invasion by numerous ethnic empires – Mongolians and Manchus being the major ones. With every invasion, the pattern seems to repeat itself: a small ethnic population stayed, adapted, and/ or assimilated into the city. The example of the Manchus who ruled during the Qing Dynasty from the seventeenth to the early twentieth century best illustrates this case. For political purposes the early Manchurian emperors often intermarried with Mongols, so that their descendants would also be seen as legitimate heirs of the previous Mongolian-ruled Yuan Dynasty. It was this interaction between Hans and Manchus throughout the Qing Dynasty that tested the resolve of Manchurian ethnic management in Beijing. On the one hand, the Manchu rulers sought to preserve a distinct Manchurian ethnic identity. However, to keep power they had to respect the existence of various ethnic groups, notably the Han, who were the majority population (see Rawski 2001). One tactic the Manchus utilized was a system of dual appointments in which all major imperial offices in Beijing would have a Manchu and a Han member. In the late nineteenth century, Manchus assimilation with Hans became apparent to the extent that they began adopting Han customs and language. Spoken Manchu declined in the Imperial Court and in the streets of Beijing. This shift in assimilating towards Han culture played a major role in overthrowing Manchurian control of Beijing in 1912; and ultimately, to the creation of the Republic of China led by Sun Yat-sen.[13]

At present, Beijing's Manchurian population is around 250,000. In fact, unknown to many, even some locals, Beijing's demographics encompass 55 ethnic minority groups, who total nearly 600,000 legal residents as elaborated in Table 6.1. As one of China's largest urban communities, Beijing is dominated by a Han population where many are descendants of ethnic minority groups, but identify themselves as Han. For example, although 42.8 percent of the ethnic minority population are officially Manchu, this number could be significantly higher as many with Manchurian ancestry choose to identify themselves as Han in

---

12   Intermarriage occurred in spite of many local sayings discouraging the practice. For example, one local saying warned: "cattle don't herd with water buffalo; immigrants shouldn't join with locals".

13   The legacy of Manchurian rule in Beijing can be seen today in the wider Han cultural context. The *qi pao*, a Manchurian dress, has been popularly adopted by Hans.

order to protect themselves from the stigma of being seen as "outside colonizers" (as Manchus were initially portrayed by Sun Yat-sen) or "imperialists" (as depicted by the CPC, particularly in the early PRC years) (see Li 1951). Ethnic identification other than Han was so common, in the 1982 census there were still lingering doubts about the government's true intention for registering nationalities (see Gladney 1994b). During the Cultural Revolution (1966–1976), a ten-year period when any types of ethnic, religious, cultural or political differences were suppressed by the CPC, mosques, temples, churches and other cultural institutions had been torn down in the name of erasing the "four olds" – old custom, culture, habits and ideas. By the early 1990s, it had become clear that those identified as an official ethnic minority were receiving real benefits, as outlined earlier, leading to a greater propensity for non-Hans to identify themselves as such. Indeed, it was not uncommon to hear reports in the outskirt districts of Beijing, where a sizeable ethnic Manchurian population exists, of those who are mixed Han/Manchu or have strong Manchurian ancestry attempting to re-identify themselves as Manchu in present-day. Most are often not successful due to strict government policy and for some, a lack of formal records to prove ethnicity.

While the Cultural Revolution sought to remove markers of ethno-cultural traditions, many ethnic minority groups such as Tibetans and Uyghurs continue to strongly resist. As a result, members of both groups in Beijing harbour resentment against the dominant majority Han, due in large part to the CPC's treatment of their large populations in the Western provinces (see Baranovitch 2003; Moneyhon 2004; China Development Brief 2006). In contrast, certain other groups such as ethnic Koreans have adapted well to Beijing's urban milieu. Yoon (2006) suggests ethnic Koreans historical experiences in China can account for their highly successful accumulation of economic capital and social integration

Table 6.1   Ethnic Composition of Total Population in Beijing, 2000

	Population	**%**
Han	**12,983,696**	**95.7**
Ethnic Minority Total	**584,692**	**4.3**
Manchu	250,286	2.8
Hui	235,837	40.3
Mongol	37,464	6.4
Korean	20,369	3.5
Tujia	8,372	1.4
Zhuang	7,332	1.3
Miao	5,291	0.9
Uyghur	3,129	
Tibetan	2,920	
Other	13,692	
Total Population	**13,568,388**	

Source: National Bureau of Statistics (2005)

in Beijing. Their migration to the city was due to famine and war in the Korean peninsula from the 1860s onwards. Most notoriously, the Japanese who occupied Manchuria in the 1930s, organized a series of collective labour migration from southern Korea to parts of Northeastern China, which eventually lead to thousands of ethnic Koreans settling in Beijing (see Kim 2003). After the Sino-Japanese war and civil war between the Communists and Nationalists during 1945–1949, Koreans in China who allied with the Communists were granted formal citizenship and were encouraged to maintain their ethnic language, education and culture. However, during the Cultural Revolution, Koreans encountered setbacks as an ethnic minority group when the Communists sought to abolish bureaucracy and feudalistic "old" elements of society. Having realized the vulnerability of being a minority group and the danger of nationalism, many ethnic Koreans in Beijing adopted a strategy of full accommodation to the authority of the central and local Beijing government. They even obeyed the population control policy so enthusiastically that most ethnic Korean families interviewed have opted to have just one child. As a result, their birth rates and population growth statistics are much lower than Han and all other ethnic minorities.

With widespread economic reforms in the 1980s and 1990s, South Korean firms began entering Beijing markets. Ethnic Koreans, who were relatively successful in retaining their native language through the generations, were positioned to benefit substantially from the introduction of such firms whose preferences was to hire cheaper, China-based employees who were nonetheless able to communicate in the Korean language and relate to its cultural values and practices. Widespread economic reforms in the 1980s not only encouraged greater economic activities for ethnic Koreans, coupled with reduced restrictions on mobility, it also provided an incentive for both Hans and other ethnic minorities to internally migrate to Beijing for employment and a higher standard of living. This movement of large numbers of ethnic minorities since the beginning of economic reforms initially resulted in the formation of distinct ethnic enclaves in the capital city.

One noticeable difference in the neighbourhood characteristics of Beijing, in comparison to multi-ethnic communities such as Toronto, Sydney or London, UK, is that the city lacks numerous defined and distinct ethnic enclaves in present day. This has not always been the case. Beijing has periodically received a large number of ethnic minorities and Han migrants from different parts of the nation. These migrants and their descendants developed geographically distinguishable ethnic centers in the city. For instance, Israeli (1982) points out Hui communities settled in areas separate from local Chinese, which allowed them to maintain their Islamic traditions. The seclusion was also made possible by domestic laws which protected Muslim traders, a point of custom which was also enjoyed by foreign entities such as the British and French in later centuries.

In spite of several Muslim-oriented ethnic enclaves, a small Tibetan neighbourhood in Haidian District and pockets of Manchurian communities in the city's outer districts, due to Beijing's unparalleled, rapid development and shortage of physical space, most ethnic enclaves have disappeared, making room for high-rise residential and corporate buildings. At present, there are still several original Tibetan temples (which have become "museums") and Islamic mosques intact, but in most cases they do not reflect ethnic demographics of the local area. This makes the Niujie area more remarkable as one of the last surviving, important historical ethnic enclaves in Beijing.

Niujie in Xuanwu District is one of the largest ethnic enclaves in the city, with a population of 24,088, of whom 54.1 percent are Huis. Historical documentation indicates a Hui settlement has been in this location since the Tang Dynasty (618–907) (see Weng 1992). By the Yuan Dynasty, Niujie, then called Willow River Village, was located outside but close to the main city walls. The location during this period amply reflected a separation between the Huis and the ruling Mongols living inside city walls (see Wang et al. 2002). Although Huis continued to strive in Willow River Village as distinct ethnic enclave and ethnic enclave economy, when Hans regained control over China establishing the Ming Dynasty (1368–1644), Hui communities slowly began to scatter throughout Beijing. By the Qing dynasty, Willow River Village changed its name to Niujie, which literally means "Oxen Street", and most likely took this name given the main economic activity was trading beef and mutton prepared in accordance to Islamic customs. Today, food services, including Islamic restaurants and supermarkets, continue to play a central role in the economic activities of the enclave.

Niujie still remains peripheral to the city's core area of economic growth – neighbouring Xicheng and Dongcheng districts have a higher GDP per capita and higher rates of economic growth than Xuanwu district, where Niujie is located. Perhaps in reaction, since 1997, the Beijing Municipal Government has redeveloped both commercial and residential areas of Niujie, affecting over 7,500 households. By 2000, approximately 3,000 households moved into new apartment buildings painted in green and white paint (to emphasize "Islamic colours") and decorated with Islamic symbols. In 2002, the second phase provided apartments for the remaining households. With a return rate of more than 90 percent according to the Niujie street administrative office, the majority of household members who did not return to Niujie were Hans, suggesting that the enclave continues to retain its ethnic characteristics. The municipal government has also spent over 10 million yuan (~ US$1.47 million) renovating the 1,000-year-old Niujie mosque. It has revitalized Oxen Street into a Muslim-style commercial street, home to numerous Muslim restaurants, a major supermarket with halal goods, a Hui Primary School, and Islamic-Chinese styled buildings (from apartment blocks to the post office). In CPC fashion, there are signs and murals present, reminding the locals about the recent historical achievements of the community and the role the municipal government has played in improving water, electricity and gas supplies to the area.

Compared to the well entrenched Hui communities in Beijing, the influx of labour migrants during the past few decades has led to the emergence of relatively new 'home' province-based and ethnic-based enclaves emerging, such as Zhejiang Village and Henan Village. For Uyghurs from Xinjiang, the early migrants concentrated in the Ganjiakou and Weigongcun, collectively known as Xinjiang

Village in Haidian District, and located near an ancient Uyghur enclave.[14] Similar to the Huis, the primary ethnic enclave economy in Xinjiang Village revolved around the food industry. Baranovitch (2003, 731) vividly recalls, at the time, that young Uyghurs sold Xinjiang-style, barbecue mutton from food stalls. In fact, Uyghurs who were better financially positioned opened restaurants which offered Xinjiang style food.[15] During the mid-1990s, the popularity of ethnic cuisine soared to such an extent that Xinjiang Village had more than 40 restaurants (see Ma and Xiang 1998).

The Uyghur ethnic enclave in Xinjiang Village did not last long. In 1999, the Village was demolished due to an official position taken by the municipal government that the action will effectively curb illegal street vending and remodel Beijing into a modern metropolis.[16] A more sinister explanation is the municipal government demolished the Village due to severe criminal activities such as drug dealing and violence (see Baranovitch 2003). Moreover, the demolition was part of a municipal strategy to "deport" Uyghurs back to Xinjiang, which, not by chance, coincided with the general crackdown of Uyghur separatists.

This begs the question, what makes one ethnic enclave thrive and another disappear in Beijing? In large part, the central and municipal government policies and attitudes are an important factor in the development and survival of ethnic enclaves in the capital city. For example, the CPC's relatively favourable policies towards ethnic minorities have provided an impetus for improving the Hui-dominated Niujie enclave and tentatively provided the space for Xinjiang Village to develop. Yet, the CPC's distrust of Uyghur activities in Beijing, during a period of heightened separatist activities in the late 1990s, resulted in the demolition of Xinjiang Village. An additional element to consider in the survival of an ethnic enclave in Beijing lies in its administrative location. The development of an enclave is improved if it is located wholly within one administrative district,[17] such as Niujie, and unlike Xinjiang Village which combined two neighbourhoods. Since the street administrative office is responsible for overseeing the residential and economic development of urban neigbourhoods, an administrative unit that solely oversees a particular ethnic enclave will be more inclined to represent the enclave's interests especially in a climate of accelerated investment in urban development. For instance, the outcomes of the redevelopment of the Niujie area

---

14   According to Zhuang (2000), during the Yuan Dynasty Uyghur intellectuals and merchants of Islamic faith settled in the Weigongcun area. However, when Hans began to rule during the Ming Dynasty, there was a gradual decline of Uyghur population in the area, with many electing to move back to Xinjiang.

15   The usual Uyghur dishes at Xinjiang style restaurants include fried, spicy mutton, flat breads, square noodles (which is often served with tomato sauce) and pilaf rice.

16   Interestingly, the area has now been replaced with numerous small ethnic restaurants, including Tibetan, Korean, Dai, Yi and Mongolian.

17   In Chinese cities, there is hierarchical administrative system which extends down as far as the neighborhood and household levels.

suggests that street administrative office played a crucial role in preserving the Hui character and ethnic-specific economic activities of the enclave; which in turn, provided a greater incentive for Hui residents to return.

Also, it is quite possible that the municipal government may have endorsed the redevelopment of the Niujie area with strong Hui and Muslim characteristics as a means to attract tourism to the area, as well as providing a showcase to illustrate the CPC's continued efforts to preserve and respect ethnic minorities in the capital. On this point, the Beijing Municipal government has designated his mosque as an important place for international leaders from Islamic nations to attend. In sum, the role of the municipal government in showcasing the Niujie area and the mosque has enhanced the possibilities of preserving the unique ethnic characteristics of the enclave.

Representation

The CPC has often depicted ethnic minorities to the general public as exotic, practitioners of "backward" traditions (especially marriage customs and the role of women) and prone to poverty and illiteracy (see Harrell 1995; Hoddie 2006). This is contrasted to the dominant majority Han who are seen as united, modern and, as Blum (2001, 68) controversially writes, "superior". The commodification and objectification of ethnic minorities by the CPC have led to Han stereotypes which inevitably play a role in Han-minority interactions.

One of the major vehicles in forging and reinforcing Han stereotypes of the ethnic minority is their portrayal in the official state media, amply demonstrated in the China Central Television's (CCTV) widely watched broadcast of the annual Chinese New Year's program. Over one half of the evening's broadcast is normally devoted to Tibetans, Mongols, Zhuang, Uzbek, Wa, Hui and other ethnic minorities happily singing in their native languages (with simultaneous Chinese translation) and performing traditional dances (see Gladney 1994b).[18] Non-minority hosts and performers exclusively wear Western-style suits and dresses, a marker in China for sophistication and respectability. At the same time, this juxtaposes the colourful and less modern costumes of minority entertainers, further reinforcing the "exotic" and "backward" image of ethnic minority groups. In many ways, minorities are also represented in official media sources by emphasizing the feminine. It is not uncommon in variety shows, such as the New Year's program, for the majority of ethnic minority performers to be female. This has lead to suggestions that

18   One of the most recent examples of these performances was during the 2008 Beijing Olympics' Opening Ceremony. Notwithstanding the fact that the 56 ethnic groups on display were actually only Han Chinese members, the "minorities" paraded cheerfully into the Bird's Nest stadium in brightly colour cultural costumes (hats, dresses and robes), while carrying the Chinese flag in an effort to signify national harmony.

feminizing minorities reinforces a perception that they are subordinate to Hans (see Hoddie 2006; Schein 2000).[19]

The media is not the only source for commodifying ethnic minorities. Cultural institutions such as the National Ethnic Palace, near *Minzu* Hotel and State Ethnic Affairs Commission (SEAC) on Chang An Avenue in Beijing, is the site of an enormous hall which stores minority artifacts, books and temporary exhibitions on ethnic minorities. Indicative of the majority of content on display is the iconographic image of ethnic minorities (mostly females) which greets visitors upon entering. Cues denoting the "primitive" and traditional livelihoods of ethnic minorities are contrasted with Han modernity.

It is further intriguing that certain ethnic minority groups such as Koreans are seldom exoticized and commodified in the media, in exhibitions such as the National Ethnic Palace, or in the wider Beijing context to the same extent as other ethnic minority groups. For the most part, it is ethnic minority groups with large populations in the relatively less-developed provinces, e.g. Tibetans, Uyghurs, Zhuang, who are usually portrayed in an exoticized and commodified fashion, whereas ethnic minority groups with relatively higher aggregate education outcomes enjoy contrasting experiences.

In typically East Asian manner, daily interactions between ethnic minorities and Hans, often revolve around food. Many Hans visit ethnic restaurants to try different cuisines and to experience an exotic and "foreign" environment. This fascination is further heightened by popular ethnic minority restaurants decorating both their exterior and interior with stereotypical ethnic designs (i.e. ethnic language scripts) and offering ethnic musical performances. For instance, despite the dismantlement of Xinjiang Village, Uyghur culture has thrived in other parts of the city where Xinjiang restaurants appear. One of the most famous and popular in Beijing is the 400 person capacity Afanti restaurant situated in an old alley in Dongcheng district. Co-owned by a ethnically mixed married couple, a Uyghur woman (daughter of the former provost of the Central University for Nationalities) and Han husband, one of its main stated objectives is to break down barriers of ethnicity and to "create a warm atmosphere of equality and harmony" (Quoted in Baranovitch 2003, 741).[20] How this manifests itself is fascinating: After dinner, typically around 8pm, a band performs both traditional and contemporary Uyghur music with an accompanying dancing troupe on stage in traditional ethnic costume. As the performance matures, patrons are encouraged to participate by dancing on their own tables, which are long and sturdy for several individuals to

---

19   This analysis does not completely factor gender role differences and the patri-/matri-archal structure of various Chinese ethnic groups, including Hans. These differences can potentially affect one interpretation of the performance and groups portrayed.

20   In many ways their marriage is a living testament to the restaurant's stated objective of breaking down barriers of ethnicity. Baranovitch (2003) reports there were initial objections to their marriage given that the husband was not Muslim. The couple eventually married only after he agreed to convert to Islam and accepted a Uyghur name.

stand on. Afanti has gained such popularity that many high ranking (
foreign government officials, business persons, and other famous figu
the restaurant.

In many respects, Afanti can be seen as a case of appropriating minority culture
into a commodity and financially profiting from it.[21] Arguably, its successes are
partially due to the tacit approval by the CPC – indicative by high ranking officials'
visits, and the invitation of Afanti's minority performers to CCTV's variety shows,
akin to the New Year's program. From another perspective, the restaurant serves
the interest of the CPC by embodying the intended image of ethnic harmony and
tolerance in the capital. As the Tibetan vice-director of the State Ethnic Affairs
Commission, Dainzhub Ongboin, reiterates, like Hans "people from different
ethnic groups help each other and their relations are harmonious" (Beijing Review
2007).

The increasing popularity of ethnic food notwithstanding, religious and ethnic
traditions can potentially be a barrier for minorities to integrate and fully interact
with Hans, especially among Tibetans and Islamic minorities such as Hui, Uzbek
and Kazak who have strong clerical traditions. A matter as differing diets due to
varying ethnic traditions and customs with Hans can be a barrier for interactions
with ethnic minorities, especially given food is so central to social life in China.
For example, since Islamic diet requires meat to be prepared in accordance to
religious practice, and it strictly prohibits the consumption of pork – a staple among
Hans – there is the potential for reduced social interactions between Islamic ethnic
minority groups and Hans. In fact, deep rooted ethnic Hui identity and religious
traditions, centered with the Mosque and Islamic food, have for many generations
separated Huis from Hans in Beijing (Wang et al. 2002).

Perhaps the most culpable barrier for minority group interactions with Hans is
the institutionalization of an ethnic group by the CPC itself. The official system
of categorization constantly reminds ethnic minorities that they are members of
a fixed and specific ethnic group differing from the dominant majority Hans.
Clarifying the boundaries between ethnic minority groups and Hans creates a host
of issues, especially when history or 'home' province issues mix within the politics
of ethnic minority representation. This can potentially lead to continued negative
stigmas of Mongolians who are historically portrayed in Chinese textbooks as
barbarians, or Manchus as imperialists. This may mean Han-ethnic minority
relations in Beijing can be affected by far away frictions between Uyghurs from

---

21　While Afanti restaurant was used as an example, the lessons from this case can be
transferred to many other ethnic minority restaurants in the capital. For instance, King Gesar,
a Tibetan restaurant in Chaoyang District has a similar setup to that of Afanti. Decorated
with traditional ethnic Tibetan style frescos and waiters in full Tibetan costumes, customers
are offered traditional Tibetan food such as yak meat, cheese and butter tea. Traditional
Tibetan performances, akin to Afanti, are also performed from 8 to 10 pm.

Xinjiang or Tibetans from the Greater Tibetan Area.[22] For example, just prior to the demolition of Xinjiang Village, many Hans decided not to frequent the Village on the grounds that is unsafe and dangerous due to growing disturbances in Xinjiang (see Baranovitch 2003). Even in March 2008, protests and demonstrations by ethnic Tibetans in the Tibet Autonomous Region and Greater Tibet Area marking the forty-ninth anniversary of the Tibetan uprising, can potentially lead to a growing distrust of Tibetans living in Beijing. What makes both Uyghurs and Tibetans communities particularly vulnerable in Beijing is that they are more easily identified as 'outsiders' due to their physical appearance.[23]

While the popularity of all things ethnic, from music, dance and food, remains at its highest levels in the capital city, the contradictory nature of the inter-ethnic representation and interactions remains rooted in stereotypes perpetuated by the CPC controlled media and ironically, in part, by ethnic minority oriented restaurants such as Afanti.

Conclusion

The evidence presented in this chapter suggests that despite the contrasting histories of Beijing with recent immigrant-receptive communities such as Toronto and Sydney, ethnic enclaves in the capital city continue to serve as a potential source of social networks and livelihoods for members of ethnic minorities. In an environment of rapid urban expansion, Beijing's ethnic enclaves serve a more critical role as a location where minorities' practices can be preserved and protected. Unlike ethnic enclaves in Canada, Australia and the United Kingdom, minorities in Beijing tend to leave their enclave for reasons not primarily involving socio-economic advancement or assimilation, but rather, due to forced dispersement caused by urban development.

From another viewpoint, the institutionalization of ethnic relations may be a double- edged sword. On the one hand, celebratory festivals and events showcasing ethnic traditions and culture serve as a mechanism to promote minority groups to the mainstream. Yet, similar to Reiss' chapter, harsh criticism can be levied when a packaged and commodified version involving song, dance and foods is presented of a particular ethnic minority group. The central concern is that the socio-economic struggles of many ethnic minority groups are being masked when

---

22 The Greater Tibet Area incorporates historic Amdo in the northeast (in present day Qinghai, Gansu and Sichuan provinces) and Kham in the east (in northern Yunnan, Qinghai and Sichuan).

23 The worry that ethnic minority issues may result in growing dissension has led to the creation of a monitoring body (proposed in the ethnic minorities affairs eleventh Five-Year Plan, 2006–2010, and approved by the State Council) that aims to "clamp down separatism so as to safeguard ethnic unity, social stability and national security" n Beijing Review 2007).

a celebratory version of their culture and traditions is presented. This becomes a topic of concern in the next chapter.

References

Ando, K. 1974. Sun Yat-sen's Nationalism and the 1911 Revolution – Its Anti-Imperialist Significance. *Rekishigaku Kenkyu (Journal of Historical Studies)* 407.

Attane, I. and Y. Courbage. 2000. Transitional Stages and Identity Boundaries: The Case of Ethnic Minorities in China. *Population and Environment* 21(3): 257–80.

Baranovitch, N. 2003. From the Margins to the Centre: The Uyghur Challenge in Beijing. *The China Quarterly* 175: 726–50.

Beijing Review. 2007. *China has no Racial Discrimination.* March 30.

Blum, S. 2001. *Portraits of Primitives: Ordering Human Kinds in the Chinese nation.* USA: Rowman and Littlefield.

Brown, M.J. 2002. Local Government Agency: Manipulating Tujia Identity. *Modern China* 28(3): 362–95.

China Development Brief. 2006. *Miao, Yi, and Tibetan Migration.* Available at: http://www.chiandevelopmentbrief.com.

Gladney, D. 1994a. Ethnic Identity in China: The New Politics of Difference. In *China Briefing*, ed. W. Joseph, 171–92. USA: Westview Press.

Gladney, D. 1994b. Representing Nationality in China: Refiguring Majority/ Minority Identities. *Journal of Asian Studies* 53(1): 92–123.

Harrell, S. 1995. Introduction. In *Cultural Encounters on China's Ethnic Frontiers*, ed. S. Harrell, 3–36. Seattle: University of Washington Press.

Hoddie, M. 2006. Minorities in the Official Media Determinants of State Attention to Ethnic Minorities in the People's Republic of China. *Harvard International Journal of Press/Politics* 11(4): 3–21.

Hon, T.K. 1996. Ethnic and Cultural Pluralism: Gu Jiegang's Vision of a New China in his Studies of Ancient History. *Modern China* 22(3): 315–39.

Israeli, R. 1982. Muslim Plight Under Chinese Rule. In *The Crescent in the East: Islam in Asia major*, ed. R. Isareli, 227–45. London: Curzon Press.

Kim, S.J. 2003. The Economic Status and Role of Ethnic Koreans in China. In *The Korean Diaspora in the World Economy*, eds C.F. Bergsten and I.B. Choi. Washington, DC: Institute for International Economics.

Leibold, J. 2006. Competing Narratives of Racial Unity in Republican China: From the Yellow Rmperor to Peking Man. *Modern China* 32(2): 181–220.

Li, F. 1951. China: A World Power. *Fourth International* 12(1): 8–12.

Lipman, J.N. 1997. *Familiar Strangers: A History of Muslims in Northwest China.* Seattle: University of Washington Press.

Ma, L. and B. Xiang. 1998. Native Place, Migration and the Emergence of Peasant Enclaves in Beijing. *The China Quarterly* 155: 546–81.

Ma, R. 2004. *Sociology of Ethnicity: Sociological Study of Ethnic Relations.* Beijing: Beijing University Press.

Minority Rights International. 2007. *State of the World's Minorities 2007.* Available at: http://www.minorityrights.org.

Moerman, M. 1965. Who are the Lue? *American Anthropologist* 67: 1215–30.

Moneyhon, M.D. 2004. Taming China's 'Wild West': Ethnic Conflict in Xinjiang. *Peace, Conflict, and Development: An Interdisciplinary Journal* 5(5): 2–23.

National Bureau of Statistics [NBS]. 2005. *Tabulation on Nationalities of 2000 Population Census of China.* Beijing: China Statistics Press.

People's Daily. 2000. *Number of Ethnic Minority Cadres Soaring Up.* June 28. Available at: http://english.people.com.cn/english/200006/28/ eng20000628 _44161.html.

Rawski, E. 2001. *The Last Emperors: A Social History of the Qing Imperial Institutions.* Berkeley: University of California Press.

Schein, L. 2000. *Minority Rules: The Miao and the Feminine in China's Cultural Politics.* USA: Duke University Press.

Stalin, J.V. 1953. *Works 1907–1913, Volume XI.* Moscow: Foreign Languages Publishing House.

Tong, F.X. 1981. *Toward a People's Anthropology.* Beijing: New World Press.

Wang, W., S. Zhou and C. Fan. 2002. Growth and Decline of Muslim Hui Enclaves in Beijing. *Eurasian Geography and Economics* 43(2): 104–22.

Weng, L. 1992. *Beijing Hutongs.* Beijing: Yanshan Publishing.

Yoon, I-J. 2006. Understanding the Korean Diaspora from Comparative Perspectives. *Asia Culture Forum*, Kwangju, Korea, 27 October.

Zarrow, P. 2004. Historical Trauma: Anti-Manchuism and Memories of Atrocity in Late Qing China. *History and Memory* 16(2): 67–107.

Zhao, S. 2004. *A Nation-State by Construction: Dynamics of Modern Chinese Nationalism.* Palo Alto: Stanford University Press.

Zhuang, K. 2000. The Time and Space Process of Food Culture in Beijing's Xinjiang Street. *Shehuixue Yanjiu (Sociological Research)* 6: 92–104.

Chapter 7
Comparing Ethno-Development Outcomes in Toronto and Taipei

Reza Hasmath

The management of urban ethno-development can be a tricky proposition often sparking intense emotions and passion among local populations. With nearly 40 percent of its 4.6 million population represented by various visible ethnic minority groups, Toronto has become one of the most multi-ethnic communities in the world. Spurned by vast post-World War Two immigration from all corners of the globe, the city now encompasses numerous distinctive ethnic enclaves and economies. In order to manage the increased ethnic diversity, a variety of local policies and initiatives have been enacted, supported and reinforced by federal and provincial efforts. Some examples of these include changes in Toronto's 2001 Social Development and 2000 Economic Development Strategies to incorporate "tenets of multiculturalism"; financial support for annual festivals and cultural events such as Caribana described in detail by Reiss' chapter; and, through international and inter-provincial marketing efforts to promote the city's ethnic diversity to lure tourists and potential migrants. In fact, Toronto's conduct in managing ethnic diversity is seen as so successful it is often cited as exemplary and a model for other urban centres (see UNDP 2004).

While Canada have a multitude of recognized ethnic groups based on self-identification of ancestry, when it comes to ethnic differences in Taiwan the discussion is often directed towards two groups, the *dominant majority* 98 percent Chinese population and their interaction with the island's official thirteen Aboriginal groups (*yuanzhumin*), totaling nearly 458,000 persons (DBAS 2006). Great lengths have been taken by Taiwan to provide benefits to officially recognized Aboriginal groups, with annual statistics on educational and occupation outcomes used as a benchmark to monitor their social and economic development progress; and particularly outside of Taipei City where the vast majority of Aboriginals reside. Yet, similar to the previous chapter on Beijing, to examine ethno-development within a Chinese-Aboriginal dualism is to ignore the diversity, histories, and rich social and economic experiences of all ethnic groups – Hokkien, Hakka and the recent mainland Chinese population.

While it is undeniable that Toronto has been a leader in promoting multiculturalism in a programmatic manner, there are serious questions about the celebratory focus on festivals and cultural events as a mode of managing ethnic differences. While ethno-festivals and events serve as a means to promote awareness of various ethnic minority groups "culture", they may in the process, over-shadow or mask the socio-economic struggles that many ethnic minority groups face. Ironically, while the intentions of Taiwan is to promote the ethnic development of the official Aboriginal population, the lack of focus on the Hokkien and Hakka cultures, who combined constitute approximately 85 percent of Taiwan's population and referred to collectively as "Taiwanese", has created historical and contemporary tensions with the recent mainland Chinese population – who currently constitute approximately 13 percent of the total population – who migrated in mass nearing the conclusion of the Chinese Civil War in 1949. Moreover, embroiled in this political ethnic-based struggle is a lack of attention on the potential socio-economic disparities between all three ethnic groups; and in particular, those residing in Taiwan's most important financial centre, Taipei.[1]

This chapter will investigate the ethno-development of Toronto and Taipei, with a focus on the educational attainments and occupational outcomes of minority members. Empirically, one of the most compelling universal expectations is future occupational achievements and financial success based on higher educational attainments. This has been reinforced by studies that show the economic value of an education, that is, the added value a university degree has on an individual's working life earnings and occupational prospects (see Day and Newburger 2002, OECD 2004). One may argue this is the result of meritocratic selection procedures, whereby an individual's achievements in education is the main criteria for occupational advancement (Heath et. al. 1992; Young 1958). This of course assumes that occupational outcomes are based solely on merit, which is often defined by educational attainment. Moreover, studies have also suggested the higher the education and socio-economic status, the greater propensity for the individual to socially integrate within the community (see Bagley 1984, Muiznieks 1999). Measuring one's education attainment to occupational outcomes thus serves as a natural pairing for examining ethnic minority development in both communities.

What makes the Toronto and Taipei comparison compelling is the juxtaposition of similarities and contrasts of both cities. In the context of their respective communities, both Toronto and Taipei enjoy a likeness in their political and economic importance. As Taiwan's capital, Taipei is the centre of political power and can be viewed as an urban environment that has one of the highest levels of economic development relative to national standards. Without hyperbole, Toronto's importance to Canada is similarly unquestioned as a financial and cultural capital. Beyond the surface of their urban iconic status in their respected nations, both cities have very different histories, with the population of Taipei shaped by a history of colonial rule and more recently, historical events in mainland China, and Toronto being an immigrant-receptive city. Arguably as a consequence, they both define ethnic groups in sharply contrasting ways. How this ethnic categorization

---

1   Due to the extremely low number of official Aboriginal members living in Taipei City, a meaningful analysis is unable to be conducted. As such, this group is not included in the chapter's ethno-development analysis.

manifests itself in the educational and occupational market is a subject of interest. When looking at occupational differences between ethnic groups in Toronto and Taipei, there is a strong need to ask whether these differences are explained by their differing educational achievements. Thus, it could be the case that the lower occupational attainments of a particular ethnic group could be explained by the group's lower educational achievements. The concern in both cities, therefore, ought to shift to address the problem why there are so few members of this ethnic group who have high educational attainment. Alternatively, if an ethnic minority group with the exact educational attainments as the dominant group is underrepresented in the labour market, in effect fail to reap the returns on their educational investments, it may be prudent to examine and discuss possible reasons behind an ethnic penalty.

Modern Historical Ethno-Development

It is first worthwhile to expand on the modern historical development of ethnic differences in Toronto and Taipei in order to truly comprehend the ethno-development reality at present. In Toronto, the majority of residents prior to World War Two were from the Charter population, British and French descendants, who permanently settled in the city in the late eighteenth century.[2] In the first major wave of modern immigration from 1946 to the late 1960s, due to a system that encouraged family sponsorship, chain migration of Western European groups were common, with the Italians[3], Portuguese and Greeks the largest cohorts. Typically, the majority of immigrants who arrived during this period had close knit family and friend connections. In addition, many came with little formal education and economic capital upon arrival to the city. For example, Tomasi (1977, 505) indicates 40 percent of the Italian cohort who came after World War Two had only a fifth grade education. At the time, there were few public programs in place to assist immigrants to integrate to Toronto. This resulted in many first-wave immigrants relying on their close connections to assist in the integration process, which in turn, had the unintended consequence of reducing their incentive to learn English, since their main mode of communicating in their social milieu was in their native language.

---

2   The first permanent European presence in Toronto was the French who established a trading fort in 1750, however, Fort Rouille was abandoned nine years later. From 1787 onwards, a large influx of British Loyalists fleeing the American Revolution settled in the city (which at the time was known as York). The next significant wave of settlement came during the Great Irish Famine in the mid-1800s, where Catholic Irish immigration numbers were to such an extent, they became the largest single ethnic group in the city (see Benn 2006).

3   Although Italians have been immigrating to Toronto since 1880, the first major wave of Italian population movement was post-World War Two.

Due to the relatively low education levels and for many, the inability to speak English fluently, many first-wave immigrants, mostly men, filled positions as manual laborers, craftsmen, mechanics and miners. Some commentators have even suggested the manual labour skills these groups possessed is one of the predominant reasons why the Canadian government and the city of Toronto welcomed them (see Delvoie 2000). The end of World War Two brought an enthusiastic interest in revitalizing, modernizing and building Toronto through the construction of roads, railways and infrastructure. Taking advantage of the depressed economies and high unemployment rates in Western Europe, Canada encouraged immigration from this region, with many Western European governments – especially Italian and Greek – even assisting in actively promoting temporary and permanent emigration to Canada since it provided relief to their ravaged domestic economies.

In 1966, a new immigration policy based on a points system involving factors including age and occupational qualification, replaced the older system which stressed sponsorship. This sparked the second major wave of immigration to Toronto from the late 1960s to late 1990s. Not coincidentally, only a year prior to changes in the immigration policy the Canadian government commissioned the *Preliminary Report of the Royal Commission on Bilingualism and Biculturalism*, which is commonly referred to as the first use of multiculturalism as a social policy for managing ethnic differences. The change in immigration policy and the onset of a formalized multiculturalism policy signaled Canada's willingness to accept further immigrants from non-European ethnic backgrounds. The ripple effect was immediate in the visible ethnic demographics of Toronto as Table 7.1 attests. In a matter of thirty years non-European immigration from the Caribbean and Latin America (especially from the late 1960s to 1980s), and South and East Asia (mainly in the 1990s) multiplied by almost tenfold, comprising 1,845,875 residents or 39.8 percent of Toronto's 2001 total population.

With an increase in the ethnic diversity of Toronto's population, policy responses became necessary to meet the demands and concerns of the changing population, and these can be traced in three distinct phases. With the advent of the 1971 policy on multiculturalism, the first phase stressed cultural reinforcement in public activities. Facing pressures to assimilate, many ethnic groups sought public support during this phase to maintain their traditions and heritage. For example, ethnic minority groups were supported by the government to bring their "cultures" into public activities in events such as Black History Week[4] (see Canadian Heritage 2006) or Caribana (see Chapter 5).

By the late 1970s, the increasing number of ethnic groups living in close proximity to each other fostered policy responses to strengthen inter-group relations in the city. In the background, there was a growing concern that discriminatory attitudes based on negative attitudes by the dominant population towards ethnic minority groups were restricting inclusion and integration. Community institutions

4   From 1976 onwards, this was changed to Black History month which occurs in February.

Table 7.1   Ethnic Composition of Total Population in Toronto, 1971–2001

	1971 Population	%	1981 Population	%	1991 Population	%	2001 Population	%
European Total	2,475,220	95.9	2,586,860	87.5	2,838,665	73.7	2,792,740	60.2
Non-European Total	104,830	4.1	371,255	12.6	1,012,030	26.3	1,845,875	39.8
East Asian	61,785	2.4	165,685	5.6	384,585	10.0	667,520	14.4
Caribbean	15,325	0.6	54,960	1.9	77,930	2.0	278,285	6.0
African	12,135	0.5	26,635	0.9	166,850	4.3	117,845	2.5
South Asian	5,650	0.2	71,490	2.4	212,420	5.5	484,480	10.4
Middle Eastern and West Asian	2,455	0.1	16,375	0.6	70,225	1.8	147,770	3.2
South and Central American	765	0.0(3)	18,790	0.6	61,740	1.6	104,245	2.3
Total Population	2,580,050		2,958,115		3,850,695		4,638,615	

Source: Statistics Canada (2005)

from media to business were not recognizing the full participation of all. As a consequence, Toronto's public institutions were encouraged to setup and participate in diversity training programs that sensitized individuals to ethnic differences. The end goal of these programs was to "open-up" public institutions to greater ethno-cultural diversity in both the content and delivery of its service.

Finally, in the third phase from the late 1980s to mid-1990s, anti-discrimination policies were strongly emphasized. This phase is marked by public policies in Toronto that sought to combat racism, which was also particularly featured in other larger Canadian urban centres such as Vancouver or Montreal. The central issue during this phase was that racism based upon physical characteristics had not been sufficiently addressed in policies of multiculturalism. Anti-Black and anti-Asian prejudices in the workforce and in everyday life, though sometimes subtle, were present and became a public issue. Media campaigns, increased ethno-cultural activities in schools, and diversity training in the workforce were anti-discrimination initiatives initiated by both the province of Ontario and city of Toronto.

The non-European ethnic groups that dominated second-wave immigration to Toronto largely differed from the first wave, since they were more formally educated and experienced in skilled occupations. This was the result of a more stringent process in accepting immigrants based on a points system which rewarded skills and education, to the extent that 80 percent of newcomers to Toronto are secondary school graduates and 40 percent have completed university (City of Toronto 2001). However, upon arrival many found they were not readily employable in the profession of their home country. Professional degrees such as medicine and engineering were not recognized by professional associations in the Province of Ontario. This has lead to strong undertone among many first-generation, second-wave, non-European group members that they feel "cheated" upon settlement in Toronto.[5] Like the first-wave, many felt they were brought here to undertake jobs that Torontonians no longer wanted. In this context, immigrants have become the new "job-makers" through investment and business formation, and significantly, they participate in the entrepreneurial sector at a higher rate than individuals from Charter group backgrounds.

In contrast to Toronto, ethnicity in Taipei has historically been contested and rife with controversy. In this respect, ethnicity has often been constructed within general terms that arguably speak more to political aspirations. Since the two main groups of Chinese living in Taipei are either long-time immigrants or newcomers from mainland China at different periods of historical time, they have different memories of mainland China and Taiwanese history. For instance, Hokkiens and Hakkas have experienced events such as the colonial occupation by Dutch and Japanese governments and vast struggles during the early years of the Republic of Taiwan.

---

5   This observation should be tempered by Perlmann and Waldinger's (1997, 918) note that the children of immigrants with higher education are more likely to succeed in the education and occupational market than previous generations.

After Japan's defeat in World War Two, Taiwan was put under the administrative control of the Republic of China Kuomintang (KMT) government in 1945 by the United Nations Relief and Rehabilitation Administration. At the time, the KMT was fighting a bloody civil war with the Communists in mainland China. By 1949, with the defeat of the KMT in mainland China and the establishment of Taipei as a provisional Republic of China capital, nearly 2 million mainlanders – predominantly supporters and families from KMT political and military personnel – migrated to Taiwan.

The tensions between Hokkiens and Hakkas and the recent mainland population increased tremendously from 1949 to 1987, a period marked by KMT-imposed martial law. In one form or another, the island was engaged in national Sinification projects to promote the Mandarin language and the "purification of identity" (Lin 2007). In this effort, Mandarin Chinese was installed as the official language to be taught in schools. Local Hakka and Hokkien "dialects" were prohibited from being spoken in public institutions – suggesting speaking Mandarin could make one become a "real Chinese".

One re-interpretation for the *raison d'etre* for these projects is offered by Yang (2007), who argues the Taiwanese were seen as "slaves" who had been occupied and colonized by Japan, thus, anything Japanese was regarded as imperialistic. As a result, authorities began to suggest that Taiwanese people needed to learn Mandarin Chinese in order to remove Japanese colonial influences. Another interpretation is that the "Sinification policy" was based on the premise of forging a nation-building project to ensure that the differences in cultures on the island will mesh and be easily ruled by appealing to a common "Chinese" background. That is, similar to the experiences in the previous chapter, by employing the term Chinese, the KMT essentially brought together large groups of ethnicities into one superimposed nationality, that is, a new imagined community of Chinese.

Notwithstanding the rationale behind the KMT's Sinification policies, in effect, what it accomplished was to put "Chinese-ness" and "Taiwanese-ness" in conflict with each other – setting up an unusual clash of cultures. For instance, during the "Chinese Cultural Renaissance Movement" in the 1960s the conceptual understanding of "Chinese culture" was strengthen through different kinds of "national cultural projects". These "national cultural projects" were contrasted by the local Hakka and Hokkien "low culture" which was presented through the concepts of "local dialects", "local operas" and "local customs". While under the official KMT view, these policies were for the purpose of reviving Chinese culture and the 'Chinese race', the consequence was to present the Hakka and Hokkien peoples at the level of "local culture" and fostering a strong potential for ethnic tensions. Given the long dominance of the KMT and mainlanders in political, cultural and social affairs in Taipei, with only a brief end to their rule in 2000–2008 with the election of Chen Shui-bian, an assessment of differences in education attainment and occupational outcomes is our subject of interest to assess potential differences in contemporary ethno-development.

Ethno-Development Outcomes

In both Toronto and Taipei, formal education is seen as the long-term equalizer for all groups, when it comes to ensuring their future economic and social security. As such, it is not surprising that in both communities the educational attainments of ethnic minorities is relatively high. For instance, Table 7.2 shows that ethnic minorities in Toronto have achieved relative parity with or even exceeded the level of educational attainments with European groups. In fact, ethnic minorities are more likely to be university graduates (at the undergraduate level) than the European groups, with an odds ratio of 1.21. Moreover, at the graduate school level, there is relative parity between European groups and ethnic minorities.[6] While this may indicate the relative success of initiatives to improve access to ethnic minorities at the university level, what is disconcerting is the level of ethnic minorities having "some university" education, with an odds ratio of 3.39. This may suggest there is a disproportionate number of ethnic minorities who start, but fail to complete their university education.

Furthermore, before praising Toronto's high level of ethno-development support throughout the public education system, the extent to which this relative success is attributed to Canada's immigration policies – which are based on labour skills and age – has to be taken into account. Herein lies the utility of disaggregating the educational attainment statistics based on ethnic minority groups that have a 20 and 40 percent population that is Canadian born, roughly serving as a proxy for capturing the realities of the one and a half, and second generation ethnic minority Canadians. It is fascinating to observe that ethnic minorities who are predominantly 20 and 40 percent Canadian born have achieved rapid educational attainment convergence with the European groups, namely in their rates of return at the university level.[7] The growth of non-European migrants to Canada since the late 1960s has challenged the traditional dichotomy that once explained patterns of migrants and their offspring's educational attainments. Perhaps the second wave of migrants who reside in Toronto, who came to the city voluntarily, and often under a selection system that favours high educational attainment, is finding that their offspring are benefiting from the quality and quantity of their parental inputs.

---

6   When the statistics are not disaggregated between the age categories of 25–34 and 35–54, the younger population is more educated than the older population. In fact, young persons in every ethnic category have a university graduate rate that is higher than the older age group; an 8.2 percent overall difference between the 25–34 and 35–54 age groups. This trend may reflect the growing importance of education in the competitive, Toronto labour market.

7   This may not necessarily be the case for the Canadian-born segment of the Caribbean population, who have an aggregate total of 10.2 percent attaining a university (undergraduate) qualification.

Table 7.2 Educational Attainment and Odds Ratio (in parentheses)* by Ethnic Population in Toronto, Ages 25–54, 2001

	Did Not Finish High School %	High School %	Trade %	College (Technical Institute) %	Some University %	University (Undergrad) %	Graduate School %	Z
European Total	20.7	22.4	8.8	19.8	2.4	19.2	6.8	1,324,490
Non-European Total	23.2	21.0	7.5	15.9	4.4	21.2	6.8	858,295
	(1.26)	(0.88)	(0.72)	(0.65)	(3.39)	(1.21)	(0.99)	
Non-European (> 20%)⁺	24.6	21.1	7.6	16.0	4.2	20.1	6.4	692,950
	(1.41)	(0.89)	(0.75)	(0.65)	(3.06)	(1.10)	(0.89)	
Non-European (> 40%)⁺	15.1	20.4	9.5	23.0	4.1	22.6	5.3	65,820
	(0.53)	(0.83)	(1.17)	(1.35)	(2.92)	(1.39)	(0.61)	
Middle Eastern & West Asian	21.3	20.3	6.0	12.1	5.4	26.3	8.7	70,160
	(1.06)	(0.82)	(0.46)	(0.37)	(5.06)	(1.88)	(1.64)	
South Asian	25.6	21.6	6.9	12.0	3.2	21.4	9.2	227,145
	(1.53)	(0.93)	(0.61)	(0.37)	(1.78)	(1.24)	(1.83)	
East Asian	22.6	18.4	5.1	14.1	5.5	26.8	7.3	334,705
	(1.19)	(0.67)	(0.34)	(0.51)	(5.25)	(1.95)	(1.15)	
African	23.5	26.0	11.1	19.6	3.8	11.8	4.3	49,250
	(1.29)	(1.35)	(1.59)	(0.98)	(2.51)	(0.38)	(0.40)	
Caribbean	21.0	23.6	13.3	27.1	2.8	10.2	2.0	126,035
	(1.03)	(1.11)	(2.28)	(1.87)	(1.36)	(0.28)	(0.09)	
South & Central American	24.8	25.5	9.5	19.5	4.7	12.1	3.8	51,000
	(1.44)	(1.3)	(1.17)	(0.97)	(3.84)	(0.4)	(0.31)	

* The odds ratios compare the odds of educational attainment [p(attainment) / (1 – p(attainment)] for the selected non-European group (numerator) and Europeans (denominator). An odds ratio value of 1 thus indicates group equity; an odds ratio value that is > 1 indicates the educational attainment segment is more likely to occur among the selected non-European group; conversely, an odds ratio value that is < 1 indicates the educational attainment segment is less likely to occur among the selected non-European group.
+ Represents non-European ethnic minority groups that have a demographic of 20 percent and 40 percent Canadian born respectively.
Source: Calculations based on Statistics Canada Census 2001

Table 7.3   Educational Attainment and Odds Ratio (in parentheses)* by Ethnic Population in Taipei City, 2007

	Self-Educated %	Elementary %	Junior High %	Senior High %	College %	University %	Graduate School %
Mainland	-	5.8	8.7	24.6	14.5	33.3	13.0
Chinese	1.3	16.9	11.7	32.5	15.6	19.4	2.6
		(8.47)	(1.81)	(1.74)	(1.16)	(0.34)	(0.04)
Hokkien							
Hakka	-	10.5	10.5	36.8	21.1	15.8	5.3
		(3.30)	(1.46)	(2.24)	(2.11)	(0.22)	(0.16)
Average	**0.6**	**11.5**	**10.3**	**29.7**	**15.8**	**24.9**	**7.3**

* The odds ratios compare the odds of educational attainment [p(attainment) / (1 – p(attainment)] for Hokkien and Hakka groups (numerator) and Mainland Chinese (denominator). An odds ratio value of 1 thus indicates group equity; an odds ratio value that is > 1 indicates the educational attainment segment is more likely to occur among the selected Hokkien or Hakka group; conversely, an odds ratio value that is < 1 indicates the educational attainment segment is less likely to occur among the selected Hokkien or Hakka group.
Source: Calculations based on author's sample survey of 172 respondents (Hokkien, N=77; Hakka N= 19; Mainland N=69; Other = 7)

In Taipei City, the survey results reveal that the Mainland group has a higher education attainment, on average, at the university and graduate school level, than other groups. In fact, over 60 percent surveyed from the Mainland group had attained a form of tertiary education. Although still subject to contestation, this trend may reflect the structural advantage the recent mainland Chinese group may have had from 1945 to the late 1980s. While the survey sample size may not be suitable for making comprehensive age group comparisons, the majority of respondents in all ethnic groups in the 18–30 age category achieved significantly higher education attainments than the older age categories. This signifies that there is a growing parity among ethnic groups' education attainments in Taipei City; however this may not be reflected in the general population sample for another generation.

It is a widely accepted view that high education outcomes bode well for employment possibilities. As we see in Taipei this belief holds true, in Toronto the reality is slightly different. Income and ethnic participation by occupational sectors have historically been reliable measures for discerning an ethnic penalty in the labour market. The existence of observable ethnic concentration in certain occupational sectors may suggest differential access to the labour market. Thus, Table 7.4 examines occupational sectoral distribution by European and ethnic minority groups to ascertain whether there are patterns of concentration. What

Table 7.4 Occupation and Odds Ratio (in parentheses)*, and Mean Salary per Annum by Ethnic Population in Toronto, Ages 18–64, 2001

	High Level Manager (%)	Mid-Level Manager (%)	Professional (%)	Skilled Non-Manual (%)	Skilled Manual (%)	Less Skilled Non-Manual (%)	Less Skilled Manual (%)	Mean Salary (CAD)	N
European Total	2.3	12.7	20.2	19.5	8.1	26.8	10.4	54,131	1,602,504
Non-European	0.9	8.8	17.2	16.6	6.3	32.3	18.0	38,356	949,579
	(0.15)	(0.48)	(0.73)	(0.72)	(0.60)	(1.45)	(2.98)		
Non-European Total (>20%)+	0.8	8.0	16.9	16.4	6.5	32.1	19.4	37,785	767,326
	(0.12)	(0.40)	(0.70)	(0.71)	(0.64)	(1.43)	(3.48)		
Non-European (>40%)+	1.5	9.9	19.4	19.4	5.3	35.1	9.4	44,701	83,550
	(0.43)	(0.61)	(0.92)	(0.99)	(0.43)	(1.72)	(0.82)		
Middle Eastern & West Asian	1.6	13.2	19.8	16.4	6.9	29.9	12.2	42,675	72,670
	(0.48)	(1.08)	(0.96)	(0.71)	(0.73)	(1.24)	(1.38)		
South Asian	1.0	8.4	15.7	14.7	6.2	30.7	23.2	37,825	249,055
	(0.19)	(0.44)	(0.6)	(0.57)	(0.59)	(1.31)	(4.98)		
East Asian	0.9	9.8	20.7	17.7	4.9	30.2	15.9	39,413	361,080
	(0.15)	(0.6)	(1.05)	(0.82)	(0.37)	(1.27)	(2.34)		
African	0.6	6.5	14.0	15.5	6.2	37.4	19.8	35,761	52,145
	(0.07)	(0.26)	(0.48)	(0.63)	(0.59)	(1.95)	(3.62)		
Caribbean	0.5	6.6	13.8	17.4	7.7	37.7	16.2	36,880	156,640
	(0.05)	(0.27)	(0.47)	(0.8)	(0.9)	(1.98)	(2.43)		
South & Central American	0.5	6.9	11.6	16.2	10.0	36.2	18.6	34,970	57,989
	(0.05)	(0.3)	(0.33)	(0.69)	(1.52)	(1.82)	(3.2)		

1 USD = 1.04 CAD

* The odds ratios compare the odds of working in an occupational sector [p(outcome) / (1 – p(outcome)] for the selected non-European group (numerator) and Europeans (denominator). An odds ratio value of 1 thus indicates group equity; an odds ratio value that is > 1 indicates that the selected non-European group is more likely to work in that particular occupational sector; conversely, an odds ratio value that is < 1 indicates the selected non-European group is less likely to work in the respected occupational sector. + See Table 7.2 note on demographic breakdown.

Source: Calculations based on Statistics Canada Census 2001

is observed is that the higher the managerial ladder, the less ethnic minority representation. Among mid-level managers ethnic minorities have an odds ratio of 0.48, their chances decrease further when examining high level managers, with an odds ratio of 0.15. Essentially in all occupational categories which required skilled labour, ethnic minorities fared worse than European groups. Furthermore, an analysis of the data also reveals a worrying income disparity of approximately CA$16,000 between European and non-European group earners. This suggests the possibility of a significant income inequality in Toronto's labour market.

In Taipei City, education attainment, in general, parallels the employment destination type and subsequent gross income one enjoys. Among all ethnic groups, those with tertiary level education have a gross income nearing NT$480,000 per annum; and those with high school or below nearly half that amount. Although the recent mainland Chinese group does have a slightly higher average gross income per month in both education categories, given the age trend in the survey data, this gap is expected to be closed significantly in the near future. Even more revealing in Table 7.5 is the employment destinations by ethnic groups. Perhaps again due to the legacy of the structural ethnic imbalance from 1945 to the late 1980s, we

Table 7.5 Occupation and Odds Ratio (in parentheses)*, and Gross Income per Annum by Ethnic Population in Taipei City, 2007

	Managerial %	Professional %	Skilled Manual %	Skilled Non-Manual %	Less-Skilled Manual %	High School and Below (NTD)	Tertiary Education (NTD)	Average (NTD)
Mainland Chinese	68.6	53.7	30.6	24.1	20.8	249,144	489,912	**395,700**
Hokkien	2.9	9.8	8.3	10.3	33.3	229,200	444,888	**307,872**
	(0.00[2])	(0.03)	(0.07)	(0.18)	(2.56)			
Hakka	28.6	36.6	61.1	65.5	45.8	246,012	453,660	**333,444**
	(0.17)	(0.46)	(4.00)	(7.37)	(4.84)			

1 USD = 31.4 NTD

* The odds ratios compare the odds of working in an occupational sector [p(outcome) / (1 − p(outcome)] for Hokkien and Hakka groups (numerator) and Mainland Chinese (denominator). An odds ratio value of 1 thus indicates group equity; an odds ratio value that is > 1 indicates that the selected Hokkien or Hakka group is more likely to work in that particular occupational sector; conversely, an odds ratio value that is < 1 indicates the selected Hokkien or Hakka group is less likely to work in the respected occupational sector.

Source: Calculations based on author's sample survey of 172 respondents (Hokkien, N=77; Hakka N= 19; Mainland N=69; Other = 7)

still see at the managerial and professional level a high dominance by the recent mainland Chinese group.

Potential Steps for Improvement

Both Canadian and Taiwanese education is highly subsidized. Thus, governments at all levels have a significant stake ensuring ethnic minorities in Toronto and Taipei realize their potential in the labour market and to minimize the economic losses that come with the under-utilization of their human capital in the form of education. Public institutions, at all levels, must promote a more active approach to improving ethnic representation in the public and private sectors.

While Toronto has sought to instill federal employment equity legislation, which in theory should reduce the ethnic penalty, the success of these policies is in doubt. After two decades of implementing employment equity, ethnic minority inequities in the labour market in Toronto are still prevalent and perhaps even worse from a historical standpoint. The effectiveness of employment equity legislation is severely reduced since it is rarely implemented in a manner in which it was intended. Unfortunately, there is a lack of convincing evidence at this juncture to suggest that most employers fully comply with employment equity legislation in Toronto, other than reporting basic workplace data (see CRRF 2005). For example, in a 2002 public service employee survey, only 37 percent reported that they met legislated standards of employment equity; and an additional 5 percent reported exceeding these standards (Government of Canada 2004). Few employers actively maintained programs designed to remove barriers to workplace recruitment and advancement, and crucially, to change the working culture that acts as an important determinant in perpetuating the ethnic penalty.

Perhaps the situation can be mitigated if Equity Officers in Toronto are provided with improved incentives to be more aggressive in implementing and monitoring employment equity. If municipally-funded organizations and departments do not, in a reasonable time, take steps to attain employment equity parity, there has to be the threat of real repercussions from higher levels of government.[8] In short, more severe penalties should be imposed when employers fail to implement employment equity legislation requirements. Admittedly, in the private sector this is a more difficult proposition to execute as regulatory bodies could only extend so far. Yet, governments at all levels can provide tax incentives to promote employment equity in Toronto's private sector.[9] This is feasible in principle and could work similar to existing tax incentives to "go green" (promoting environmental initiatives) currently in practice. Moreover, by targeting big business and large corporations,

---

8   Potential repercussions in the public service can derive from negative evaluations by the Director General or the Auditor General's Report.

9   By targeting major corporations to promote and practice employment equity, it is hoped that this message can be delivered through their supply and partner chains.

one will hope that this employment equity message will be delivered through supply and partner chains.

As for Taipei? There is still an institutional culture dominated by the recent mainland Chinese group in the public sector. As hinted earlier, this is the legacy of Kuomintang dominance over a fifty year period. In fact, while conducting the survey the recent mainland Chinese group often voiced a greater willingness to have their children enter government than the Taiwanese groups – as it was perceived to foster more stable careers. Whether there is an old-boys network is debatable and difficult to discern given the favourable preference of the mainland Chinese group for the public sector. Nevertheless, we must be mindful that there is a structural imbalance in ethnic representation in employment destinations and gross income. If this is kept unchecked, it can lead to further social and political strains based on ethnic lines in Taipei. These imbalances are often the key traits that cause long-term ethnic conflict, so addressing this is an important priority. In this vein, it may be prudent to monitor education attainments and employment outcomes by ethnicity in Taipei to ensure that indeed one's education matches one's employment destination. If it fails to do so, then public policy responses ought to be conducted.

Whether there is sufficient political capital or motivation necessary to enact these policies is another question. Non-action in these regards can be explained if governments embrace the idea that the market is the final arbiter of social justice, i.e. the market can determine the fair distribution and compensation for labour. In line with this process, one potential fear if the government intervenes is that they may effectively distort market conditions. Yet this must be tempered by the fact that there are significant market failures having little to do with statistical discrimination as traditionally understood, which play a powerful role in perpetuating the ethnic penalty. Conversely, educational and occupational experiences are influenced by social and psychological externalities, notably within the social contexts of opportunity within which ethnic minority groups are embedded. Thus, government's legitimacy and motivation to enact policies to curb potential ethnic penalties and integration failures stem from this realization.

References

Bagley, C. 1984. Education, Ethnicity and Racism: A European-Canadian Perspective. *Currents* Fall 1984: 8–12.

Benn, C. 2006. *The History of Toronto: An 11,000 Year Journey*. Toronto: City of Toronto Museums and Heritage.

Canadian Heritage. 2006. Multiculturalism. Available at: http://www.canadianheritage.gc.ca/progs/multi/.

Canadian Race Relations Foundation [CRRF]. 2005. *The Labour Market Experience of Social Work Graduates: Exploring the Role of Affirmative Action in Education*. Toronto: Canadian Race Relations Foundation.

City of Toronto. 2000. *An Economic Development Strategy for the City of Toronto 2000.* Toronto: City of Toronto Press.

City of Toronto. 2001. *A Social Development Strategy for the City of Toronto 2001.* Toronto: City of Toronto Press.

Day, J. and E. Newburger. 2002. The Big Payoff: Educational Attainment and Synthetic Estimates of Work-Life Earnings. *Current Population Reports.* US Department of Commerce.

Delvoie, L. 2000. Canada and Italy: A Steady State Relationship. *International Journal* 55(3): 463–74.

Government of Canada. 2004. *Employment Equity in the Federal Public Services 2002–2003.* Available at: http://www.tbs-sct.gc.ca/report/.

Heath, A.F., C. Mills, and J. Roberts. 1992 Towards Meritocracy? Recent Evidence on an Old Problem. In *Social Research and Social Reform*, eds C. Crouch and A.F. Heath, 217–44. Oxford: Clarendon Press.

Lin, C.S. 2007. *Citizenship after 288.* LSE Workshops of Ethnicity, Citizenship and Taiwan.

Muiznieks, N. 1999. *Human Development and Social Integration.* UNDP Reports.

Organization for Economic Co-operation and Development [OECD]. 2004. *Education at a Glance 2004.* Paris: OECD Publishing.

Perlmann, J. and R. Waldinger. 1997. Second Generation Decline? Children of Immigrants, Past and Present: Reconsideration. *International Migration Review* 31(4): 893–922.

Statistics Canada. 2005. *2001 Census of Canada.* Available at: http://www12. statcan.ca/ english/census01/home/Index.cfm.

Taipei City Government. 2006. *Taipei Statistical Yearbook.* Taiwan: Taipei City Department of Budget, Accounting and Statistics.

Taipei City Government Department of Budget, Accounting and Statistics (DBAS). 2006. *Survey of Family Income and Expenditure of Taipei City.* Available at: http://w2.dbas.taipei.gov.tw.

Thompson, R. 1989. *Theories of Ethnicity: A Critical Appraisal.* USA: Greenwood Press.

Tomasi, L.F. 1977. The Italian Community in Toronto: A Demographic Profile. *International Migration Review* 11(4): 486–513.

United Nations Development Programme (UNDP). 2004. Globalization and Cultural Choice. *Human Development Report 2004.* Available at: http://hdr. undp.org.

Yang, C.C. 2007. *Ethnic Conflict since 228.* LSE Workshops of Ethnicity, Citizenship and Taiwan.

Young, M. 1958. *The Rise of the Meritocracy: 1870–2023.* London: Thames and Hudson.

Chapter 8
"Cooling Out Troublesome Constituents": The Politics of Managing "Isms" in the Antipodes

Augie Fleras

To say we live in a multicultural world is surely an assertion of understated proportions. Our world is characterized by immigrant-driven demographic diversity, a growing commitment to multiculturalism as basis for living together differently, and the codification of inclusiveness protocols for managing diversity. To be sure, the post 9/11 and 7/7 epochs have played havoc with the principles and practices of multiculturalism, with reactions ranging from outright hostility to studied indifference, as conveyed by the following questions: Can an official multiculturalism provide a bulwark against the sense of alienation and exclusion by disaffected second generation youth that may mobilize into anti-social activities? Can multiculturalism be held accountable for so called integration failures related to home grown terrorism (Jakubowicz 2007; also Biles and Spoonley 2007)? Is multiculturalism a move to address racialized and immigrant inequality, or a cynical ploy to disguise inequities behind a façade of orchestrated platitudes (Pearson 2001)? How potent is multiculturalism as an instrument of change: Does it promise more than it can deliver ('a kind of sheep in wolf's clothing') or, alternatively, does it do more than its willing to admit ('a wolf hiding in sheep clothing') (Fleras 2007)? Are evolving references to multiculturalism more a matter of semantics than a substantive transformation – in effect reinforcing its status as a kind of 'floating signifier' that can mean everything, yet nothing? Responses to these questions puts the onus on exploring the differences between what an official multiculturalism says its doing and (1) what it really is doing; (2) what people think its doing; (3) what people think it should be doing; and (4) what it can really do under the circumstances.

The dearth of consensus over these questions makes it abundantly clear: A theorizing of multiculturalism has proven an enigmatic and elusive exercise insofar as the concept rarely means what it says, or says what it means. Consensus is virtually non-existent because of political and philosophical disagreements over multiculturalism – ranging from questions of how to balance collective with individual rights, to debates over establishing a framework for equality between groups without sacrificing individual freedoms within groups. Even more problematic is a theorizing of an official multiculturalism. Except to acknowledge a condition in which numerous ethnicities coexist, together with a belief that this condition is preferred and should be promoted official multiculturalism rarely strikes a responsive cord, largely because of seemingly limitless possibilities under its umbrella. Consider the range of options: Some versions of multiculturalism believe that a society of many cultures is possible, but only if differences are rejected so that everyone is treated the same regardless of race or ethnicity, akin to the case of France in Adsett's chapter. Another variation argues that a society of many cultures is possible so long as peoples' cultural differences do not stand in the way of full democratic participation and equal citizenship treatment. Differences are tolerable under this model, but should neither hinder nor help in sorting out outcomes. A third multicultural model proposes a society of many cultures as one that treats everyone the same as a matter of course, but takes cultural differences into account when necessary to ensure more equitable outcomes. A final version contends that a true multicultural society of many cultures is possible – at least in theory if not practice – but only when group specific differences are taken seriously up to and including the creation of separate institutions, support for segregated ethnic enclaves with values and practices at odds with mainstream, or recognition of minorities as legally constituted entities that justify the allocation of societal rewards (May 2004).

Such a spectrum of meanings and applications complicates any theorizing of official multiculturalism falters. Except to acknowledge the necessity of diversity management for cooperative coexistence, there is virtually no agreement regarding the status and role of multiculturalism, its magnitude and scope of expression. Yet consensus or not, approve or disapprove, democratically diverse societies confront an unmistakable multicultural challenge: How to manage diversity by making society safe *from* differences as well as to make society safe *for* differences (Schlesinger 1992). Or phrased alternatively, how to construct a cohesive yet prosperous society without undermining either the interconnectedness that holds it together or the diverse parts that compromise the totality (May 2004)?

Nowhere is the challenge more contested than in immigrant societies. Namely, those societies with policies in place to regulate the intake of immigrants, who see immigrants as a society-building asset, who expect immigrants to take out citizenship, and who endorse programs like multiculturalism or employment equity for improving newcomer integration (Fleras and Elliott 2007). As Lenard (Chapter Two) concedes, multiculturalism can contribute to the society's (nation)-building project through policies and programs that themselves focus on fostering mutual trust. This inextricable link between society-building and official multiculturalism underscores its political centrality: Insofar as it reflects, reinforces, and advances both state and government interests, an official multiculturalism is ultimately a political act to achieve political goals in a politically acceptable manner. In that multiculturalism is primarily about 'ruling elites' controlling 'unruly ethnics', its fundamental logic is patently pragmatic, with national and vested interests prevailing over those of immigrant minorities.

No one ever said that living together with differences was easy. No more so than now, thanks to the proliferation of indigenous peoples politics, politicized minorities, identity politics, and the politics of diversity. According to Robinson (Chapter 3), institutional accommodations (from special rights to immunities) pose a problem of justification for those liberal-democratic societies who want to balance cultural identification with social equality without caving in to moral relativism, cultural essentialism, or social chaos. The emergence of an official multiculturalism has proven both an opportunity and challenge in coping with these emergent realities, especially in those contexts contesting the liberal ideals of colour blind state neutrality and formal equality before the law (Bader 2007). The conclusion seems inescapable: Inasmuch as an official multiculturalism is primarily a discourse in defence of dominant ideology, it constitutes a *branding* strategy for conflict resolution and impression management. Insofar as immigrants and racialized minorities are implicitly framed as problem people who have problems or create problems that are costly or inconvenient, the multicultural challenge is unmistakable: That is, 'cooling out' these so-called 'troublesome constituents' by fostering the illusion of change and inclusiveness without substantially disturbing prevailing patterns of power and privilege.

The verdict on multiculturalism is mixed writes Marangozov (Chapter 10). For some, multiculturalism represents a good idea gone badly because of religious extremism, growing inequalities and politicized ethnicity. For others, it's a bad idea that has unfolded according to plan by encouraging cultural separatism or ideological extremism – to the detriment of national unity. To deconstruct the how and why behind these oppositional dynamics, this chapter explores the politics of managing 'isms' in the Antipodes. Federal multiculturalism in Australia is shown to be a pragmatic exercise that acknowledges the reality of diversity without taking unnecessary risks in undermining society-building. By contrast, the politics of 'isms' in New Zealand are situated within the context of an 'official' biculturalism against the backdrop of a de facto multiculturalism (Fleras and Spoonley 1999). Even the discursive framework is shown to be shifting: Whereas the 'isms' in the Antipodes were once concerned with managing diversity and reasonable accommodation, the emphasis now is on managing the 'isms' to ensure an appropriate narrative for living together differently within limits and without undue hardship. That makes it doubly important when theorizing multiculturalism in Australian and New Zealand to focus on the dynamics of diversity management without ignoring the politics of managing the 'isms'.

Multiculturalism Down Under: Australian Perspectives

Canada and Australia have much in common despite their positioning at opposite ends of the globe. Both countries originated as British-driven colonies, confronted an indigenous peoples who were divested of land and authority to facilitate the colonisation project, perceived themselves as resolutely "white" societies with a civilizing mission, embarked on vast immigration programs for society-building purposes, and are now compelled to rethink the challenges of living together with differences in a globally interconnected world. The politics of immigration also reveal powerful parallels: Australia flung open its doors to immigration from so-called non conventional sources (Non English Speaking Backgrounds, NESB) such as Asia – in contrast to its historical past when an openly racist immigration policy blocked entry to most non-whites. As seen in the next chapter, the postwar infusion of immigrant women and men has escalated to the point where the Commonwealth (central) government has had little option except to intervene in pursuing social cohesion and national unity (Jayasuriya 2000). The emergence of an Australian model of multiculturalism has proven an intriguing if imperfect branding strategy for managing the challenges of living together with differences.

Several post-World War Two trends contributed to the origins of an official multiculturalism. Most notable of these was the termination of the White Australia policy, largely because of large-scale and diverse immigration to fuel the post War economic boom. With 23 percent of its population now foreign born, Australia is the world leader in this regard followed by New Zealand and Canada both at 19 percent. Another 40 percent of the population is comprised of foreign born, if including at least one immigrant parent, with Asia the most significant source of new immigrants. In the hope of making virtue of necessity, the main political parties formally adopted multiculturalism in the 1970s as official policy in "appreciation of cultural diversity and [to] maintain the languages and cultural traditions of minority groups". Official Multiculturalism was further bolstered when Australia signed the International Convention on the Elimination of all Forms of Racial Discrimination, followed by the passage of its own Racial Discrimination Act in 1975. In essence, the Act made it "unlawful for a person to do any act involving a distinction, exclusion, restriction, or preference based on race, colour, descent, or national or ethnic origin which has the purpose or effect of nullifying or impairing the recognition, enjoyment, or exercise, on an equal footing, of any human right or fundamental freedom in the political, economic, social, cultural or any other field of public life" (cited in Hudson 1987, 97).

A 'Fair Dinkum' Multiculturalism

Multiculturalism sought to improve the social, economic, and political integration of new Australians from different cultural backgrounds. An initial emphasis on protecting ethnic minority rights eventually evolved into an awareness to include all Australians for multiculturalism to work (Kerkyasharian 2005). Too much emphasis on specific considerations for minorities posed a governance danger. Not only did it erode the legitimacy of multiculturalism in the eyes of the general public; it also fostered the potential for social isolation and political fragmentation. Not surprisingly, multicultural policy quickly shifted to facilitate the settlement of immigrants through racial tolerance, equal opportunity, and full participation

(Kerkyasharian 2005). In response to the 1978 Report on the Review of Post-Arrival Programs and Services for Migrants (the Galbally Report), the Australian Institute of Multicultural Affairs was established with the following goals in place:

- enhancing public awareness of Australia's diverse cultures, including an appreciation for their contribution to the enrichment of Australian society and national identity;
- promoting intercultural harmony and sharing among the various ethnic groups in Australia;
- fostering societal cohesion through understanding and tolerance of diversity;
- facilitating an environment that encouraged full and equal participation for all minorities while enhancing opportunities for minority women and men to achieve their own potential.

In addition to the creation of this Institute, the government accepted the recommendations of a report directed at improving ethnic broadcasting on multicultural television. A Special Broadcasting Services (SBS) established a government-funded, nationwide television and radio network, with a mandate to offer a variety of foreign language programs. A review panel had also recommended the teaching of languages and cultures in schools and universities. These objectives were consistent with the National Language Policy of 1987 with its advocacy of second language learning as critical for cultural and intellectual enrichment, economics (foreign trade and tourism), equality (social justice and equity), and external affairs (foreign policy) (Foster and Seitz 1989). Clearly, then, the promotion of linguistic diversity was not about diversity per se, but about managing diversity as a marketing strategy to take advantage of an emergent global market economy.

The profile of multiculturalism in Australia was firmly grounded in July 1989, with the establishment of a National Agenda for Multicultural Australia. The national multiculturalism agenda embraced three objectives: *cultural identity* – the right of all Australians to express (within limits) their language and culture; *social justice* – the right of all Australians to equal treatment and opportunity through removal of all discriminatory barriers; and, *economic efficiency* – the need to capitalize on the skills and resources of all Australians. Particular attention was aimed at promoting multiculturalism as a marketing asset to meet the global challenge of trade, investment, and financial linkages. Eight basic goals were articulated in advancing multicultural objectives: (1) freedom from discrimination, (2) equality of life-chances, (3) equality of access and resources, (4) equal participation in society, (5) development of potential for all, (6) sharing of cultural heritage, (7) institutional responsiveness, and (8) acquisition of English and community languages (Foster and Seitz 1989). The National Agenda also articulated a set of limits to Australian Multiculturalism:

An overriding commitment to Australian society and its national interests had to prevail. Diversity was acceptable; nevertheless, any primary attachment belonged to Australia alongside a corresponding endorsement of basic institutions, principles, and core values. And while diversity is valued, it is not a case of anything goes, according to the National Agenda, but a multiculturalism constructed around core values of mutual respect, tolerance and harmony, the rule of law, and protection of individual rights.

Under the recently defeated Howard Government, in power since 1996, a commitment to multiculturalism underwent the equivalent of continuity in change (Robbins 2007; Hawthorne 2008). To one side is the diminishment of multiculturalism as a national narrative (Healey 2007). The term itself is being phased out, including its removal from the immigration portfolio and replaced with citizenship, so that government policy is increasingly focused on concept of shared commonality rather than multicultural diversity. Instead of an ethnic particularism, a focus on civic universalism (reflecting majority Australian values) prevails, based on the social, cultural, political and economic rights of all citizens of a democratic polity (Pearson 2001, 2004). To the other side, multiculturalism continues to play a pivotal role in Australia's fortunes, as articulated in the New Agenda for a Multicultural Australia (originally 2000 but updated in 2003), namely, to build on Australia's success as a culturally diverse society that is united in diversity and a shared community and commitment. Four principles underpin Australia's current multicultural policy:

a. Civic Duty (*responsibilities of all*) – all Australians must support those basic structures, values, and principles of freedom and equality of Australian society;
b. Cultural Respect (*respect for each person*) – All Australians have the right to cultural expression as long as this expression does not break the law or deny this right for others;
c. Social Equity (*fairness for each person*) – All Australians are entitled to equality of treatment and opportunity in enhancing Australia's social, political, and economic life;
d. Productive Diversity (*benefits for all*) – All Australians benefit from the social and economic dividends of a productive diversity.

The conclusion seems obvious: In seeking to balance unity with diversity, responsibilities with rights, Australia's multicultural policy established the limits of an inclusive society. The freedom of all Australians to express and share their cultural heritage is respected; ultimately, however, this right depends on endorsing mutual civic obligations, including an overriding loyalty to Australia, its people, and the basic structures and principles informing its democratic governance, namely, the Constitution, Parliamentary democracy, freedom of speech and religion, English as the national language, the rule of law, acceptance, and equality (Commonwealth of Australia 2003). Strategies and programs are thus designed to (1) make institutions more respectful of, more reflective of, and more responsive to diversity (2) promote intergroup harmony, (3) ensure delivery of services that are available, accessible, and appropriate, and (4) optimize benefits of cultural diversity for all Australians. Emphasis is focused on fostering harmonious community relations; after all, national security begins with domestic community harmony fostered by Australian multiculturalism (Commonwealth of Australia 2003).

Despite the downturn in profile and political popularity, Australia remains a de facto multicultural in principle, programs, and practice. According to the then Minister of Citizenship and Multicultural Affairs, Peter McGauran (2005), Australia embraces a multiculturalism that disavows promoting diversity or special privileges to minorities of non-English backgrounds. Policies and services are endorsed that enable all Australians to reach their full potential in contributing to Australia's development, while respecting Australian values (freedom of speech, rule of law, equal opportunities). Or as ex-Prime Minister John Howard writes in the introduction to the New Agenda, "All Australians, regardless of their ethnic, cultural, or religious background are encouraged to participate fully in the wider Australian community to show a commitment to our nation, its democratic institutions and its laws." The values and principles that underpin multiculturalism extend to all Australians, including indigenous Australians and their unique culture and the contributions it makes to Australia. To be sure, Australia has no intention of formally enshrining multiculturalism in legislation (as does Canada), although the principles of multiculturalism are arguably safeguarded in existing legislation like the Racial Discrimination Act of 1975. Rather, as McGauran argues, multiculturalism is properly expressed as a lived reality – a sentiment reinforced by the new Prime Minister, Kevin Rudd, in his speech to an Ethnic Small Business Awards ceremony in Sydney "in Australia diversity is a fact of life, multiculturalism is a way of life" (FECCA eNews 2008).

Interestingly, while commonwealth multiculturalism as governance appears to be on hold, Australian states are strengthening a commitment to multiculturalism as policy and practice (Fleras 2009). The state of Victoria introduced a government policy statement in 2002 in that articulated four multicultural themes, including: valuing diversity, reducing inequality, fostering participation, and promoting the economic and cultural benefits of diversity for all Victorians. Passage of the Multicultural Victoria Act in 2004 proved pivotal: It not only established the state's cultural diversity, but also endorsed a vision of Victoria as united community with shared commitments without loss of a people's cultural heritage (Victoria Multicultural Commission, *Annual Report 2006/2007*). The state of Queensland has likewise reinforced its commitment to a policy of multiculturalism (Queensland Government 2004). Passage of the Multicultural Queensland – Making a World of Difference policy in 2005 confirmed the principle of equal rights, opportunities, and responsibilities of Queenslanders, regardless of race or ethnicity. In seeking to secure an inclusive and harmonious society, the policy secured a blueprint for managing and maximizing Queensland's diversity for the social and economic well-being of all its citizens (Queensland Government, Multicultural Highlights

2006/2007). As is the case with Victoria's commitment to a 'productive' multiculturalism, there is no question about divided loyalties. Minorities and migrants must display an overriding and unifying commitment to Australia, its values, interests, and prosperity.

Not surprisingly, multiculturalism continues to elicit strong reactions from all sides of the political spectrum (Longley 1999). Many praise multiculturalism as one of Australia's great success stories (Kerkyasharian 2005). Supporters acknowledge that its role in conflict management should not be discounted because of a white Australia image, history of exclusionary immigration programs, and commitment to assimilation. Yet criticism abounds. Critics have attacked multiculturalism for everything – from selective amnesia over its racist past in confirming a national monoculture, to little more than a 'pork barrel' for buying ethnic loyalties (Povinelli 1998). Those on the left have been disillusioned by the failure of this 'white supremacist' discourse to eradicate racism; those on the right fear it as a threat to the coherence of a white settler identity. Aboriginal Australians have positioned themselves outside this discursive framework since their interests as descendants of the original occupants are fundamentally different from immigrants and multiculturalism. The multicultural project has also been accused of being too contradictory an ideology to attract enduring support, too limiting because of its cultural approach to structural problems of racism and inequality, and too reductionist by fossilising cultural differences into an imagined and coherent community (Vasta and Castles 1996). Or as Nicolacopoulos and Vassilacopoulos conclude in the next chapter, in its role in containing cultural diversity, Australia's multiculturalism devalues the social status of some new Australians to that of the 'perpetual foreigner within'. Thus, the politics of multiculturalism remain sharply contested, in part because of government moves to diffuse the Muslim challenge, in part to defuse the threat of terrorist attacks and security concerns. In acknowledging Ghassan Hage's (2003) contention that official multiculturalism cannot address a politicized Islam, the Muslim presence exposes a multicultural conundrum, namely, should Australia be tolerant of those who are intolerant of tolerance (Dunn 2003)?

In short, Australia possesses an active if conflicted commonwealth multicultural policy, together with a comprehensive range of cultural and language programs that bear some resemblance to comparable initiatives in Canada. Differences are evident, of course. Multiculturalism in Australia exists as policy rather than being entrenched in law or the constitution. For historical reasons, Australia's commitment to community languages are more active than the passive support for heritage languages in Canada. And Australia's commitment to multiculturalism appears to be more explicit about drawing the line between what is acceptable or not. Diversity is fine, in other words, as long as it does NOT imperil national interests and national unity, break the law, violate individual rights, or contravene core cultural values. The political profile of multiculturalism continues to shrink as governments look for ways to pare costs while pandering to international capital and investment. Fear of being seen as catering to special interests groups such as Asian migrants or Muslim radicals has also contributed to the diminishment (Pearson 2001). No less unmistakable are the similarities. As in Canada, an official multicultural policy is directed at managing diversity by putting it to work on behalf of Australia's national and vested interests. The focus is on disadvantage rather than diversity through the mainstreaming of minorities and removal of discriminatory barriers. Emphasis is not on what Australia can do for diversity, but what diversity can do for Australia.

Duelling Isms in Aotearoa New Zealand

Aotearoa/New Zealand has long enjoyed an international reputation for its harmonious management of 'race' relations (Crothers 2007). This assessment is accurate to some extent, even if the outcome has been tarnished in recent years and conceived by accident rather than design. Yet the challenge in crafting an inclusive governance that recognizes and rewards differences has proven both elusive and daunting, with biculturalism narratives clearly dominating over alternative 'isms' (see Spoonley et al. 2004, Liu et al. 2005, O'Sullivan 2006). To the extent that many Pakeha (non Maori) New Zealanders waffle over an openly monocultural framework, yet are wary of any fundamental constitutional changes for fear of losing control of the national agenda, they vaguely endorse a preference for multiculturalism – at least in principle if not always in practice. In that government policy embraces a bicultural commitment as a basis for cooperative coexistence, there are grounds for optimism, although this biculturalism may not go far enough in acknowledging Maori constitutional status as the 'nations within'. In that neither multiculturalism nor biculturalism as currently articulated can constructively engage the politics of Maori indigeneity, with its focus on challenge, resistance, and transformation, a more politicised biculturalism is proposed. In that neither indigenous rights nor more complex notions of equality and inclusion have attracted much serious national debate under biculturalism (Barclay 2005), the politics of bi-nationalism are gaining traction as a preferred framework for democratic governance (Maaka and Fleras 2005).

The politics of 'isms' in New Zealand are sharply contested (Fleras 1998). The ideology of multiculturalism is problematic because it negates the primacy of Maori as 'tangata whenua' (peoples of the land). Conversely, a bicultural ideology rooted in the principles of the Treaty of Waitangi (partnership, protection, participation, and autonomy) is no less dismissive of immigrant cultures (see DeSouza 2007). Minorities resent replacing a monocultural supremacy with a bicultural exclusion, while Pakeha are known to reject biculturalism and endorse multiculturalism – not necessarily out of principle but from fear of bicultural demands or as a dissembling device to secure the status quo (May 2004; Pearson 2001).

Complicating the situation are challenges to this country's semi-official biculturalism: To one side are growing demands for recognizing multiculturalism as preferred framework for living together with differences (Liu 2005). This anxiety is not surprising: the flow of Asian immigrants and Pacific Islanders superimposes new ethnic "fault lines" upon increasingly politicized dualities, resulting in mounting pressure for a multiculturally based democratic governance (Spoonley 2005; Ward and Masgoret 2008). To the other side is a politicized Maori assertiveness that dismisses both a nascent multiculturalism or state sponsored biculturalism as grounds for constructive engagement. In embracing a bi-national blueprint that realigns the national discourse towards a two-nation state, each of which is partnered as part of a power-sharing relationship, tribal models of self determining autonomy are proposed consistent with Maori status as the 'nations within' (O'Sullivan 2006; Maaka and Fleras 2008). To yet another side is the reassertion of monoculturalism as national identity – at least judging by enthusiastic political and public acceptance over a 'we are one people' discourse (Seuffert 2006). The government response? A review of all policies and programs to ensure they are based on individual need rather than on race or indigenous rights.

Monoculturalism? Multiculturalism? Biculturalism? Binationalism? Some would argue that the differences between multiculturalism and biculturalism are minor and inconsequential. Others disagree, and acknowledge fundamental differences in scope, objectives, underlying rationale, strategies, and proposed outcomes. Still others concede the possibility of major differences between the two "isms". Nevertheless, repeated and often imprecise use has rendered biculturalism virtually indistinguishable from its multicultural counterpart. Still others contest that neither multiculturalism nor biculturalism adequately captures the logic underlying ethnic politics in New Zealand. Proposed instead is a binational governance structure that privileges the indigenous rights of Maori tribes as tangata whenua. Yet others are casting about for a compromise, including a governance arrangement that balances the agenda setting rights of Maori and Pakeha, with the multicultural rights of immigrants and descendents of immigrants. Failure to find a workable compromise in securing a balance between the competing rights of the 'tangata whenua' and the 'tangata tauiwi' ('immigrants') is not without consequences. The delay has prompted a Race Relations conciliator, Dr Rajen Prasad (1997, A-9), to go on record in pleading for "another way of thinking about ourselves as a multi-ethnic society with an indigenous culture, and with a founding document that regulates the relationship between Maori and Crown". It remains to be seen if a biculturally based multiculturalism within a binational framework can evolve from this welter of 'isms'

Biculturalism vs Multiculturalism: Competing Governances as Conflicting Discourses

New Zealand as a Treaty-based Pacific nation has proven a site of contestation in sorting out the politics of "isms". In shifting from monoculturalism to multiculturalism and biculturalism, and back again (Fleras 1984, Fleras and

Spoonley 1999, Pearson 2001, Seuffert 2006), New Zealand has evolved from a monocultural British enclave to one that acknowledges the bicultural legitimacy of Maori as founding peoples. But while initial interest in multiculturalism quickly dissipated because it compromised the biculturality of New Zealand (May 2004), a multicultural and increasingly politicized demographic has emerged. Consider the numbers: According to the 2006 Census, about two-thirds of the population identified as European, just under a third as Maori, Pacific Islander, and Asian. Nearly a quarter of the people living in New Zealand are foreign born. With the entry of Asian immigrants from Hong Kong, Taiwan, Korea, the Philippines, and Japan, New Zealanders of Asian origins now comprise approximately 9 percent of the population, Pacific Islanders at 6.4 percent of the population, Maori at about 14 percent, and European based whites at around 70 percent. Compare this with figures from 1976 when 86 percent identified as European, 9.2 percent Maori, and Pacific and Other at less than 2 percent (Human Rights Commission 2006). Immigration numbers suggest a continued diversification. In 2005/2006 a total of 51,236 migrants were approved for permanent residence, with the largest group from the United Kingdom, followed by China, South Africa, India, Fiji, and South Korea. As a result, as a percentage of total population, New Zealand has more overseas-born than any other country except Australia, while Auckland is home to more foreign-born than any other Australasian city (Spoonley 2007).

New Zealand has never formally endorsed multiculturalism as policy or program (McGrath et al. 2005). Unlike other countries, it typifies an unwillingness to accommodate its expanding diversity though a commensurate institutional recognition of its diverse languages and cultures (May 2004). Nevertheless, a de facto multiculturalism prevails for accommodating diversity, with government initiatives responding to increasing ethnic diversity, including ratification of international human rights conventions and domestic legislation to ensure equal opportunity and reduce disparities (Singham 2006). Additional initiatives range from the establishment of a Ten Point New Zealand Diversity Action Programme in 2004 for improving race relations (available online at www.hrc.co.nz) and programs like 'Connecting Diverse Communities and Building Bridges' project (for details, see NZ Parliament, 7 August 2008), to the introduction of a new educational curriculum that confirms New Zealand's multicultural commitments without reneging on its bicultural foundational principles (Fleras 2009).

Establishment of an Office of Ethnic portfolio within the Internal Affairs Department Affairs in 1999 eventually led to the creation of a stand alone unit in 2001. With the Office of Ethnic Affairs to provide policy advice in promoting the advantages of ethnic diversity, the popularity of multicultural discourses is secured, particularly among state elites, minority leaders, and non Maori academics (Pearson 2004). According to the Office of Ethnic Affairs (Ethnic Affairs 2006) new initiatives include more pre-arrival information for immigrants, training programs in the public sector to improve intercultural communication, and a national statement on religious diversity to enhance interfaith understanding. Admittedly, much of what passes for New Zealand multiculturalism rarely involves major public resources, does little to make Pakeha uncomfortable, and puts the onus on minority communities to preserve their culture (Spoonley 2005). Still, the re-emergence of multiculturalism as a complimentary national narrative has complicated an already complex balancing act of democratic governance (Race Relations Conciliator 2000).

In light of this emergent multicultural turn for framing cultural diversity, a bicultural reading of New Zealand has come under fire. A survey involving a random sample of 2,020 New Zealand households indicated strong support for a multicultural ideology, including 89 percent who believe diversity is good for the country (Ward and Masgoret 2008). Advocates of multiculturalism not only criticize a bicultural commitment for failing to recognize New Zealand's emergent multicultural reality (Ip and Pang 2005, 186; Eaton 2007). They also believe it is both unfair and unjust to encourage immigration without a corresponding commitment to multiculturalism for facilitating acceptance and integration.

Others disagree with any privileging of multiculturalism. Many point to the irrevocability of Aotearoa as a bicultural partnership between Treaty signatories, with its guarantee of collective rights that supersede the individual rights of recent immigrants (Sibley and Liu 2007). Biculturalism assumed the status of government policy in 1986 following passage of the State Owned Enterprises Bill which read: "Nothing in the Act shall permit the Crown to act in a manner that is inconsistent with the principles of the Treaty of Waitangi" (The Treaty of Waitangi signed in 1840 between the British Crown and many Maori chiefs is widely regarded as New Zealand's foundational constitutional document). The 1987 Court of Appeal ruling reaffirmed the bicultural partnership between the Crown and Maori, with each partner expected to act reasonably and in good faith toward the other. Passage of the State Services Act in 1988 confirmed the shift from a monocultural national identity to the 'biculturality' of Aotearoa by instructing state institutions to incorporate the Treaty obligations of partnership, participation, and protection into the delivery of service (Seuffert 2006).

Put bluntly, Maori bicultural rights as original occupants must take precedence over the multicultural rights of immigrants. Otherwise there is a danger of conflating Maori concerns with immigrants' aspirations, with a corresponding diminution of Maori foundational status as tangata whenua (original occupants). Dislodging biculturalism for multicultural commitments is dismissed as irresponsible, colonizing, and contrary to the spirit of Treaty partnership (Walker 1995; Ip and Pang 2005). Only when biculturalism is securely entrenched as the ruling paradigm for defining who gets what, can multiculturalism assume its rightful place. Not surprisingly, Maori attitudes toward immigration appear to have hardened in recent years, according to a Massey University Study, primarily because of Maori perceptions that New Zealand bi-culture is being eroded by newcomers, that immigration adversely affects Maori in terms of employment and access to services, and that immigrants may compromise Maori indigenous rights under the Treaty of Waitangi (Eaton 2007; Massey News 2007).

Multiculturalism vs biculturalism? To what extent are multiculturalism and biculturalism competing frameworks of governance discourse. In theory, multiculturalism as a political governance ideal differs from biculturalism. Multiculturalism is concerned with the principle of institutional inclusiveness through reasonable accommodation. By contrast, biculturalism ideally acknowledges the centrality of Maori as tangata whenua whose indigenous rights as embodied in the Treaty of Waitangi must be incorporated as grounds for democratic governance. In reality, however, the politics of biculturalism in New Zealand falls short of the mark. Biculturalism as currently employed barely addresses the possibility of power-sharing by way of Maori models of self-determining autonomy ('tino rangatiratanga'). It tends to focus instead on institutional accommodation in two ways (May 2004). First, by incorporating a Maori *dimension* into state practices and national symbols for Maori needs, including, the adoption of Maori names for government departments, increased use of Maori language and protocols for ceremonial occasions, and inscription of official reports in the official languages of Maori and English (Spoonley 1993, Durie 1995, Poata-Smith 1996). Second, by creating specific Maori institutions to address distinctive Maori needs without, however, departing from a state-scripted agenda. In both cases, biculturalism constitutes an accommodative exercises in state-determination. Or as Dominic O'Sullivan (2006, 4) concludes when contrasting state-determination with Maori self determination:

> [B]iculturalism cannot realize greater autonomy because its primary concern is with relationships among people in institutional settings, and within and among bureaucratic institutions. Self-determination is in contrast concerned with creating, to the greatest extent possible, independence and autonomy for groups, not necessarily in isolation from wider society, but certainly apart from the controls and regulations imposed from outside.

Later, he confirms the rift between state-biculturalism and Maori self-determining biculturalism:

> Biculturalism offers colonial dependence. Self-determination at least legitimises and to some extent offers autonomy, not as an act of government benevolence, but as an inherent right of indigeneity ... Biculturalism is a state strategy to manage resistance and a limited concession seeking strategy for Maori. It modifies assimilation, while protecting the nation's state assumed exclusive jurisdiction. It offers cultural space, while self-determination is more concerned with wider issues of citizenship, language, and political participation. Biculturalism misses the point of overlapping and interdependent Maori/Pakeha relationships and ignores the possibility of non colonial relationships beyond Pakeha, which makes it inevitably limiting (2006, 209)

The conclusion seems inescapable: Insofar as the objective is make institutions more respectful of Maori diversity, more reflective of this diversity, and more responsive to it, what passes for biculturalism is really a multiculturalism for Maori – one that reduces Maori to individuals with needs or a population with problems, rather than a peoples with rights. But even a bicultural multiculturalism is insufficiently politicized. In that the political claims of Maori are of a different magnitude than that of immigrant New Zealanders, this conflating of divergent political orders poses a severe governance problem.

Towards a Bi-national Governance: Truth to Power?

A paradox informs the policy basis of Maori-Crown relations. To one side is a continuing commitment to the principles and practices of a state-defined biculturalism. To the other side is a growing commitment to a Maori-determined biculturalism involving a bi-national agenda that endorses the unique status of the original occupants as "nations within" with inherent and collective rights to self-determining autonomy over jurisdictions related to land, culture, and political voice (Fleras and Elliott 1992). The relational status of Maori to society is not that of minority groups or ethnic communities. As nations within, Maori tribes constitute fundamentally autonomous political communities who are autonomous in their own right, yet jointly sharing jurisdictions in areas of mutual concern (Maaka and Fleras 2008). In that an appropriate governance framework is neither an exercise in institutional inclusiveness nor a discharge of Crown obligations by righting historical wrongs through grievance settlements, two outcomes can be discerned: First, the re-crafting of a new constitutional agenda along the lines of post-colonial social contract; second, a bi-national multiculturalism that challenges the foundational principles of New Zealand's constitutional order (Johnson 2008).

The politics of 'isms' are glaringly obvious. To the extent that Maori-Crown relations are increasingly articulated around a bi-national partnership of two founding nations within the framework of a single state, its opposition to multiculturalism could not be more forcibly stated. Consider the ways in which binationalism and multi/biculturalism differ as ideals for democratic governance:

- Multiculturalism strives to improve institutional accommodation; bi-nationalism entails creation of new constitutional space for living together differently.
- Multiculturalism involves a discourse about disadvantage and needs; under bi-nationalism, the language of rights prevails.
- Multiculturalism is concerned with grafting bits of diversity onto a mainstream core; bi-nationalism endeavours to restructure the constitutional order to foster power sharing, partnership, and participation.

- Multiculturalism deals with managing majority-minority relations; bi-nationalism provides a constitutional framework for engaging indigeneity along a majority-to-majority partnership.
- Multiculturalism is geared toward placement of immigrants in society through removal of discriminatory and prejudicial barriers. A bi-national agenda involves the sharing of sovereignty between two dominant cultures in complementary coexistence.
- For multiculturalism, the objective is to ensure an ordered social hierarchy in which minorities are nested into a pre-arranged system of shared goals and common means. By contrast, bi-nationalism focuses on a co-sovereign constitutional order involving a compact ("covenant") between fundamentally different political communities.
- Multiculturalism is rooted in the principle of universality and liberal pluralism: namely, that what we share in common as morally autonomous individuals is more important than any inherited differences that divide or provoke. The rationale behind bi-nationalism differs, reflecting a robust reading of diversity in which indigenous difference constitute the basis for recognition, relationship, and rewards.
- Multiculturalism endorses a commitment to working together by building bridges; bi-nationalism acknowledges the necessity to stand apart before the possibility of working together differently.
- Bi/multiculturalism in Aotearoa is essentially an accommodative exercise for preserving the status quo. The de-politicizing of differences through institutional inclusion seeks to make New Zealand safe from diversity, safe for diversity. Compare this with the ideal of bi-nationalism, with its notion of challenge and change though the politicization of differences, thereby making indigeneity *safe from New Zealand as well as safe for society.*

Clearly, then, neither multicultural nor bicultural discourses cannot possibly address the demands and claims of indigenous peoples as foundationally autonomous political communities who claim they are sovereign in their own right yet sharing in societal sovereignty by way of shared jurisdictions. More is involved than the inclusion of few bicultural bits – from increased use of Maori language and protocols at official levels to the inclusion of Maori in drafting local legislation that is protective of Maori interests or even the discharging of Crown obligations by righting historical wrongs through grievance settlements. Such a commitment hardly alters the balance of power in terms of who gets what as long as the state continues to define what differences count, and what counts as difference (Johnson 1994). Nor do multiculturalism or biculturalism comply with the recognition of two nations who share power through constitutional arrangements. With its roots in consensus, conformity, and control, any multiculturalism is poorly equipped to handle the highly politicized discourses of challenge, resistance, and transformation associated with the politics of indigeneity (O'Sullivan 2006).

Not surprisingly, the isms tend to talk past each other. Inasmuch as governments are largely content with institutional accommodation and grievance settlement rather than reforging the constitutional basis of society, central authorities will continue to misread the politics of Maori indigeneity and their implications for a binational coexistence. As long as the Crown defines indigenous peoples as multicultural minorities rather than autonomous and self-determining political communities, it will continue to misfire by applying inappropriate solutions to incorrectly defined problems. A de facto monoculturalism will remain intact as long as the constitutional order is anchored in Eurocentric values and structures as the normative standard by which policies are formulated, actions are judged, prevailing patterns of power and privilege are perpetuated, and priorities are assigned. These miscalculations are not without costs: In that a bi-national agenda constantly interrogates the colonial structures and mindset that organise indigenous people-Crown relations, its potential for disrupting the status quo is potent.

Nevertheless a multi-dimensional reality is inescapable: New Zealand constitutes a bi-national society composed of two founding peoples who continue to exercise control over the national agenda. But a commitment to binationalism should not be invoked to diminish the rights of multicultural minorities or recognition of ethnic diversity (Fleras 1998). Neither binationalism nor multiculturalism need to be mutually exclusive of each other, but can work in tandem to sustain a political climate and social partnership consistent with Treaty principles and multicultural realities (Ip and Pang 2005, Ward and Lin 2005). An official multiculturalism may yet succeed if it goes beyond a set of instructions imposed on minorities but re-emerges as a dialogue between different communities (Jakubowicz 2007), while focusing on inequities rather than identities (Bader 2007; Biles and Spoonley 2007). And for a country that is no stranger to remaking itself, its institutions and policies (Spoonley and Trlin 2004), the challenge is relatively straightforward – at least in principle if not in practice: A pluralistic governance that acknowledges a commitment to multiculturalism at peace with a priority to Maori as tangata whenua (May 2004). Time will tell if political governance that properly captures the duality of a bi-national society without forsaking multicultural realities – a multicultural New Zealand within a bi-national framework – can generate the political traction to capture public attention.

The Politics of "Isms": Antipodean Perspectives

Society building is a difficult and elusive challenge in the best of times. No more so than in settler societies like Canada and the United States, New Zealand and Australia (Pearson 2001). Consider the conflicts of interest involving the interplay of three exclusive yet interrelated dynamics. First, the process of colonization with its dispossession of indigenous peoples; second, the process of settlement involving establishment of the colonizers agenda and displacement of others; third, the process of immigration with its varying benefits and costs. The fractured allegiances of each of these three dynamics – indigenous, colonizer, immigrant – posed a challenge in constructing a unified society of commitment, consensus, community, and citizenship. Responses varied, but invariably focused on creating a universal (read: homogeneous) and centralized nation-state – namely, one people in one polity in one territory – through assimilationist initiatives that fostered exclusivity, racism, and ethnocentrism.

Both opportunities and challenges inform the politics of managing diversity 'down under'. Antipodean nation/state-building narratives shifted in response to immigrant demographics, identity politics, and increasingly politicized minorities. With increased emphasis on a commitment to flexibility, inclusiveness, and de-racialized pluralistic frameworks, governments in Australia and New Zealand have embraced the principles of "isms" as basis for managing diversity. Australia was first off the mark by focusing on official multiculturalism to accommodate immigration dynamics. New Zealand addressed the challenge of unity within diversity by opting for a biculturalism framework, given the size and political potency of its indigenous Maori population, in effect relegating multiculturalism to a political limbo. But the emergence of an alternative bi-national discourse clearly demonstrates the containment and control implicit in a state sponsored bi/multiculturalism.

In other words, appearances are deceiving. Debates over biculturalism versus multiculturalism notwithstanding, both of these "isms" constitute a form of institutional accommodation that fosters the appearance of inclusiveness without posing a threat to prevailing patterns of power and privilege. Or as Russell Bishop (1996) explains, neither multiculturalism or biculturalism are unlikely to work unless the domineering group stops dominating. In that the politics of 'isms' are a politically astute branding (or marketing) strategy for cooling out troublesome constituents – both indigenous and immigrant – their role in society-building is unmistakable. Depending on where one stands on the political spectrum, this assessment is a cause for contentment or source of dismay.

References

Bader, V. 2007. Defending Differentiated Policies of Multiculturalism. *National Identities* 9 (3): 197–215.

Barclay, K. 2005. Rethinking Inclusion and Biculturalism: Towards a More Relational Practice of Democratic Justice. In *New Zealand Identities*, eds J. Liu, T. McCreanor, T. McIntosh and T. Teaiwa, 118–39. Wellington: Victoria University Press.

Bedford, R. 2003 *New Zealand: The Politicization of Immigration.* Migration Information Source. Available at: http://www.migrationinformation.org/Profiles/display.cfm?ID=86.

Biles, J. and P. Spoonley. 2007. National Identity: What Can It Tell Us About Inclusion and Exclusion. *National Identities* 9(3): 191–95.

Bishop, R. 1996. *Collaborative Research Stories*. Palmerston North, NZ: Dunmore.

Butcher, A. and L. Hall. 2007. Immigration and Social Cohesion: From policy goal to reality? Paper to the ESOL Home Tutors Conference. May 19.

Commonwealth of Australia. 2003. *Multicultural Australia. United in Diversity. Updating the 1999 New Agenda for Multicultural Australia: Strategic Directions for 2003–2006.* Available at: http://www.immi.gov.au/media/publications/settle/_pdf/united_diversity.pdf.

Crothers, C. 2007. Race and Ethnic Studies in New Zealand. *Ethnic and Racial Studies* 30(1): 165–70.

DeSouza, R. 2007. New Zealand Today. Biculturalism and Immigrants. Available at: http://www.wairua.co.nz.

Dunn, K. 2003. *Representations of Islam in Australia*. Research Institute for Asia and the Pacific. Diversity of Islam Seminar Series 2. University of Sydney.

Durie, M. 1995. Tino Rangatiratanga. *Te Pukengo Korero* 1(1): 66–82.

Eaton, D. 2007. Migrant Study Backs Turia. *Christchurch Press*. Feb 28.

Ethnic Affairs 2006. *Government Develops Programme to Strengthen Community Relations.* Published by the Office of Ethnic Affairs, Wellington NZ. Available at: http://www.dia.govt.nz/oeawebsite.nsf/wpg_URL/Whats-Happening-Message-Board-Government-develops-programme-to-strengthen-community-relations-Media-Statement?OpenDocument.

FECCA eNews 2008. *PM Kevin Rudd: Multiculturalism is a Way of Life. Federation of Ethnic Communities Councils of Australia.* Available at: http://www.fecca.org.au/Media/2008/eNews_200811.htm.

Fleras, A. 1984. Monoculturalisnm, Multiculturalism, and Biculturalism: Managing Diversity in New Zealand. *Plural Societies* 15(1/2): 52–74.

Fleras, A. 1998. Working through Differences: The Politics of 'Posts' and 'Isms' in New Zealand. *New Zealand Sociology* 13(1): 62–96.

Fleras, A. 2007. Multiculturalism Across the Divide: Canadian and European Perspectives. Paper presented to the Universities of Siegen, Augsburg, Erlangan Germany, June.

Fleras, A. 2009. *The Politics of Multiculturalism: Multicultural Governance in Comparative Perspectives.* New York: Palgrave Macmillan.

Fleras, A. and J.L. Elliott. 1992. *The Nations Within*. Toronto: Oxford University Press.

Fleras, A. and J.L. Elliott. 2007. *Unequal Relations* 5/e. Toronto: Pearson/Prentice Hall.

Fleras, A. and P. Spoonley. 1999. *Recalling Aotearoa*. Melbourne: Oxford University Press.

Foster, L. and A. Seitz. 1989. The Politicisation of Language Issues in 'Multicultural' Societies: Some Australian and Canadian Comparisons. *Canadian Ethnic Studies* 21(3): 55–73.

Hage, G. 1998. *White Nation: Fantasies of White Supremacy in a Multicultural Society*. Sydney: Pluto Press.

Hage, G. 2003. *Against Paranoid Nationalism: Searching for Hope in a Shrinking Society.* Sydney: Pluto Press.

Hawthorne, L. 2008. *The Impact of Economic Selection Policy on Labour Market Outcomes for Degree Qualified Migrants in Australia and Canada.* Montreal: Institute for Research on Public Policy.

Healey, J. (ed.) 2007. *Immigration and Citizenship.* Sydney: The Spinney Press.

Hudson, M. 1987. Multiculturalism, Government Policy, and Constitutional Entrenchment – A Comparative Study. In *Multiculturalism and the Charter: A Legal Perspective*, ed. Canadian Human Rights Foundation, 59–122. Toronto: Carswell.

Human Rights Commission. 2006. *Tui Tui Tuituia: Race Relations in 2006.* Wellington, NZ.

Ip, M.Y. and D. Pang. 2005. New Zealand Chinese Identity: Sojourners, Model Minority, and Multiple Identities. In *New Zealand Identities*, eds J. Liu, T. McCreanor, T. McIntosh and T. Teaiwa, 174–90. Wellington: Victoria University Press.

Jakubowicz, A. 2005. Multiculturalism in Australia: Apogee or Nadir? *Canadian Diversity* 4(1): 15–18.

Jakubowicz, A. 2007. Political Islam and the Future of Australian Multiculturalism. *National Identities* 9(3): 265–80.

Jayasuriya, L. 2000. *Welfarism and Politics in Sri Lanka.* Perth: University of Western Australia.

Johnson, J.T. 2008. Indigeneity's Challenge to the White Settler State: Creating a Third Space for Dynamic Citizenship. *Alternatives* 33(1): 29–52.

Johnson, P.M. 1994. Examining a State Relationship: "Legitimation" and Te Kohanga Reo. *Te Pua* 3(2): 22–34.

Kerkyasharian, S. 2005. Multiculturalism in Australia: Finding or Losing our Way? *Canadian Diversity* 4(1): 109–11.

Liu J.H. 2005. History and Identity: A System of Checks and Balances for Aotearoa/New Zealand. In *New Zealand Identities*, eds J. Liu, T. McCreanor, T. McIntosh and T. Teaiwa, 69–87. Wellington: Victoria University Press.

Longley, K. 1999. Beyond Multiculturalism: Australia and Canada. *Australian-Canadian Studies* 17(2): 75–83.

Maaka, R.and A. Fleras. 2005. *The Politics of Indigeneity.* Dunedin: Otago University Press.

Maaka, R.and A. Fleras. 2008. Contesting Indigenous Peoples Governance. The Politics of State Determination vs Indigenous Self-determining Autonomy. In *Aboriginal Self Government in Canada*, ed. Y. Belanger, 69–104. Saskatoon: Purich Publishing.

Massey News. 2007. Study Finds Maori Views On Immigration Hardening. Available at: http://www.masseynews.massey.ac.nz.

May, S. 2004. Accommodating Multiculturalism and Biculturalism: Implications for Language Policy. In *Tangata Tangata: The Changing Ethnic Contours of New Zealand*, eds P. Spoonley, C. Macpherson and D. Pearson, 247–64. Palmerston North NZ: Dunmore.

McGauran, P. 2005. Interview. *Canadian Diversity* 4(1): 6–8.

McGrath, T., A. Butcher, J. Pickering, and H. Smith. 2005. *Engaging Asian Communities in New Zealand*. Asia:NZ Foundation.

Munshi, D. 1998. Media, Politics, and the Asianisation of Polarized Immigration Debate in New Zealand. *Australian Journal of Communication* 25(1): 97–110.

O' Hare, N. 2004. *The Unfriendly Isles*. Carter Centre. Available at: http://www.cartercenter.org/news/documents/doc1889.html.

O'Sullivan, D. 2006. *Beyond Biculturalism*. Wellington NZ: Huia Publishers.

Pearson, D. 2001. *The Politics of Ethnicity in Settler Societies: States of Unease.* New York: Palgrave.

Pearson, D. 2004. Rethinking Citizenship in Aotearoa/New Zealand. In *Tangata Tangata: The Changing Ethnic Contours of New Zealand*, eds P. Spoonley, C. Macpherson and D. Pearson, P. Spoonley, 291–314. Palmerston North NZ: Dunmore.

Poata-Smith, E. 1996. The Evolution of Contemporary Maori Protest. In *Nga Patai: Racism and Ethnic Relations in Aotearoa/New Zealand*, eds P. Spoonley, D. Pearson and C. Macpherson, Palmerston North, NZ: Dunmore.

Pearson, D. 2005. Citizenship, Identity, and Belonging: Addressing the Mythologies of the Unitary Nation State in Aotearoa/New Zealand. In *New Zealand Identities*. eds J. Liu, T. McCreanor, T. McIntosh and T. Teaiwa, 21–37. Wellington: Victoria University Press.

Povinelli, E.A. 1998. The State of Shame: Australian Multiculturalism and the Crisis of Indigenous Citizenship. *Critical Inquiry* 24: 575–610.

Prasad, R. 1997. New Cultural Issues Face the Race Relations Office. *Otago Daily Times.* 19 September.

Queensland Government 2004. *Multicultural Queensland – Making a World of Difference*. Brisbane: Queensland Government.

Queensland Government. 2008. *Multicultural Highlights 2006/2007*. Brisbane, Queensland Government.

Robbins, J. 2007. The Howard Government and Indigenous Rights: An Imposed National Unity. *Australian Journal of Political Science* 42(2): 315–18.

Schlesinger, A. Jr. 1992. *The Disuniting of America: Reflections on a Multicultural Society.* New York: W W Norton.

Seuffert, N. 2006. *Jurisprudence of National Identity: Kaleidoscopes of Imperialism and Globalisation from Aotearoa New Zealand.* Burlington VT: Ashgate Publishing.

Sibley, C.G. and J.H. Liu. 2007. New Zealand – Bicultural? Implicit and Explicit Associations between Ethnicity and Nationality in the New Zealand Context. *European Journal of Social Psychology.* 37(6): 122–24.

Singham, M. 2006. Multiculturalism in New Zealand – the Need for a New Paradigm. *Aotearoa Ethnic Network Journal* 1(1) Available at: http://www.aen.org.nz/journal/1/1/AENJ.1.1.Singham.pdf.

Spoonley, P. 1993 *Racism and Ethnicity in New Zealand*. 2nd ed. Auckland: Oxford University Press.

Spoonley, P. 2005. Multicultural Challenges in a Bicultural New Zealand. *Canadian Diversity* 4(1): 19–22.

Spoonley, P. 2007. He Iwi Tahi Tatou? *Massey News*. April. Available at: http://www.massey.ac.nz/~wwpubafs/magazine/2007_Apr/stories/06–22–07.html.

Spoonley, P. and A. Trlin. 2004. *Immigration, Immigrants, and the Media: Making Ssense of a Multicultural New Zealand*. Massey University. New Settlers Program.

Vasta, E. and S. Castles. 1996. *When the Teeth are Smiling*. Sydney: Allen & Unwin.

Victoria Multicultural Commission. 2007. *Annual Report 2006–2007*. Available at: http://www.multicultural.vic.gov.au/resources/publications/annual-report.

Ward, C. and E. Y. Lin. 2005 Immigration, Acculturation and National Identity in New Zealand. In *New Zealand Identities*, eds J. Liu, T. McCreanor, T. McIntosh and T. Teaiwa,155–73. Wellington: Victoria University Press.

Ward, C. and A-M. Masgoret. 2008. Attitudes Towards Immigrants, Immigration, and Multiculturalism in New Zealand: A Social Psychological Analysis. *International Migration Review* 42(1): 227–48.

Walker, Ranginui 1995 Immigration Policy and the Political Economy of New Zealand, in *Immigration and National Identity in New Zealand*. S Greif (ed.). Palmerston North: Dunmore.

Chapter 9

Australian Multiculturalism: Beyond Management Models

Toula Nicolacopoulos and George Vassilacopoulos

In 1897, on the eve of Australia's Federation, a handful of migrants from Greece gathered together to form a community organization, the *Greek Orthodox Community of Melbourne and Victoria*. The Community's founders were eager to maintain their distinctive cultural heritage in the British colony where they lived as foreigners who had become successful businessmen. In forming their association, however, the foreigners also gave institutional shape to a certain principle of *ethno-cultural diversity* and this during times that following the dispossession of the Indigenous peoples, gave rise to a newly federated *White Australia*. Surprisingly, a form of association that presupposes cultural pluralism took shape and flourished just as the white Australian state, which came into being by denying equal citizenship status to Aboriginal peoples, was busy setting up the machinery to enforce race-based immigration restriction controls in the name of maintaining the racial purity of its British people. The Greek community leaders saw no contradiction in their actions. Absolute devotion to their own Greek national origins did not bar them from demonstrating their genuine political allegiance to the Australian state or from showing respect for the presumed higher status of its British people as was expected of the foreigners. On the contrary, as if to anticipate Lenard's claim concerning the link between a society's nation-building efforts and its reliance upon multicultural policies and programs oriented towards fostering trust relations, they took the view that to render public the precise nature of their dual loyalties was to supply evidence of a *moral character* and *integrity* in the foreigners that rendered them trustworthy and hence worthy of the British-Australian authorities' acceptance (Nicolacopoulos and Vassilacopoulos 2004, 55–118).

The principle of cultural pluralism that the foreigners' actions exemplified had to wait until the close of the twentieth century before becoming a central feature of Australian migrant settlement policy. Following the election of the conservative Howard Government in 1996, and in the aftermath of a resurgence of public expressions of overt racism against both Aborigines and various immigrant groups from Asia and the Middle East, the Howard Government pursued a restrictive immigration policy with regard to family reunion and a notoriously controversial refugee policy (Baringhorst 2004). It also introduced its *New Agenda for a Multicultural Australia* in 1999 and subsequently proceeded to set tri-annual

'Strategic Directions' with its *Multicultural Australia: United in Diversity* document (DIMIA 2003). As Fleras' chapter outlines in greater detail, this reformulation of Australia's multicultural policy drew explicit links between the recognition of Australia's cultural diversity, the maintenance of community harmony and national security imperatives. But in insisting that migrants show allegiance to Australia's core values – the English language, parliamentary democracy, the rule of law, tolerance, a fair go – as their overriding commitment, the Howard Government also made explicit the link between these values and Australia's British heritage (Hirst 2005, 22–3). The Howard Government's rule in this 'post-multicultural era' is thus marked, not by a desire to move beyond multiculturalism, but by a broad appeal to the unifying power of a certain difference, namely the ethnicity associated with Australia's British national origins. Implicit in this formulation of the multicultural policy agenda is a focus on *depoliticized* cultural differences. In contemporary Australia, at the symbolic level such inequalities are affirmed and perpetuated through persistent socio-historical processes that position designated migrants as perpetual foreigners within the state's control or what we term 'perpetual-foreigners-within'. Characteristically, when addressing Australia's Muslim communities in 2004, the then Prime Minister Howard insisted on reminding the communities of Australia's European origins and of the status of the British as the 'host' culture. Since, by comparison to the 'astonishing variety in world Islam', Australian cultural diversity is the product of British Australians' *choice*, Muslim Australians must be reminded of their indebtedness to 'old Australia', that is, dominant white Australia.[1] Thus the policy's appeal to the maintenance of social harmony in the interests of national security translates into the expectation that Muslim Australians conduct themselves in accordance with their subordinate position as perpetual-foreigners-within.

The Multicultural Success Story and Twentieth Century Patterns of Continuity

Our suggestion that perpetual foreigner communities remain an integral part of Australian life today is at odds with the dominant representation of Australia's twentieth century development towards the post-multicultural state of affairs. The history of the past century is more often represented in the terms of a great epic story of advancement, social change and collective enlightenment. Indeed, with some variation both critics of multiculturalism and its defenders represent Australia in such terms, focusing on the transformation from an overtly racialized Anglo-centric national identity to a multi-ethnic nation unified by shared civic ideals and the toleration of cultural differences.[2] Australia boasts the supposedly

---

1   Cited and discussed further in Nicolacopoulos and Vassilacopoulos 2005.

2   See, for example, Castles 2000 and MacIntyre 2004. Within a shared framework of agreement with the representation of white Australia as a success story, Castles laments that

conflict-free implementation of an extensive mass migration program from 1945 supported by the adoption of multiculturalism as official policy from 1973. The adoption of official multiculturalism marked the transition to a society in which the racism and xenophobia that underpinned the earlier institutionalization of *White Australia* would no longer be tolerated publicly. This change in official policy is sometimes associated with the view that Australians progressively became a less racist and xenophobic people (Chesterman and Galligan 1999, Jupp 2002).

The story of success, which usually includes a chapter on the gradual incorporation of Indigenous Australians as equal citizens, has been well received internationally. For example, noting that countries like Australia have given up on their earlier policies of genocide, Will Kymlicka goes so far as to appeal to Australia as one of the great multicultural success stories of the modern western world to develop a highly problematic argument in favour of exporting western liberal capitalist models of ethno-cultural diversity to other parts of the world (Nicolacopoulos 2007, 106–8). As Fleras (Chapter 8) argues, in so far as it reflects and reinforces state and government interests, official multiculturalism is ultimately a political act whose underlying pragmatic logic pushes towards "fostering the illusion of change and inclusiveness" in order to control 'unruly ethnics' in the interests of 'ruling elites'.

This said, to ask whether there are any actual or potential tangible benefits of a multicultural Australia to its population is to pose a question both as to the legacy of the policy's twentieth century implementation and as to whether the meaning of multiculturalism is unavoidably restricted to such a state management model. For obvious reasons, we need to examine this question against the background of the dynamics of three inextricably linked processes, those of Australian colonization, Indigenous sovereignty and the history of Australian immigration (Curthoys 2001). Moreover, in assessing multiculturalists' claims regarding the benefits of multiculturalism over and above the deployment of multiculturalism as an effective marketing strategy we must ask who, precisely, is affected by the policies and how are they affected, particularly, at the symbolic level? Relatedly, to whom are multicultural discourses typically directed and to what effects?

If we think of the last century's developments in terms of two main periods broadly distinguished by the state's response to the cultural diversity of Australia's

---

following the transition to multiculturalism the dominant structures of power within Australian society have not sufficiently changed to facilitate a more equal sharing of privileges and resources with non-Anglo Australians (Castles 2000, 147–52), whereas MacIntyre objects that 'in their arraignment of the host culture, they [Australia's multiculturalists] failed to explain how it had accommodated the transformation' (MacIntyre 2004, 277–8). On this issue MacIntrye, an historian of the Left, is in full agreement with the conservative historian John Hirst who argues that it is absurd to think that Australia's immigration program could have succeeded in the absence of the tolerance of "old Australians" (Hirst 2005, 11–23). So the primary difference between the multiculturalists and multicultural critics is that each credits different historical agents with the achievements of the times.

population initially as one of the *denial* of a place for difference and subsequently as a matter of its *management* then symbolically we can mark these two periods by the moment in 1945 when, without abandoning the *White Australia* policy, Australian government ministers nevertheless decided to drop the *White Australia* slogan from future public discourse. The decision was understandably prompted by an acute awareness of the potentially damaging effects of the policy on Australia's international standing and immigration plans (Tavan 2005, 236). Thanks to the progressive bureaucratic dismantling of race-based immigration selection criteria, that began in the 1950s and continued from 1966 to 1975 (Jordens 1997), Australia saw a gradual increase in immigration initially from the non-preferred sources of Southern Europe and later from non-European countries. In the 1950s and 1960s the need for official management of cultural differences arose both from the mass arrival of non-British European migrants and from the continued presence of the Aboriginal people who did not become extinct in accordance with the authorities' expectations.

Initially this management proceeded with the adoption of the well known policy of assimilationism, the idea that non-British Australians were to be absorbed into "the [British] Australian way of life" (Murphy 2000, 149–67). Its deeply problematic nature notwithstanding, assimilationism is sometimes credited with at least two significant advances on the road to Australian multiculturalism. Firstly, according to Stephen Castles (2000, 137–8), it benefited the migrants in granting them formal citizenship rights through naturalization – a case we saw with diverging outcomes in Austria, Germany and Canada throughout the collection of chapters. Secondly, according to Jon Stratton and Ien Ang the 'cultural nationalism' that assimilationism implies, "had the consequence of freeing Australia from its colonial shackles and, in the end, forcing it to distinguish itself from British racial/ cultural identity" (Stratton and Ang 1998, 152–3).

These suggestions seem to miss the impact of the policy's implementation, when viewed from the standpoint of the emerging migrant and Aboriginal rights activism that characterizes this period.[3] Whereas for Aboriginal people the policy of assimilation translated into the authorities' forced removal of their children from their homes and their violent placement in white living conditions, for migrant peace and labour movement activists it meant intimidation by the Australian security services and repeated refusals by government agencies to grant them the security of citizenship status (HREOC 1997; Nicolacopoulos and Vassilacopoulos

---

3   Although the dominant view of researchers is that Australia's European immigrant communities entered the public, political landscape only *after* the state adopted a policy of multiculturalism this view is based on a lack of research in the area. For example, Lopez (2000, 131–55) under-represents the political involvement of migrants and fails to identify any connections to Indigenous activism because he is completely unaware of the latter. See Jupp (2002, 27–34), Moreton-Robinson (2000, 150–171) and Nicolacopoulos and Vassilacopoulos (2004, 2004d, 2007a and 2007b).

2007a, 149–53). So in both cases assimilationism served as a basis for collective organization in opposition to the state.

To be sure, the shift in the understanding of Australia's British identity from a racial one to one capable of being fully acquired through individuals' self-conscious adoption of 'an Australian way of life', would certainly have challenged the conflation of Australian national identity with British origins. But, although this challenge was indeed a precondition for the emergence of multiculturalism, its emergence need not be attributed to the operation of the policy of assimilationism. In fact, non-British migrant activists had already insisted upon the differentiation of citizenship from British ethnicity in advocating their own ideals of multicultural citizenship well before Labor Government Minister Al Grasby pronounced the *White Australia* policy dead and buried in 1973 and officially introduced the term 'multiculturalism' into Australia's Anglophone public political discourse (Nicolacopoulos and Vassilacopoulos 2002, 2004a, 2007a). Equally so, when the Hawke Labor Government adopted the *National Agenda for a Multicultural Australia* (OMA 1989) it effectively instituted an ideal of multicultural citizenship along the lines already embodied in the political lives of the migrant activists. In the light of the 1950s and 1960s history of popular demands for equal rights and social justice, it should come as no surprise that migrant and ethnic minority groups enthusiastically embraced both the term 'multiculturalism' and the state's gesture towards the inclusion of minorities. Many saw this as proof that the Australian state could be moved along the road to recognizing the cultural diversity of its citizenry as a value rather than as a problem to be either eliminated or managed and contained.

Management Models of Multiculturalism and their (Mis)Management

However, against these popular aspirations, Australia's multicultural era has revealed the limits not only of management models of multiculturalism in general, but also of critical multiculturalists' attempts to identify practical benefits with the model they consider most adequate, namely one that relies upon a universalist mainstreamed conception of multiculturalism. For the purposes of illustrating these points, let us consider more closely the form that multicultural policy took in its heyday, that is, in the period from 1973 to 1996. This is the period in which progressive governments redefined multiculturalism in terms of three distinct yet inter-related models (Castles 2000, Kalantzis 2000). At the outset, the Whitlam Government's pronouncement of Australia as officially multicultural conformed to a *minority rights* model that recognized the need to address socio-economic disadvantage on the basis of ethnic group difference. Here, the policy's objective was to implement migrant welfare programs aimed at redressing social imbalances.

From 1975 to 1982 the Fraser Government adopted and implemented a second, *cultural pluralist* model of multiculturalism. This model recognized the place of ethnic communities within the domain of civil society and gave them a role in the provision of welfare services. Here we have the institutional shift from the recognition that cultural difference impacts upon social disadvantage to the acceptance of the value of diversity. On this second model the recognition of cultural diversity served as a means to ensuring social cohesion and unity on the organizational level of representing diverse interests through state accommodation of ethnic lobby groups and the formation of advisory bodies such as the *Australian Ethnic Affairs Council* (Jordens 1997, 226–41; Jupp 2002, 61–82). Although at this time the term 'Anglo-Celt' was also introduced into the Anglophone public discourse to register the view that Australians of British origins were also one ethnic group amongst a plurality (Inglis 1999, 186–218), nevertheless the model made no structural changes to the system through which dominant white Australia continued to supply the substance of Australia's core values. For example, Anglo-Australians continued to hold senior decision-making public service positions within the 'Ethnic Affairs Branch' of the 'Immigration Department' which was responsible for interpreting and implementing the government's migrant settlement and multicultural programs (Bostock 1984, Jupp 2002, 43). Indeed they still retained the power to define the parameters of research and community education with regard to multicultural Australia when the Fraser Government established bodies such as the *Institute of Multicultural Affairs* in 1981. Australians of non-British origins certainly played an important *advisory* role in formulating the link between the government's multicultural policy and the values that were to inform Australia's national identity – social cohesion, individual freedom to maintain one's cultural identity, equal opportunity and equal social participation – as was the case with the preparation of the 1982 Ethnic Affairs Task Force's report, *Multiculturalism for All Australians: Our Developing Nationhood* (Galligan and Roberts 2004, 81–4). However, like its predecessors, this task force continued to report to the dominant white Australian group that held decision-making power.

With its *National Agenda* the Hawke-Keating Government instituted a third model of Australian multiculturalism based on the *universal rights* of all Australians. As Fleras' chapter outlines, this model of multicultural citizenship re-oriented the policy from its original focus on migrant and ethnic minority groups to an articulation of the rights and responsibilities of all citizens in relation to cultural, social justice and economic advancement issues. The policy thus formalized the historic disengagement of ethnicity from citizenship, a process whose beginnings can be traced back to 1949 when the legal status of 'Australian citizen' replaced that of 'British subject' (Davidson 1997). In this new framework of multicultural citizenship ethnicity was reconceived as part of the range of the choices available to citizens who, regardless of differences stand in a formally equal relationship to the state. The state in turn had to represent itself in terms of a corresponding neutral relationship towards the variety of cultures comprising the society, including the British Australian.

What was the significance of this model for the lives of the people affected by it? Although the model retained elements of its predecessors, namely recognition of the link between ethnicity and social disadvantage and a role for ethnic community networks, on a practical level government service delivery was reformulated in terms of generalized and often ineffective access, equity, and equal opportunity programs. In addition, governmental co-option of ethnic community organizations resulted in their re-orientation towards bureaucratic goals and, hence, their depoliticization (Castles 2000, 150–52; Jupp 2002, 81–2). Here much like the case of Afro-Caribbean political dissent that Reiss describes following Caribbean immigration to Canada, multiculturalism provided the means to obscure the race issues that arose with the increase in Asian immigration and took the form of popular fears of the 'Asianization of Australia' (Ang 2001).

Of course on a symbolic level, the assessment of the model of multicultural citizenship is less straightforward. Internationally, from as early as the 1980s critical multiculturalists have drawn attention to the tendency of state multiculturalism to manage and contain cultural differences rather than recognizing, celebrating or allowing them to flourish freely in the best interests of culturally diverse societies (Goldberg 1994, Gunew 2004). Surprisingly, however, when it comes to the assessment of the multicultural citizenship model, Australia's multiculturalists, such as Mary Kalantzis and Stephen Castles who otherwise object to multiculturalism's disciplining effects, nevertheless manage and contain their own object of inquiry. Kalantzis and Castles advocate ethno-cultural pluralist ideals of multicultural citizenship that each represents as a measure of the degree to which immigration countries, like Australia, are succeeding in managing cultural diversity in the globalized world. For Castles (2000, 138–40), the strength of an ethno-cultural pluralist model of multicultural citizenship lies with its potential to promote social harmony in so far as it accepts "immigrant populations as ethnic communities which remain distinguishable from the majority population with regard to language, culture and social organization" and whose members are still entitled to equal citizenship rights. The important thing for Castles (2000, 145–6) is that multiculturalism secures an important link between cultural pluralism and social justice, even as it does little to promote ethnic community members' access to economic justice. Similarly, for Kalantzis (2000, 107) Australia's post-nationalist approach to managing diversity has two main strengths: "diversity becomes a genuinely mainstream issue" and it makes possible the emergence of a "new collaborative politics" in which "managing diversity is a key principle of nationalism that crosses the different realm of indigenous differences, immigrant differences, gender differences, and so on".

Even though Kalantzis appeals to the interests of potentially self-determining groups that are marked by difference, her discussion of the potential value of an efficient top-down management of 'productive diversity' shows that her speech is directed, first and foremost, to the interests of the policy makers (Kalantzis 2000, 107–8). Just as multicultural policy manages cultural diversity, so too the multicultural theorist manages the policy makers. But what interests are the multicultural policy makers actually serving? Relatedly, how has the mainstreaming of multiculturalism affected the position of ethnic communities and their members? To the extent that the Australian state no longer conflates citizenship with the substantive norms deriving from an exclusively Anglo-centric monolingual monoculture it has achieved a level of maturity in that the state explicitly manifests a liberal democratic principle of formal equality. Even so, this assertion of relative state neutrality towards diversity has ushered in a new logic according to which Anglo-Australia rightfully retains its privileged position of power. The appearance of state neutrality in the abovementioned sense did not result from any redistribution and sharing of power with ethnic minority groups.[4] Rather, having repositioned itself as *the guarantor* of the state's neutrality, the dominant Anglo-Australian group now serves a dual function. Firstly, within the apparatus of the state and in their capacity as efficient diversity-managing individuals, the members of this group continue to implement multicultural policy albeit neutrally, that is, in accordance with the policy's re-orientation towards the mainstream. Secondly, within the wider public-political culture in its capacity as bearer of Australia's British heritage, the dominant Anglo-Australian group assumes the role of the rightful guardian and protector of the nation's identity in virtue of its privileged historical knowledge (Nicolacopoulos and Vassilacopoulos 2004, 269–80; 2005). To be sure Kalantzis acknowledges that multiculturalism has not divested the dominant group of its privileged power. She advocates the inclusion of non-Anglo Australians in positions of power and her model of multicultural citizenship enables this form of inclusion. But she fails to realize that although ethnically diverse individuals may well participate in the exercise of state power, either in their capacity as individuals or as spokespersons for their communities, this form of participation does not challenge, but instead presupposes the very cultural hierarchy to which Kalantzis objects (Davidson 1997, 149–87).

So, with the official adoption of the model of multicultural citizenship the cultural hierarchy that defined white Australia from the outset remains intact. Now all citizens can potentially participate in the exercise of power at the highest levels, but the business of regulating the exercise of power itself continues to remain the exclusive privilege of one ethnic group. This, however, is not an incidental effect of the implementation of multicultural policy but an outcome of the model's underlying logic, a logic that in rendering the universality of citizenship in merely formal terms unavoidably leaves it open for one particular ethnicity to continue to dominate elsewhere and otherwise. On this reading, with the election of the Howard Government the transition to the post-multicultural era did not require the abandonment of the model of multicultural citizenship since the changes merely rendered the very same logic explicit through the now *public* re-assertion of the privileged role of 'old Australia' as bearer of Australia's British heritage. Although Fleras' chapter correctly observes that in the Howard era multiculturalism diminished as a national narrative, this had less to do with a re-orientation of government policy toward shared commonality in preference to multicultural

---

4 For evidence that the implementation of multicultural policy did not result in the redistribution of power to (im)migrant groups see Davidson (1997).

diversity and more to do with the fact that it became necessary to abandon the claim that the multicultural era heralded a new national beginning and a radical break from Australia's racist past. This was the logical extension of the operative model of multiculturalism – one that recognizes the *formally* specified shared commonality of multicultural citizens – in the socio-historical circumstances of its implementation. For, the dominant Anglo-Australian group retains its cultural-political position of power in shaping the nation even as it shifts from opposing the recognition of cultural diversity to toleration and ultimately to recognition of its value for Australia. As today's guardian of the framework in which ethnic minorities may function, dominant Anglo-Australia continues to play the role of the regulator of what is to be considered properly *Australian*. This is why as Prime Minister, Mr Howard seldom missed an opportunity to "speak for all Australians" in order to explain "the Australian way" of doing things in his dealings with ethnic minorities (Hage 2001, Nicolacopoulos and Vassilacopoulos 2005, Rundle 2001).

It is perhaps not surprising then that, Kalantzis' discourse recognizes the disciplinary power of government, media and education but outside of these she implicitly attributes active political, economic and symbolic agency only to the more or less adequate embodiments of the dominant culture, albeit *in the name* of the interests of other groups with worthy powers of self-determination (Kalantzis 2000, 109). This discourse effectively reduces Australian multiculturalism to a disciplinary mechanism in the form of official institutional policy. The exclusive attention to a top-down management model of multiculturalism allows no room for the emergence of the voices of the supposed beneficiaries of the policy, the ethnic minority groups and the Indigenous peoples along with their respective articulations of the meaning and value of multiculturalism for them. In this sense Australian multicultural discourse uncritically conforms to a restrictive management model of analysing multicultural policy.

On the other hand, Castles does acknowledge Indigenous peoples' representations of the meaning of multiculturalism for them. He notes Indigenous opposition to being included in multicultural policies and programs on the ground that this would be to deny the special status of the continent's original inhabitants since they would thus "seem like one group among others" (Castles 2000, 147). However, in keeping with his approval of the adoption of a universalist model of multicultural citizenship, Castles views the practice of focusing multiculturalism on "immigrants and their descendants" as a weakness and calls for his preferred model of multicultural citizenship to be made relevant to Aboriginal people through the establishment of "more vigorous anti-racist policies" and "effective means of overcoming discrimination and exclusion" (Castles 2000, 148).

Although on the face of it, Castles appears responsive to the Indigenous position, on closer inspection his suggestion that the solution lies in more efficient multicultural programs implies that the issue is as at base a strategic concern about resource allocation between competing groups. Here Castles misreads the point of Indigenous opposition to multicultural management. This opposition and, indeed, the assertion that Indigenous peoples are not ethnic minorities on a par with other Australian minority groups, ultimately derive from resistance to the exclusive whiteness of the Australian state, that is, to the incorporation of the Indigenous peoples through the denial of their sovereignty rights (Moreton-Robinson 2007). So the source of Indigenous opposition to multiculturalism is akin to that of New Zealand's Maori peoples that Fleras aptly describes in the previous chapter. In contrast, Castles fails to appreciate the potential merits of viewing multiculturalism as strictly in relation to *post-migration* poly-ethnicity (Modood 2007) because he remains committed to a discourse of Australian multiculturalism that is grounded in a European white-centred conception of the nation-state (Hage 1998). In Australia, whiteness has been historically and socially constructed through processes that at once position Indigenous peoples as non-Australian and designated migrant groups as what we have called white Australia's perpetual-foreigners-within. These positions come into play quite apart from the formal status or self-understandings of the groups in question. They are an effect of the impact that the on-going violent dispossession of the Indigenous peoples has on the nature of white Australian ways of being, including no less being as Australian (multicultural) citizens. (Nicolacopoulos and Vassilacopoulos 2003/4; 2004b).

Whiteness as an Onto-Pathological Condition

The claim of white Australia to ownership of the country *as if* Australian territory had not already belonged to other sovereign peoples rests on the fact of Indigenous peoples' *continued* dispossession (Reynolds 1996). Significantly, what is at issue in this question of rightful ownership is not just a question about the legal or moral right of the white Australian nation-state to occupy and control the territory. Nor is it just a question of acknowledging past injustices against the country's original owners, as with Prime Minister Kevin Rudd's historic delivery of a formal apology to the stolen generations on behalf of the white Australian state and people. Rather, the nature of the relationship between the modern western European concepts of property and subjectivity has given rise to a deeper tension at the ontological level of our constitution as a nation. This tension is first and foremost reflected in what it means for us to be as *Australian* subjects. As members of a modern western liberal order we are encouraged through social institutions, whether legal, political or economic, to relate to the world as private property-owning subjects. That is, quite apart from the multiple effects of cultural diversity, in order to act effectively in societies such as Australia that are organized around the global market economy we must rely upon our property-owning power not merely in the strict juridical sense, but also in the ontological sense of functioning as beings for whom everything in the world has the potential to be reduced to a property item. Although we may choose not to think of everything in private property terms – as items in relation to which ownership is a non-issue – this can be our choice in so far as we are empowered to think of everything in precisely these terms. According to the philosopher G.W.F. Hegel, a fundamental division that marks the modern western world is that between individual subjects who are empowered to transform mere 'things' into property items and the things that exist in their external world. Through the act of taking possession of something accorded the status of an otherwise will-less thing the will of an individual subject is thereby embodied in the thing in question and consequently this act binds both subject and object in the property relation. Today, nothing is inherently immune to this power of embodiment of a will in a thing in this Hegelian sense of these terms (Nicolacopoulos and Vassilacopoulos 1999, 79–97). So, property-owning subjectivity in the ontological sense conforms to a logic that underpins the separation and ultimate commodification of every aspect of social life. Indeed, we function in our capacity as private property-owning subjects to the extent that we are implicated in the global network of commodity circulation and in the current conditions of the globalized world effective agency depends upon being thus implicated.

Just because it has the power to inform every aspect of our being as social actors, our private property-owning identity is at the heart of what it means to be a member of a modern western poly-ethnic society like Australia. Yet dispossession denies this very form of subjectivity to Australia's Indigenous peoples. The point here is not just that white Australia fails to give adequate weight to the historical connections between Indigenous peoples and their lands. To be sure, as is the case of Canada's Aboriginal communities, prior occupancy, prior sovereignty and the loss of self-determination set Indigenous communities apart from other visible minorities. But unlike the Aboriginal peoples of Canada, and indeed unlike the situation that gave rise to the biculturalism of New Zealand that Fleras' chapter examines, the unique position of Australia's Indigenous peoples by comparison with other Australian minorities has to do with the fact that the denial of their sovereignty rights has taken the form of the white state's refusal to enter into a treaty (Langton 2001) and hence to recognize the property-owning power whose source is the sovereign nations of Australia's Indigenous peoples. This is a key factor in understanding both the position of the Indigenous peoples in white Australia and the reason why a governmental policy of multiculturalism inevitably obscures the complex nature of race-relations in Australia. For the Indigenous peoples have been denied the very identity on which the collective being of white Australians has been founded and socially instituted. Because Indigenous subjectivity is thus rendered as *non-Australian*, for Aboriginal people Australian citizenship status is co-extensive with a *whitening* of their identity and inevitably perpetuates the myth of their inclusion as equals.

The denial of property-owning subjectivity to the Indigenous peoples in their own right has in turn profoundly impacted upon the possibilities for *white Australian* ways of being. The reason for this has to do with the role that institutionally reinforced processes of inter-subjective recognition play in structuring modern western social relations. Specifically, in order to exercise orderly possession and control of our property people need to be recognized as rightful owners. But the Indigenous peoples who remain dispossessed are not in a position to supply white Australians with this indispensable form of recognition. To be sure, on an individual level Indigenous Australians may be sufficiently integrated into the white Australian institutional order so as to engage in the various types of property relations that consumer capitalism makes possible.[5] Nevertheless, they have still been denied the possibility of engaging in the mutual recognition of property-owning subjects in their capacity as members of their distinct sovereign nations whose sovereignty they continue to insist was never ceded (Moreton-Robinson 2007). White Australia's collective failure to give and to receive this basic form of recognition gives rise to what we call an 'ontological disturbance'. This refers to a disturbance of the very conditions that render coherent our being as white Australian. Moreover, precisely because dominant white Australia is unwilling to recognize its occupier status it has had to invoke a suitable 'Other' to play the role of legitimating its authority and alleviating the anxiety that the occupation of stolen land produces for an ontologically disturbed subjectivity. This Other is 'the migrant' who is positioned as white-non-white and/or white-not-white-enough. To play a dual legitimating and anxiety-relieving role for dominant white Australia, certain migrant groups are periodically positioned as the perpetual foreigners-within, akin to Herzog-Punzenberger and Rao's analysis in Austria and Yue's chapter on Germany. So, as a direct outcome of the willful exclusion of Indigeneity from Australianness, dominant white Australia has rendered indispensable a perpetual positioning and repositioning of its foreigners-within as white-non-white and/or as white-but-not-white-enough. These are the conditions of the white Australian onto-pathology.

White-Non-White and White-Not-White-Enough as the Perpetual-Foreigners-Within

The white Australian onto-pathology – the willful perpetuation of a failure to recognize the subjectivity and sovereignty of the Indigenous peoples and the consequent reliance on a perpetual-foreigner-within – provides the key to understanding how the institutions and multicultural policies of dominant white Australia ambiguously position certain migrant ethnic groups. But how precisely does the process of positioning ethnic migrants as perpetual-foreigners-within work?

Dominant white Australia positions designated migrant and ethnic minority groups within the control of the white Australian state as social inside-outsiders. It does this by reference to the interplay of their dual identity as private property-owning subjects (white insiders) and as bearers of a racialized difference (non-white outsiders). Whereas in their capacity as property-owning subjects the members of such groups are *like* the dominant Europeans/Anglophones who make up the white Australian population, they nevertheless always remain distinguishable

---

5   We would like to thank the anonymous reviewer of our chapter for clarification of this point.

from them by reference to their residual racialized differences. Here, the markers of racialized difference need not consist of a set of fixed essential characteristics, like 'skin colour' or 'racial affiliation', but may instead be drawn from any number of assigned group characteristics that can be relied upon to render visible the members of a designated group. Indeed the visibility of any group that suitably marks it as a perpetual foreigner group is not a pre-given state of affairs but results from the assignment process from the standpoint of dominant white Australia.

The special quality of the social groups positioned as such inside-outsiders is that their individual members remain *perpetual* foreigners irrespective of their particular histories and characteristics – such as formal citizenship status, place of birth, length of stay in the country and so on. From the standpoint of the dominant white Australian, the foreigner-within is at best *like us* in aspiring to the benefits of Australian citizenship but *unlike us* in that he or she can claim no right to such benefits. The members of groups assigned the identity and role of perpetual-foreigners-within have the status to engage in the processes of recognition that bind 'the foreigners' to their white Australian 'hosts' and directly implicate the former in the latter's denial of Indigenous sovereignty rights.

As we saw in our brief comparison of the discourse of the migrants who formed the first Greek-Australian association in 1897 to that of the Howard Government, historically, the notion of the foreigner-within operates as an ethnic minority discourse as well as cutting across and informing official and public understandings of the social status of various (im)migrant groups. We find evidence of its operation in a range of Anglophone discourses of the foreigner beyond official policy and political speeches. The media and intelligence services, the courts, trade unions and representations of public opinion more generally all have had a role to play in perpetuating foreigner discourses in relation to the legal, political, economic and social status of immigrants (Nicolacopoulos and Vassilacopoulos 2004c). Sometimes there is explicit mention of 'the foreigners' but more often the notion of the perpetual-foreigner-within operates covertly to frame and influence what comes to be seen as appropriate treatment of the classes of people who happen to fall within its scope at the particular historical moment. This covert operation of the notion of the perpetual-foreigner-within works through the dynamics of three inter-related images of the foreigner.

Three Images of the Perpetual-foreigner-within

The three images of the perpetual-foreigner-within conform to three distinct ways of relating its two defining qualities. One has been to give priority to the foreigner's racialized difference. Another has been to concentrate on the foreigner's power to exercise his or her private property-owning power. Yet a third way of relating the perpetual foreigner's defining qualities has been to attempt to balance them in some way. Prior to the adoption of the state policy of multiculturalism, the dominant white Australian discourses relied on two images of the foreigner. One was the image of the foreigner as 'subversive' and the other represented the foreigner as potentially 'compliant' (Nicolacopoulos and Vassilacopoulos 2004c). Each had a role to play in transforming the migrant into the perpetual foreigner-within since together they were responsible for socially instituting the two indispensable qualities of the perpetual-foreigner-within. Whereas the subversive foreigner image gave priority to the foreigner's racialized difference as a *group* attribute, the image of the compliant foreigner reinforced the recognition of the foreigner's property-owning identity in his or her capacity as an *individual*.

The key element of the subversive foreigner image is the idea that migrants' political allegiance is dictated by their national origins. It follows from this that all non-British nationals constitute a potential danger to the nation. Here, the actions or omissions of individuals are of no consequence since the image of the foreigner pertains to the group's non-white identity. From this perspective foreigner communities are inherently subversive just in virtue of containing their unassimilable racialized difference. Although their members' potential for danger may or may not manifest in expressions of 'disloyalty' or 'anti-social behaviour' of various forms, for dominant white Australia subversive communities constitute the *visible sites* of unassimilable racialized difference.

By contrast, at the heart of the image of the compliant foreigner is the view that since there is no necessary connection between political allegiance and national origins it is open to individual (im)migrants to demonstrate their loyalty to the nation. As individuals, rather than as members of their ethnic communities, migrants are *in principle* assimilable by virtue of the exercise of their private property-owning identities. Behaviourally, they can adopt and adapt to the ways of 'the host' society and thereby demonstrate compliance with the expectations of them. Still because they can never be collectively fully absorbed they remain not-white-enough. So whereas in the image of the subversive foreigner the foreigner's whiteness is totally eclipsed so that group membership unavoidably designates every individual as non-white, the image of the compliant foreigner admits of varying traces of whiteness though the whiteness in question is never enough for full membership.

The interplay of the images of the subversive and the compliant foreigner provide a framework in which to identify a clear pattern in Australia's treatment of non-British migrants notwithstanding the state's endorsement of multiculturalism since the 1970s. So, for example, today's asylum seekers from the Middle East retain their position as perpetual foreigners-within in striking similarity to Australia's Southern European immigrants of the 1930s (Nicolacopoulos and Vassilacopoulos 2002a). Just as the lawmakers had previously denied legal entitlements to naturalized British subjects of Southern European origins, so too, the previous Howard Government refused to conform its handling of refugees to the UN Conventions by which Australia is legally bound. In conformity with the image of the subversive foreigner, it had refused to grant any right to work to asylum seekers indefinitely confined to detention centres, not only whilst their claims were being assessed, but even potentially for life, as the case of the stateless failed asylum seeker, Al-Kateb forcefully demonstrates (Marr 2005,

221–3). The Howard Government policy thus registered its unwillingness to recognize asylum seekers' property-owning subjectivity in much the same way that Australian governments had denied equal treatment before the law to certain classes of immigrants from the 1920s to the 1940s. The parallels do not end here. In the twenty-first century the granting of fixed term temporary protection visas to asylum seekers in place of permanent visas to onshore applicants bears the very same mark of rendering a certain class of immigrant bodies as potentially available to be singled out for discriminatory treatment by the Australian state as did the association in the 1930s of all non-British born nationals with inherently subversive leftist ideas. So too, in keeping with the dual interplay of the subversive and compliant foreigner images, not all asylum seekers are positioned as subversive foreigners. Indeed, the public discourse that praises valid entry visa holders shows that multiculturalism's underlying values do not extend, as a matter of principle, to white Australia's reception of refugees.

The image of the subversive foreigner dominated across the Anglophone discourses until the early 1940s when the Curtin Labor Government began preparations for the mass migration program. Although the two images operated throughout the 1950s and 1960s, the image of the compliant foreigner came to dominate the Anglophone discourses in this period. So, for example, when in 1966 the Holt Government introduced a parliamentary Bill to conscript non-naturalized migrants for service in the Vietnam war, the Prime Minister took the view that new-comers should not be allowed to hide behind the legal technicality of not having been naturalized in order to gain an 'unfair advantage' over the Australian-born youth being conscripted. This view reflected the dominant discourse of the times that demanded from the compliant foreigner that he show his allegiance to the white Australian state and people by conforming to their expectations (Nicolacopoulos and Vassilacopoulos 2004a). Whereas throughout the pre-multicultural era migrants' public opposition to Australia's war involvement served as proof of their status as subversive foreigners, with the transition to multiculturalism the significance of such opposition has changed. So, for example, when non-British migrants distributed anti-war leaflets in the 1930s the government responded with internment to what it took to be *inherently subversive* acts. By the 1960s anti-Vietnam war activists risked rejection of their naturalization applications, not because they were considered inherently subversive foreigners, but because their actions showed them to be failing the test of conformity with the image of the compliant foreigner (Nicolacopoulos and Vassilacopoulos 2004a). In contrast, in the post-multicultural era politicians receive Muslim community concerns against Australia's involvement in the Iraq war and its role in the Middle East without inevitably reading into them any threat to national unity or evidence of subversive conduct (Nicolacopoulos and Vassilacopoulos 2005).

How then has the adoption and progressive refinement of multicultural policies from the 1970s to the post-multicultural era affected the social positioning of migrants as perpetual-foreigners-within? Far from having *overcome* the tendency to position non-British migrant communities as foreigner communities, from the 1970s with the transition to state multiculturalism, dominant white Australia has also progressively invoked a *third* image of the perpetual foreigner. This is the image of the 'submissive foreigner'. Submissive foreigner communities are ethnic minority groups who respond positively when the state calls upon them perpetually to demonstrate their willingness to recognize the white Australian state's authority and the rightful belonging of its people. At the heart of the concept of the submissive foreigner is the view that the migrants' proper response to their perpetual foreigner position is not mere compliance with the demands and expectations of the white Australian authorities and people but *submission to them with integrity*. With multiculturalism's institutional endorsement of the value of difference, migrant communities have been positioned in accordance with the logic underlying the *submissive* foreigner discourse, a logic that, as we saw in the case of the Greek community association, had already been elaborated as a migrant community discourse.

The transformation of the submissive foreigner discourse from a migrant minority discourse to the framing logic of multicultural policy has had two important implications. First, the concept of ethnicity is now open to community members' own definitions so it can no longer play the role of a racialized difference that *inevitably* marks all migrant and ethnic communities in the same way. Accordingly, as then Prime Minister Howard's address to the Muslim Australian communities illustrates, ethnic communities can no longer function as the visible sites of a racialized unassimilable difference. Instead, this role has now been assigned to Australia's refugee detention centres (Nicolacopoulos and Vassilacopoulos 2002a).

Second, in accordance with the logic of the submissive foreigner discourse, the post-multicultural era's depoliticizing effect on cultural diversity has meant that dominant white Australia positions some elements of ethnic difference as the acceptable cultural capital of its *individual* owners whilst continuing to mark other elements as potentially subversive, for example, when they are associated with the inhabitants of the refugee detention centres. The now familiar ways of Southern European migrants fall into the first category whereas Muslim religious practices fall into the second. Nevertheless, due to the disassociation of ethnicity with the images of the subversive/compliant foreigner, in the (post-)multicultural era, individuals now enter into public-political life without *presumed* loyalties to any particular ethnic community (Nicolacopoulos and Vassilacopoulos 2004, 269–80).

If our analysis is sound then state multiculturalism has acquired a covert meaning via its implication in the onto-pathology of white Australia and the latter's reliance upon the perpetual-foreigners-within. Far from doing away with migrants' ascription of their perpetual foreigner status, it reinforces the social positioning of specific ethnic minority groups as the perpetual-foreigners-within in accordance with the images of the subversive, the compliant or the submissive. So, what could multiculturalism have to offer Australians by way of tangible benefits that do not ultimately reinforce and perpetuate this pervasive underlying logic? To begin to identify the peculiar logic of the operations of these images of the perpetual-foreigner-within, is to appreciate how it is that from the standpoint of the denial of Indigenous sovereignty, non-Indigenous Australians are equally complicit in perpetuating white race privilege, regardless of the obvious asymmetries of power amongst the members of Australia's various non-white and not-white-enough migrant and ethnic communities. That is, the members of migrant and ethnic communities remain *white*-non-white and *white*-not-white-enough even if this is not always rendered fully visible. As Aileen Moreton-Robinson (2003, 23) points out, from an Indigenous perspective the most basic distinction remains that between the Indigenous peoples and the white Australians defined as 'the migrant colonizers', even if this distinction attributes whiteness to migrant groups who would otherwise fall into the racial category of non-whites, such as 'the Asians' or 'the Indians'. For this reason the possibility of tangible benefits flowing to the population of Australia calls for articulations of the ideal of multiculturalism outside of a *white state straightjacket*, that as the attire of a 'racial state' in David Theo Goldberg's (2002, 235) sense of this term, is at once all-pervasive and invisible. This is not to deny that power asymmetries, and especially the economic stratification of ethnic minority members, does not place practical obstacles in the way of implementing social change but to insist that an effective realization of multicultural values presupposes a re-imagining of the ideal.

Signs of Non-State Based Multiculturalisms

At base, to imagine the ideal of multiculturalism outside of a white state straightjacket is to understand it in Bikhu Parekh's (2006) broad sense of a perspective on human life. When we look to ethnic minority groups' own discourses of multiculturalism in this broad sense of the term, it becomes possible to identify moments in the Australian historical experience that have given rise to such conceptions. We will conclude with an illustrative case from the history of the Greek-Australian communities. From as early as the 1940s, the Greek-Australian workers' leagues, that had been formed a decade earlier, promoted an ideal of Australian citizenship that took culturally diverse values to *inform* universal citizenship values such as democracy and freedom, rather than sit alongside them in a depoliticized way. As if to anticipate the turn of the century international research debate into the question of how the cultural dimensions of citizenship impact upon its legal, political and administrative dimensions (Hudson and Kane 2000, Stevenson 2001, Turner 2001), the members of the workers leagues drew upon their internationalist discourse of solidarity to frame their concerns as non-British migrants living in Australia. With a core principle of collective self-determination at its heart, this discourse enabled the migrants to draw from their own culturally specific symbols of democratic participation in Greece's liberation struggles and to reformulate the values underpinning these symbols so as to facilitate their identification as *Australian* citizens, workers and family members without having to deny their cultural background. Thus in 1949 the representatives of Greek community organizations, who came together to form the national *Confederation of Greek Organizations in Australia*, announced the basis of their decision as follows:

> We, who strongly believe in the democratic ideals; and in the fundamental principle that the ethical, spiritual and financial advancement and success of individuals can only be achieved with the freedom guaranteed to them by a democratic state; and that for this reason every free person has *the duty* to defend *above all the institution of democracy* (cited in Nicolacopoulos and Vassilacopoulos 2007, our translation from the Greek).

Amongst other things, this defence took the multiple forms of organized participation in the wider Australian peace efforts, encouraging Greek women's participation in issues of public concern and facilitating community-based migrant settlement services that, whilst including the establishment of language learning facilities, would also inform new migrants as to differences in the Australian political culture and labour traditions. Even though historically, political memberships within national communities have been tightly associated with the definitions of cultural membership that privilege the language, culture and class of the dominant group (Turner 2001, 13), here the migrants' own representations' of their difference determined the meaning of their political responsibilities as fellow citizens. In defiance of the dominant Anglophone discourses of the times, on this occasion, as on many other occasions throughout the twentieth century, Greek-Australian migrants were called upon to take up their political responsibilities by *redefining* the meanings of democratic participation and patriotism as *Australian citizens of Greek origins*.[6]

References

Ang, I. 2001. *On Not Speaking Chinese: Living Between Asia and the West.* London and New York: Routledge.

Baringhorst, S. 2004. Policies of Backlash: Recent Shifts in Australian Migration Policy. *Journal of Comparative Policy Analysis* 6(2): 131–57.

Bostock, W. 1984. Ethno-Cultural Control in Australia. In *Ethnic Politics in Australia*, ed. J. Jupp, 97–113. New South Wales: George Allen and Unwin.

Castles, S. 2000. *Ethnicity and Globalization.* London: Sage Publications.

Chesterman, J., and B. Galligan. 1999. *Defining Australian Citizenship: Selected Documents.* Melbourne: Melbourne University Press.

Curthoys, A. 2001. Immigration and Colonization: New Histories. *UTS Review* 7(1): 170–79.

---

6 For further historical examples see Nicolacopoulos and Vassilacopoulos 2002, 2004a and 2004d.

Davidson, A. 1997. *From Subject to Citizen*. Cambridge: Cambridge University Press.

Department of Immigration and Multicultural and Indigenous Affairs. 1999. *New Agenda for a Multicultural Australia*. Available at http://www.immi.gov.au/mulitcultural/australian/policy.htm.

Department of Immigration and Multicultural and Indigenous Affairs. 2003. *Multicultural Australia: United in Diversity*. Available at: http://www.immi.gov.au/mulitcultural/australian/policy.htm.

Galligan, B. and W. Roberts. 2004. *Australian Citizenship: See You in Australia*. Melbourne: Melbourne University Press.

Goldberg, D.T. 1994. *Multiculturalism: A Critical Reader*. Oxford and Cambridge: Blackwell.

Goldberg, D. T. 2002. Racial States. In A *Companion to Racial and Ethnic Studies*, ed. D.T. Goldberg, 233–58. Massachusetts and Oxford: Blackwell.

Gunew, S. 2004. *Haunted Nations: The Colonial Dimensions of Multiculturalisms*. New York: Routledge.

Hage, G 1998. *White Nation: Fantasies of White Supremacy in a Multicultural Society*. Sydney: Pluto Press.

Hage, G. 2001. Ayatollah John's Australian Fundamentalism. *Arena Magazine* 51.

Hirst, J. 2005. *Sense and Nonsense in Australian History*. Melbourne: Black Inc. Agenda.

Howard, J. 2003. Address to the 39th Annual Congress of the Australian Federation of Islamic Councils, Sydney. 12 April. Available at www.pm.gov.au.

Hudson, W. and J. Kane. 2000. Rethinking Australian Citizenship. In *Rethinking Australian Citizenship*, eds W. Hudson and J. Kane, 1–14. Cambridge: Cambridge University Press.

Human Rights and Equal Opportunity Commission. 1997. *Bringing Them Home: Report of the National Inquiry into the Separation of Aboriginal and Torres Strait Islander Children from their Families*. Reconciliation and Social Justice Library. Available at: http://www.austlii.edu.au/au/special/rsjproject/rsjlibrary/hreoc/stolen/.

Inglis, K.S. 1999. *Observing Australia 1959–1999*. Melbourne: Melbourne University Press.

Jordens, A-M. 1997. *Alien to Citizen: Settling Migrants in Australia 1945–1975*. St Leonards: Allen and Unwin.

Jupp, J. 2002. *From White Australia to Woomera: The Story of Australian Immigration* Cambridge: Cambridge University Press.

Kalantzis, M. 2000. Multicultural Citizenship. In *Rethinking Australian Citizenship*, eds W. Hudson and J. Kane, 99–110. Cambridge Massachusetts: Cambridge University Press.

Langton, M. 2001 Dominion and Dishonour: A Treaty between our Nations? *Postcolonial Studies* 4(1): 13–26.

Lopez, M. 2000. *The Origins of Multiculturalism in Australian Politics 1945–1975*. Carlton South: Melbourne University Press.

MacIntyre, S. 2004. *A Concise History of Australia*. Second edition. Cambridge Massachusetts: Cambridge University Press.

Marr, D. 2005. Is the Media Asleep? In *Do Not Disturb: Is the Media Failing Australia?* ed. R. Manne, 216–30. Melbourne: Black Inc Agenda.

Modood, T. 2007. *Multiculturalism*. Cambridge: Polity Press.

Moreton-Robinson, A. 2000. *Talking up to the White Woman: Indigenous Women and Feminism*. St Lucia, Queensland: University of Queensland Press.

Moreton-Robinson, A. 2003. I Still Call Australia Home: Indigenous Belonging and Place in a White Postcolonising Society. In *Uprootings/Regroundings: Questions of Home and Migration*, eds S. Ahmed, C. Cataneda, A.M. Fortier and M. Sheller, 23–40. London and New York: Berg.

Moreton-Robinson, A. (ed.) 2007. *Sovereign Subjects: Indigenous Sovereignty Matters*. NSW Australia: Allen and Unwin.

Murphy, J. 2000. *Imagining the Fifties: Private Sentiment and Political Culture in Menzies' Australia*. New South Wales: University of New South Wales Press.

Nicolacopoulos, T. 2007. What's Wrong with 'Exporting Liberal Pluralism'? On the Radical Self-Denial of Contemporary Liberal Philosophy. *Philosophical Inquiry* 29(1/2): 89–111.

Nicolacopoulos, T. and G. Vassilacopoulos. 1999. *Hegel and the Logical Structure of Love: An Essay on Sexualities, Family and the Law*. Aldershot: Ashgate.

Nicolacopoulos, T. and G. Vassilacopoulos. 2002. Doubly Outsiders: Pre-war Greek-Australian Migrants and their Socialist Ideal. *Hellenic Studies* 10(2): 141–58.

Nicolacopoulos, T. and G. Vassilacopoulos. 2002a. The Concept of the Foreigner and Refugee Rights. *Social Alternatives* 29(4): 45–49.

Nicolacopoulos, T. and G. Vassilacopoulos. 2003/4. The Making of Greek-Australian Citizenship: From Heteronomous to Autonomous Political Communities. *Journal of Modern Greek Studies* 11/12: 165–76.

Nicolacopoulos, T. and G. Vassilacopoulos. 2004. *From Foreigner to Citizen: Greek Migrants and Social Change in White Australia (1897–2000)*. (Greek) Melbourne and Pireas: Eothinon Publications.

Nicolacopoulos, T. and G. Vassilacopoulos. 2004a. Greek-Australian Community Development: Diversity and Solidarity in Place of Loyalty. In *Community Development Human Rights and the Grassroots Conference Proceedings*, ed. Centre for Citizenship and Human Rights. Melbourne: Deakin University.

Nicolacopoulos, T. and G. Vassilacopoulos. 2004b. Racism, Xenophobia and the Onto-pathology of White Australian Subjectivity. In *Whitening Race: Essays in Social and Cultural Criticism*, ed. A. Moreton-Robinson, 32–47. Queensland: Aboriginal Studies Press.

Nicolacopoulos, T. and G. Vassilacopoulos. 2004c. Discursive Constructions of the Southern European Foreigner. In *Placing Race and Localising Whiteness Conference Proceedings*, eds B. Wadham and S. Scheck. Adelaide: Flinders University Press.

Nicolacopoulos, T. and G. Vassilacopoulos. 2004d. Becoming Australians by Choice: Greek-Australian Activism in 1960s Melbourne. In *Go! Melbourne in The 60s*, eds S. O'Hanlin and T. Luckins, 245–59. Melbourne: Circa Books.

Nicolacopoulos, T. and G. Vassilacopoulos. 2005. Rethinking the Radical Potential of the Concept of Multiculturalism. In *The Body Politic: Racialized Political Cultures in Australia (Refereed Proceedings from the UQ Australian Studies Centre Conference, Brisbane, 24–26 November 2004)*, ed. T. Khoo. Brisbane and Melbourne: University of Queensland's Australian Studies Centre (ASC) and Monash University's National Centre for Australian Studies (NCAS).

Nicolacopoulos, T. and G. Vassilacopoulos. 2007. The Making of a New Trans-National Integration Discourse: The Case of Greek-Australian Migrants in the 1940s. 7th Biennial Modern Greek Studies Conference, 23–25 June 2007, Flinders University.

Nicolacopoulos, T. and G. Vassilacopoulos. 2007a. Struggles to Belong: Greek Migrants' Citizenship Rights. In *Proceedings of the 6th Biennial Modern Greek Studies Conference*, eds E. Close, M. Tsianikas and G. Couvalis, 145–54. Adelaide: Flinders University Press.

Nicolacopoulos, T. and G. Vassilacopoulos. 2007b. The Greek-Australian Unemployed Movement and the Construction of the Migrants Rights Discourse. In *Proceedings of the 6th Biennial Modern Greek Studies Conference*, eds E. Close, M. Tsianikas and G. Couvalis, 135–44. Adelaide: Flinders University Press.

Office of Multicultural Affairs. 1989. *National Agenda for a Multicultural Australia: Sharing our Future*. Canberra: Australian Government Publishing Service.

Parekh, B. 2006. *Rethinking Multiculturalism: Cultural Diversity and Political Theory*. Second edition. London: Palgrave Macmillan.

Reynolds, H. 1996. *Aboriginal Sovereignty*. Sydney: Penguin Books.

Rundle, G. 2001. The Opportunist: John Howard and the Triumph of Reaction. *Quarterly Essay* 3: 1–65.

Samad, Y. 1997. The Plural Guises of Multiculturalism: Conceptualising a Fragmented Paradigm. In *Politics of Multiculturalism*, ed. T Modood and P. Werbner, 240–60. London: Zed Press.

Stevenson, N. (ed.) 2001. *Culture and Citizenship*. London and Thousand Oaks California: Sage Publications.

Stratton, J. and I. Ang. 1998. Multicultural Imagined Communities: Cultural Difference and National Identity in the USA and Australia. In *Multicultural States: Rethinking Difference and Identity*, ed. David Bennett, 135–64. London and New York: Routledge.

Tavan, G. 2005. The *Long Slow Death of White Australia*. Melbourne: Scribe Publications.

Turner, B. S. 2001. Outline of a General Theory of Cultural Citizenship. In *Culture and Citizenship*, ed. N. Stevenson, 11–32. London and Thousand Oaks California: Sage Publications.

Chapter 10
Sold Out?
The Understanding and Practice of Multiculturalism in the United Kingdom

Rachel Marangozov

Throughout the chapters, we have seen many different understandings of the term 'multiculturalism'. Indeed, it can be argued that multiculturalism "has different implications and meaning depending on its social, political and disciplinary location" (Samad 1997, 240) and that "no amount of abstract philosophical or legal reasoning can prescribe a single 'just' model" (Werbner 1997, 263). Multiculturalism is associated with many – sometimes divergent and overlapping – discourses, institutional frameworks and policies invoking the term in rather different ways. Multiculturalism may refer to a demographic description; a broad philosophical and political ideology; specific policy tools for accommodating minority cultural practices; specially created governance frameworks to ensure the representation of immigrant and ethnic minority interests; and, a variety of support mechanisms for assisting ethnic minority communities to celebrate and reproduce their traditions.

For the purposes of this chapter, the term 'multiculturalism' is understood, first and foremost, as a description of the understandings, strategies and policies adopted to govern and manage the problems of diversity and multiplicity within multicultural societies. This descriptive definition has made multiculturalism an easy target and a loaded term. It is a classic floating signifier, attached to different sets of ideological baggage by its critics and defenders. This chapter adopts an understanding of multiculturalism that is underpinned by three key ideas:

- Equality. In the context of multiculturalism, proponents argue that equality refers to the idea of equal dignity. Equal dignity appeals to people's humanity or to some closed membership, such as citizenship. However, it applies to everybody in a relatively uniform way.
- Respect for difference. Alongside equal dignity, many proponents of multiculturalism also promote the idea of equal respect, which appeals to the idea that minority identities ought to be recognized in the public sphere. This recognition of difference is not a dualistic black/white, but a 'multi'. Minorities have multiple and different identities, combining aspects of religion, ethnicity, culture and socio-economic position.

- Integration. Integration here means not assimilation but something more interactive, recognizing that the process involves mutual negotiation on the part of both the settled and new community. This understanding is consistent with the most evidenced public policy statement on multiculturalism in the UK: the Commission for Multi-ethnic Britain report (Parekh 2000). This understanding also forms the basis against which the success of multicultural policy is judged later on in this chapter.

At a time when multiculturalism has been widely judged to be insubstantial by its critics, this chapter examines the evidence behind this claim. First, this chapter outlines the history of multiculturalism in order to identify its policy precedents and assess the strength of its historical standing. What follows from this is a discussion of the academic and philosophical underpinnings of multicultural theory and an assessment of its influence and strengths. The final part of this chapter examines how successful multicultural policy has been in delivering greater equality, respect for difference and integration. The chapter draws to a conclusion by pulling together the evidence, assessing the overall success of multiculturalism and asking whether critics have 'sold out' on multiculturalism in haste.

The History of Multiculturalism in the UK

A discussion of the history of multiculturalism in the UK highlights how multiculturalism represents something more substantial than superficial rhetoric, designed to promote the benefits of diversity. The history of multiculturalism in the UK is grounded in the concepts of integration and equality. These two concepts characterized and shaped the period of immigration settlement between 1948 and 1976 – a period which has been widely held up as a positive phase of multicultural integration in the UK. During this time, post-colonial Britain made significant efforts to try to integrate immigrant communities through nondiscriminatory treatment in healthcare, in social security and even in voting rights. These rights were embedded in the concept of the race relations model, which was enshrined in several laws in the 1960s and 1970s, culminating in the 1976 Race Relations Act. This longstanding legislation goes a long way in explaining how the UK has earned a reputation as a country largely at ease with its diversity.

Indeed, in contrast to the history of immigrants in Germany, France and other parts of Europe discussed in the latter chapters, there has been much to celebrate in the British achievement of giving legal immigrants their economic, social and political rights as rapidly as possible in order to facilitate their integration into British life. For example, the shortcomings in policing that were linked to Britain's riots in 1981 in Brixton and Birmingham, were addressed in a visionary move led by Lord Scarman, who headed an inquiry into the riots and blamed "racial disadvantage that is a fact of British life" (Scarman 1982). While there have been ingoing challenges around racial disadvantage, the key point here is that there has been a persistent engagement with the agendas of equality and integration, long before 'multiculturalism' became a popular slogan.

Between 1979–1997, when the Conservatives were in power, multicultural rhetoric and policies were largely confined to left-leaning councils. Between 1997 and 2001, multiculturalism was asserted more consciously through a range of policies and statements by the Labour Government, such as the 'Cool Britannia' agenda. 'Cool Britannia' was largely a media term used to describe the contemporary culture of the UK in the mid-1990s and was closely associated with the early years of New Labour, a relatively young Prime Minister and his platform of modernization. However, the riots in some northern towns in 2001 marked something of a turning point for the Labour Government's emphasis on multiculturalism. In less than four years, against the pressures generated by the hostility to the report of the Commission on the Future of Multi-Ethnic Britain (2000), the sharp increase in asylum claims, and the fallout from September 11, 2001, this policy has marked something of a volte-face. Increasingly, the language of 'Cool Britannia' with its promise of "communities of communities" has been marginalized by the theme of a 'cohesive nation' and 'community cohesion'.

The argument against multiculturalism is nothing new. However, its post-2001 manifestation was new in a crucial respect: it came from the pluralistic centre-left, and was articulated by people who previously rejected models of race and class and were sympathetic to the 'rainbow', coalitional politics of identity and the realignment and redefinition of progressive forces that it implied.

By 2004, it was common to read or hear that the cultural separatism of Muslim migrants represented a challenge to Britishness, and that a 'politically-correct' multiculturalism had fostered fragmentation rather than integration. The general tone of this shift was summarized by Trevor Phillips who, in 2004, declared that multiculturalism had been once useful but was now out of date, for it made a fetish of difference instead of encouraging minorities to be truly British. This line of argument and its charge of cultural essentialism in particular, has acquired even more vigour and force after the London bombings of July 7, 2005.

Despite such criticism, this brief history of multiculturalism in the UK highlights a clear set of precedents in earlier policies of integration and race equality in the UK, going back as far as the 1960s. These concrete developments in integration policy and equality legislation can be taken as evidence that multiculturalism amounts to far more than just political rhetoric around issues of diversity.

The Understanding of Multiculturalism in the UK

The period from the late 1960s through the late 1990s represents a period in which multiculturalism held a great deal of sway. During these decades, populations in Canada, Australia and the UK became more diverse through increased levels of immigration and the increased participation of minority ethnic groups in public life. Alongside these political developments, it is possible to identify contributing academic developments in political theory that questioned the adequacy of Enlightenment ideas in dealing with questions of diversity and in understanding cultural ties between individuals. Political developments in the 1960s touched the imagination of postmodern social theorists like Jacques Derrida and Michel Foucault in France. Enlightenment ideas, such as rationality and individualism were tarred with the brush of Eurocentrism, racism and domination, and increasingly gained currency within the humanities and social sciences.

Much of this critical thinking has involved identifying those features of liberalism which have obscured or distorted questions surrounding culturally diverse societies. In political philosophy, the abstract liberal-egalitarianism of John Rawls' "Theory of Justice" was subjected to a sustained attack in the 1980s and 1990s by communitarians like Michael Walzer and Charles Taylor, and liberal multiculturalists like Will Kymlicka. These have been accompanied by multicultural theories such as the "politics of difference" (Young 1990), the "politics of recognition" (Taylor 1994), liberal-egalitarian multiculturalism (Kymlicka 1995), dialogical multiculturalism (Parekh 2000), multicultural constitutionalism (Tully 1995) and libertarian multiculturalism (Kukathas 1998).

Many of these critical ideas have been collectively termed 'conventional multiculturalism' by some (Vertovec 2001) and can be described as "abandoning the myth of homogenous and monocultural nation-states" and "recognizing rights to cultural maintenance and community formation, and linking these to social equality and protection from discrimination" (Castles 2000, 5). The development of these theories, their strengths and their collective significance are discussed in more detail below.

The Theoretical Underpinnings

Laden and Owen (2007) identify three key features of liberalism which have important implications for culturally diverse societies such as the UK. The first is the idea of state neutrality. Similar to Adsett's arguments (Chapter 4), this originated from historic ideas around religious tolerance that ultimately developed into liberal ideas of the separation of the church and state. The second feature is the strong protection of individual liberties. Historically, this idea is grounded in the belief that individual citizens have particularly strong and deep ties to their religion, and these ties generate non-negotiable ends. The state can only respect its members, then, if it gives them the space to pursue those ends, and it does this by protecting a number of individual liberties. Finally, and importantly, liberalism offers an argument about human equality and similarity to justify the protection of individual liberties and state neutrality as the just response to diversity. This idea varies according to different liberal theories, but the basic idea is that while people may belong to different cultural and religious groups, they are ultimately the same underneath these differences. So while citizens may have different "conceptions of the good", beneath this, their concept of a "meaningful life" to borrow Robinson's term (Chapter 3), is that they are all the same in their claim and desire to be treated equally; whereby this involves having a fair share of the same basic goods, such as liberty, opportunity, income and respect.

Multicultural theorists have identified a number of problems associated with the idea of state neutrality – namely that it works to cover up a variety of ways in which the state favours majorities, especially cultural, national and linguistic majorities. In this way, liberalism turns a blind eye to inequality that takes the form of domination, especially when that domination takes place through social structures and actions, rather than directly via state action. Many critics have focused on the workings of social power, which does not rest directly in the control of the state, but which can serve to systematically disadvantage minority or other socially oppressed groups. Advocates of what Young calls a "politics of difference" have done much to expand the understanding of how that power functions, and its role in undermining the possibility that state neutrality could provide a proper path to justice in a culturally diverse society.

The last two features make liberalism strongly individualistic, not in the sense that it ignores or is hostile to collectivities, but in the sense that it sees these as outcomes of individual choices, as things that are chosen or joined by individuals who pre-exist them. Thus the identity of the individual is at once pre-given, in the sense of being prior to its ends, and also 'chosen', in the sense that the individual 'makes' his/her identity through his/her choices (associations joined, the values embraced, and so on). This type of individualism, which characterizes the liberal subject, makes it possible to treat cultural bonds as a matter of individual consciousness and to conceive of human equality in terms of similar treatment.

The liberal subject can be traced back to a neo-Kantian theoretical heritage that defines moral subjects on the basis of autonomy, rationality and an uncompromising distinction between reason and affectivity. Given Kant's conviction that moral legislation is contingent upon the freedom and equality of rational beings, the deliberations of those in the 'original position' must in turn, be the product of rational choice rather than bias, ascriptive or achieved characteristics (Rawls 1971). Subjects within this Kantian ideal are thus akin to "geometricians in different rooms who, reasoning alone for themselves, all arrive at the same solution to a problem" (Benhabib and Cornell 1987, 91). Rawl's theory of liberal justice is clearly indicative of this strand of liberal thought. Hence, the Rawlsian subject, much like its Kantian predecessor, inhabits a unitary subject position which occludes subjectivity outside of itself:

> In his attempt to do justice to Kant's conception of noumenal agency, Rawl's recapitulates a basic problem with the Kantian conception of the self, namely, that noumenal selves cannot be individuated. If all that belongs to them as embodied, affective, suffering creatures, their memory, their history, their ties and relations to others, are to be subsumed under the phenomenal realm, then what we are left with is an empty mask that is everyone and no one (Benhabib and Cornell 1987, 89).

The problem with the liberal subject, therefore, is that it projects a universal notion of abstract, genderless, colourless sovereign subjects without regard to their social positioning. Such criticism has revealed that liberal theories do not create much room for collectivities, much less for culture. As Sandel (1998, 150) points out, membership of a community and the shared values and goals that may go with it are, for most individuals, "not a relationship they choose (as in a voluntary association), but an attachment they discover, not merely an attribute but a constituent of their identity". In other words, culture and cultural belonging, is not merely a set of 'values' that people choose, but a force that shapes the sort of beings that people are and the moral choices they are likely to make. This kind of interrogation of the Rawlsian subject, therefore, reveals no "plurality of perspectives in the Rawlsian original position, but only a definitional identity" (Benhabib and Cornell 1987, 90). Hence,

> the judgments are those of the philosopher himself, the construction of the original position having served only to obscure, to neutralize, substantive assumptions which should have been spelled out and defended. Far from being the product of an abstract, transcendent process of reasoning, the theory of justice is revealed as chosen from a very specific social position, that of a white, middle-class, liberal American male (Frazer and Lacey 1993, 55).

From the discussions above, it is possible to conclude that the basic liberal framework is inadequate for handling questions of diversity in the UK and beyond. It can be argued, therefore, that the strength of multicultural theory has been in detailing just how inadequate this framework has been in comprehending diversity in the modern world. However, it has not been without its critics and it is important to outline their arguments before drawing conclusions about the strength of multicultural theories.

Critics of Multicultural Theory

Two features of multicultural theory have been identified as particularly problematic: the emphasis on a bounded nation state and the problem of cultural essentialism. For example, Favell (1998, 52) observes the following about the idea of a bounded nation-building project:

> Ethnic minorities are offered cultural tolerance, even 'multicultural' rights and institutions, in exchange for acceptance of basic principles and the rule of law; they are imagined as culturally-laden social groups, who need to be integrated and individualized by a public sphere which offers voice and participation, transforming them from 'immigrants', into full and free 'citizens'; they are to become full, assimilated nationals, in a nation-state re-imagined to balance cultural diversity, with a formal equality of status and membership.

Implicit in this process is what Favell sees as "an under-theorized, elite re-production of a long-lots idea of national political community; papering over inequality, conflict and power relations with a therapeutic, top-down discourse of multicultural unity". He is critical of the way such an approach reappropriates a 'functionalist, Parsonian idea of social integration' purporting to "unite all classes, and all groups – whether majority or minority – around some singular ideas of nationalist political culture' (Favell 1998, 52).

The premise here is what we might call the 'container model' of the nation state, in which social cohesion, cultural belonging and political participation are mutually defined within the geographical and administrative boundaries of the state (see Faist 2000; Turner 1997). Critical analysis of multicultural theory suggests that in the UK, the hegemonic idea of the nation as a representative container of cultural differences not only papers over inequality and power relations, but also relies on the conceptual repression of the historical impact of the fusion between imperialism and liberalism. In other words, conventional multiculturalism is constituted not only through universal elaborations – rationality, liberty, tolerance, plurality – but also through disavowal of the formative contamination of its universal ideas. Some critics have argued that it is this 'unthought dimension' which has not been theorized and is generally displaced outside the traditional problems of political theory (Gasché 1986).

Hence, while conventional multiculturalism has done away with the expectation of assimilation and acculturation, the expectation of common attachment to the encompassing nation-state has largely gone unchallenged. This is problematic because the container model of the nation state assumes a high degree of neutrality or indifference on the part of the state. This, in turn, implies "coming into the game after the rules and standards have already been set, and having to prove oneself according to those rules and standards" (Young 1990, 164). These standards are not seen as culturally and experientially specific among the citizenry-at-large, because privileged groups invoke the ideal of an unsituated, neutral, common humanity of self-formation in which all can happily participate without regard to social differences.

Grillo (1998, 195) has identified a number of other problems with multiculturalism. Arguably the most significant of these has been perceived to be multiculturalism's implicit essentialism and the system of categorization that underpins it. There are two important implications of such essentialism. The first is a form of consumer or boutique multiculturalism which tends to "keep diversity in a box" (Alibhai-Brown 2000) and may end up doing more harm than good in its simplification. Closely associated with this is a celebratory or consensual form of multiculturalism. This is characterized by the idea of a 'level playing field' which dictates that no-one is to be estranged, offended or perturbed. According to this idea, multiculturalism represents a political utopia through which it is possible to please all diverse groups all of the time.

The second important implication of cultural essentialism is that it has created a sense of white exclusion by a focus on ethnic minorities. As whiteness studies has so readily and rightly trumpeted as one of its central insights, whiteness remains unquestioned as the arbiter of value, the norm of acceptability, quality and standard of merit. Non-white subjects are thus identified precisely in the default mode of racial terms. As Richard Dyer suggests, "white power secures its dominance by seeming not to be anything in particular" (Lipsitz 1998, 66). As the unmarked category against which difference is constructed, whiteness never has to speak its name and never has to acknowledge its role as an organizing principle in social and cultural relations. This is problematic because 'whiteness' does not exist outside of culture, but constitutes the prevailing social contexts in which social norms are made and remade.

It has been this cultural essentialism that many have seen played out in the practice of multiculturalism, and which has been attributed to the failure of multicultural policy in the UK. Before turning to the details of this, it is possible to draw the following conclusions from the discussion in this section: The theoretical development of multiculturalism indicates that it is not merely a superficial marketing strategy which has been deployed to promote increasing diversity in the UK. Instead, multiculturalism has philosophical tenets that are grounded in an identifiable body of critical political theory. Multicultural theories have successfully highlighted how liberal ideas exclude considerations of minority groups and questions of diversity. To account for these exclusions, multicultural theories have stressed the concepts of equality, respect for difference, and integration. In this way, political theory has played an important role in the theoretical development of multiculturalism and has greatly informed academic and policy understandings of multiculturalism. For example, the Commission on the Future of Multi-ethnic Britain consulted many academics, such as Stuart Hall, who were highly critical of the essentialized notions of cultural difference and community. The resulting Parekh Report publicly emphasized non-essentialized understandings of culture which took multiculturalism many strides forward in trying to interpret rapid social change. Multicultural theory, therefore, has been a much-needed contribution to liberal understandings of diversity at a time when diversity and its related challenges have become pressing issues in both domestic and international affairs. Nevertheless, critics of multiculturalism have highlighted a number of problems with multicultural theory. Of these, the charge of 'cultural essentialism' has been seen as the most problematic. Many have interpreted this as a "respect for difference" which has gone too far and have held this responsible for the failure of multicultural policy in the UK.

The Practice of Multiculturalism in the UK

Having established the historical and theoretical roots of multiculturalism, this section assesses how successfully the idea of multiculturalism has manifested itself in practice and policy. 'Success' is judged here by examining the following: How well multiculturalism's three underpinning ideas have manifested themselves in practice and in policy. In policy terms, these key ideas of equality, respect for difference and integration frame procedures, processes and resources in almost every public institutional sphere in the UK, particularly at the level of local government. These ideas are upheld largely through legislations to promote equality (race equality in particular). However, they are also upheld through a public, legal and cultural commitment to respecting cultural differences, as well as through public policies and rhetoric on integration.

Equality – Has Multiculturalism Delivered?

As there is no legal or constitutional commitment to multiculturalism in the UK, equality and equality of opportunity are heavily based on the race equality legislation that the UK has had in place for over 30 years. Critics of multiculturalism often point to the lack of progress that has been made on this front. Equality of opportunity, equal access to goods, services and welfare provision remains inadequate for minority ethno-racial groups. For example, reviews of the entire provision of welfare and specific aspects of it within the UK suggest that access to welfare provision is unequally available (Craig 2003; Modood et al. 1997; Parekh 2000; Platt 2003). These reviews show that opportunity to access various aspects of welfare – housing, education, the labour market, social services, health service – is shaped strongly by the dimension of ethnicity (Heath and Cheung 2007). Although this is not the case for all ethnic groups, certain minority groups – particularly those from Afro-Caribbean, Bangladeshi and Pakistani origins, and those from more recently arriving groups such as Somalians, continue to be concentrated in the most deprived housing neighbourhoods and schools with the worst conditions in terms of poorest staffing provision and least good record of attainment (Gillborn and Mirza 2000). They often have the greatest difficulty in accessing appropriate health provision; they are obstructed in terms of advancement in the labour market and their careers; and they often end up in the workplaces with the poorest working conditions, poorest pay and least security (Cabinet Office 2007; Craig 2003); and they are concentrated amongst those with the lowest incomes (Platt 2003). In education, many have argued that disadvantage and discrimination are built into the education system from a very early age. Despite the fact that each of the main ethnic groups are achieving higher standards than before, a report commissioned by the government's inspection body, The Office for Standards in Education, Children's Services and Skills (OFSTED), found that black and ethnic minority pupils are disadvantaged systematically by the education system (Gillborn and Mirza 2000). The researchers concluded that in the case of black pupils, they actually entered school 20 percentage points in advance of the average, but left it 21 points behind the average.

In the field of health, a recent survey of pay awards in the National Health Service found discrimination riddled throughout the system. In terms of mental health, black service users are more likely to be (mis)-diagnosed as schizophrenic, contained in psychiatric institutions and treated with electroconvulsive therapy

(Rai-Atkins 2002). This – along with a much wider range of evidence – demonstrated that in terms of equality of outcomes, many ethnic minority groups still do not achieve social justice. It also demonstrates that institutional racism remains prevalent to a large degree and, for many ethnic minorities, have a determining effect on their life chances.

This lack of progress in terms of equality of opportunity has been most starkly highlighted by the recent Equalities Review undertaken by the Government, which highlights the number of years it will take to obtain full equality for women and a number of minority groups in the labour market. Although there is still much progress to be made regarding the equalities agenda, this should not cloud the fact that racial equality has progressed massively in the last 30 years. For example, blatant overt racism has almost entirely disappeared. Much of this progress reflects the gradual effects of wider economic and social change. Inherited prejudices have tended to decline with familiarity, and with new generations. Globalization and global communication have made people aware of other economies and cultures, and for most businesses, rational, self interest often means hiring the best talent with high human capital regardless of ethnic background.

However, equalities legislation in the UK has also played a crucial role in defining what is acceptable, and in establishing new norms of behaviour which have become self-reinforcing. The introduction of the 1976 Race Relations Act was a landmark statement for British society. By this piece of progressive legislation Britain committed itself to a fair and just society built on the twin tracks of eliminating procedural discrimination and promoting equal opportunity. For the first time, those engaged in the fight against inequality were given the procedural tools to do the job.

Above all, the Act was an empowering instrument, which gave individuals access to justice by enabling them to take cases of discrimination on the grounds of race to the courts, including industrial tribunals. In addition, through its remit for the promotion of equal opportunities, the Act enhanced the case for positive action and cemented values of multiculturalism. While many employers were challenged by the provisions of the legislation, for trade unions the duty to comply was required on many fronts: as employers, service providers and representatives of their members. The 1976 Act established the Commission for Racial Equality (CRE) – a completely new body with wide-ranging powers to eliminate racial discrimination; promote equality of opportunity and good relations between persons of different racial groups; and to review the effectiveness of the Act. The CRE has conducted and published three reviews of the Act's effectiveness – in 1985, 1991 and 1998. In all three reviews, the CRE recommended further changes to the legislation. It argued that, besides being bound by the Act in the same way as any other employers or service providers, public authorities should be required by law to promote racial equality. The passing of the 2000 Race Relations (Amendment) Act, strengthened the 1976 Act by placing a legal duty on many public authorities to eliminate discrimination, promote equality of opportunity and promote good race relations. This attempt to address institutional racism can be viewed as a huge step forward for those seeking to promote the equal opportunities for minority communities. The UK also has a Human Rights Act, which provides basic protection to ethnic minorities and lays down the minimum standards around equality of opportunity. The new Commission for Equality and Human Rights is expected to tackle all forms of discrimination within a common conceptual and institutional framework which can also be a source of considerable help to ethnic minorities.

It is also worth pointing out that as diversity in the UK has been increasing, so has the diversity of outcomes facing ethnic minority and immigrant groups (Kyambi 2005). Indeed, the outcomes of ethnic minority and immigrant groups in the UK can no longer be easily generalized and it is worth remembering that Indians and some other ethnic minorities do better than whites at school. Thus, it is possible to conclude that significant challenges remain meaning inequality cannot be consigned entirely to the history books. The continued disadvantage experienced by many ethnic minority groups suggests that self-reinforcing cycles of economic deprivation and social exclusion can be as important a problem as straightforward racial discrimination, but the policy levers to address those barriers are less easy to identify and to implement. In this sense, multiculturalism may not appear as simple a proposition as it did 30 years ago. However, to write it off altogether is to write off the huge strides and lessons learned that have been made on the equalities front over the past 30 years. The UK's equalities legislation has actively reinforced the fight against discrimination at both the individual and institutional level through landmark developments, such as the introduction of the Race Relations (Amendment) Act in 2000. Multiculturalism has also played a key role in supporting wider cultural shifts in attitude and behaviour which many tend to take for granted in 2007. This sort of progress is hard won but all too easy to forget in the face of ongoing challenges.

Respect for Difference – Has Multiculturalism Delivered?

In recent years, critics of multiculturalism have argued that it has gone too far in its tolerance of cultural difference and has resulted in cultural essentialism at the expense of common civic values. Scrutiny of cultural essentialism in multicultural policy has been made in the UK (Anthias and Yuval-Davis 1993), as well as Australia (Castles et al. 1998), Mauritius (Eriksen 1997), United States (Turner 1993), Canada (Kobayashi 1993), Germany (Radtke 1994) and Sweden (Ålund and Schierup 1991).

This problem has been crystallized and somewhat exaggerated through widespread media coverage of particular stories, such as that surrounding the right for young women and girls to wear particular forms of clothing – the hijab and the jilbab – at school and work. More recently, tensions have arisen as a result of performances of a play, Behtzi, which portrayed murder and abuse within a Sikh Temple, and which were abandoned as a result of vigorous street protest by members of the Sikh community.

Many of these cases have received disproportionate amount of media attention, given the particularity of the incidents in question. However, this is not to say that critics are completely without grounds for their concern. In some areas, there is evidence to show that attempts to implement multicultural policies have resulted in less than progressive outcomes. In these cases, the institutionalization of multiculturalism has undermined political struggles, entrenched divisions and strengthened conservative elements within every community (Malik 2006). For example, there is evidence that too much funding has been historically and divisively been offered to community groups that only support one particular ethnic or religious group (Commission on Integration and Cohesion 2007), and tensions are often rife in places where there is competition (received or real) for public resources. Indeed, some studies have shown how competition for public-sector housing has fuelled racial strife (Solomos and Singh 1990).

However, it is worth remembering that multiculturalism does not (and never did) call for cultural separatism or cultural essentialism. Respect for difference, or the politics of 'recognition' as Taylor puts it, interprets equality to mean that non-assimilation is acceptable and minority identities ought to be included in the public sphere. This is very different from an argument for separatism which is grounded in the principal that difference should divide cultural groups, administratively and politically. Indeed, those who say that multiculturalism means separatism clearly are not talking about the multiculturalism that is found in the main texts of academics or many public policy practitioners. Thus, if the implementation of 'multicultural policy' has resulted in divisive outcomes in some policy areas, then this is not so much a failure of multiculturalism, but a failure to understand and implement its meaning, its aims and what it seeks to achieve.

This is not to say that increasing diversity in the UK has not thrown up challenges. However, these challenges – often very sensitive, contentious and political in nature – are rarely an argument for separatism, but for a renegotiation of the terms of integration and equality. Indeed, to suggest otherwise, as many critics of multiculturalism have done, is to posit multiculturalism and Britishness as exclusive choices. However, societies that have been constituted on the basis of mass migration, like Canada, Australia and New Zealand seen throughout the collection of chapters, have long understood the need for civic integration alongside diversity; based on the belief that the inculcation of a common core of political citizenship is not antithetical to the recognition of diverse beliefs and cultural identities. The Commission for Multi-ethnic Britain report, "The Future of Multi-ethnic Britain", clearly sees no inevitable incompatibility between diversity and 'Britishness' in its public emphasis on non-essentialized understandings of cultures and communities.

Moreover, there is little robust evidence, beyond particular stories that hit the headlines, that multiculturalism encourages separatism. For example, it is widely perceived among the public that the allocation of social housing unfairly priorities minority groups at the expense of white groups. However, there is very little evidence to back this up – so little evidence in fact, that an independent inquiry was launched in November 2007 to establish the credibility of such claims.

To claim multicultural policies have encouraged cultural separatism is also to ignore a whole raft of citizenship policies that have been introduced over the past few years. Citizenship education is now part of the school curriculum and new applicants for citizenship have to demonstrate a basic mastery of the English language and knowledge of British history and civic life. Local authorities now hold ceremonies for those granted citizenship – public affirmation of access to the British community have become popular occasions. Thousands of people now gain citizenship at the local town hall, rather than through an envelope in the letter box. These citizenship laws and practices have given greater content to the objective of promoting civic integration. They are familiar to many other Commonwealth democracies, not least those that proudly describe themselves as multicultural.

Integration – Has Multiculturalism Delivered?

Many critics have argued that multiculturalism has hindered efforts to integrate ethnic minority and immigrant groups in the UK, by allowing many communities to live 'parallel lives' (Cantle 2001). They often point to a lack of English-speaking skills among established and new communities, as well as the segregation of ethnic groups in many neighbourhoods as evidence of this. These are seductive arguments, but they overlook three important issues. The first is the way in which multiculturalism's detractors tend to concentrate on the easy targets. For example, it is plainly true that Britain should anathemize egregious practices such as forced marriage or 'honour killing'. It is right to emphasize the importance of English language skills as a means to improve the socio-economic prospects for ethnic minorities and immigrants. Its is also right to imply, as the Commission on Integration and Cohesion has done, that too much funding has been historically and divisively offered to community groups that cater to only one ethnic or religious group. However, much less tends to be said about what are, in the end, the most important determinants of 'segregation', namely housing, education and a lack of access to adequate English for speakers of other languages (ESOL) provision. In fact, many commentators have contrasted the importance attached to the integration agenda by the Labour Government and others with policies that have dealt severe blows to the integration agenda (Back et al. 2002). These policies include the Government's decision in 2007 to substantially cut back on the provision of free English-speaking classes and its linking of Muslim communities with several aspects of 'security' (Somerville 2007). These two conflicting directions of integration policy under New Labour have often been labeled the 'two faces' of the Labour Government (Back et al. 2002).

There is a second issue related to the evidence around integration. The most recent authoritative literature review highlights a "serious lack of data and other factual knowledge with regard to integration" (Castles et al. 2002, ii). More specifically, there is a lack of evidence from which to draw a casual link between multicultural policy and challenges that have arisen around integration. Take the issue of 'segregated' communities, for example, where there are spatially divided concentrations of particular ethnic communities in some neighbourhoods. Much of the evidence actually suggests that it is poor housing, local labour markets and poor life chances that have a greater influence on opportunities for social mixing rather than failings in multicultural policy. Other evidence has shown how indicators of segregation can often be explained simply by a growing non-white population, rather a self-segregated ethnic minority or 'white flight' (see Simpson's work in Piggott 2006). Other academics, such as Ceri Peach (1996) and Danny Dorling (2005) have even questioned whether segregation is an issue at all, highlighting that indicators of segregation are, at most, stable or declining.

   The third issue relates to the understanding of the term integration. Integration, as it is often used today, introduces other frames of reference into the debate that do not fit easily on the plane of multiculturalism, particularly at the policy level. Notably, recent integration policy includes 'social exclusion' and 'community cohesion'. Central government and statutory agencies have employed wider expressions, such as social cohesion, active citizenship, civil renewal and social inclusion when referring to the concept of integration. The still developing terminology has led to intense debate on what indicators should be used to measure integration and on policy concepts, objectives and effects (Favell 1998, Parekh 1988, 2000, Rudiger and Spencer 2003). These wider frames of references in current discourse on integration introduce an array of issues that are not always related to a multiculturalist understanding of integration (a two-way process that is to be negotiated between both settled and new communities). As such, it can be argued that the remit and expectations of multiculturalism have become somewhat overstretched to encompass a range of social justice issues that require a broader set of policy interventions.

   Critics of multiculturalism tend to overlook the evident progress that has been made on integration in recent years, such as Labour's policy on refugee integration, which has taken the form of strategic policy development, specific resources and specific government machinery. It is also worth mentioning how understandings of integration have, in many ways, lost their asssimilationist overtones in recent decades. This is not to say that integration policy is completely rid of assimilationist notions; it is merely to point to the basic assumption, shared across the political divide and accepted by public institutions that both settled and new populations have a shared understanding that change is to be negotiated. In other words, integration is a two-way process, or a 'two-way street'. This basic assumption – however entwined it now may be with newer concepts of 'community cohesion' and 'social exclusion' – was not shared by both sides in the 1960s and 1970s, when legislation was first passed through Parliament.

Sold Out? Multiculturalism in the UK

From the evidence put forward in this chapter, it is possible to conclude that multiculturalism has been far more than just a marketing exercise, deployed to sell the benefits of increasing diversity in the UK. Specifically, this conclusion is based on the strength of the following considerations: The historical roots of multiculturalism show that there has been persistent engagement, beginning well before 'multiculturalism' was a popular slogan, with the equality agenda and the treatment of all British people as equals, irrespective of their racial or ethnic origins. As far back as the 1960s and 1970s, the UK granted legal immigrants their economic, social and political rights as rapidly as possible in order to facilitate their integration. Since then, the UK has accumulated over 30 years of experience in race equality issues and related legislation. While this does not afford complacency in the current day, it does serve to highlight that multiculturalism in the UK is far more than just a fashionable term or abstract policy aspiration.

By examining the understanding of multiculturalism in the UK, it is possible to see that its theoretical underpinnings have arisen from a much-needed questioning of Enlightenment theories and out of a growing recognition of the need to take into account cultural and community rights. Multicultural theory has continued to influence academic and policy understandings of multiculturalism in many quarters, despite becoming something of a dirty word in others. In this way, multiculturalism remains a powerful corrective to liberal approaches which have failed to adequately address and respond to socio-demographic and political developments around increasing diversity.

The criticisms made against multiculturalism have tended to be problematic on a number of fronts, not least because many of the challenges the UK faces today are not a result of the failure of multiculturalism, but of a failure to understand and implement a multicultural model effectively. Given the evidence, it is possible to question why multiculturalism comes under such a sustained attack in recent years. Much of this can be explained by a widespread confusion regarding the expectations of a multicultural model. Multiculturalism is not an 'ideal', conflict-free state at which diverse communities 'arrive' (Werbner 1997). Instead, multiculturalism is about a process of management and governance in which differences are fore-grounded, whilst at the same time, there is recognition of the importance of connections and a common area of engagement across differences. Understood in this way, multiculturalism is not always about preventing conflicts and tensions, but rather ensuring such conflicts do not destroy the society as a whole, and at the same time ensuring the protection and application of social justice to all parts of society. This form of multiculturalism is capable of dealing with diversity, difference and heterogeneity without lapsing into a mere celebration of various subject positions or essentialist notions of cultural difference. It is this model – with the concepts of equality, respect for difference and integration at its core – that policymakers, academics and practitioners in the UK should be working to advance. It is a democratic model that retains as its starting point of where individuals and communities 'are', not where they 'should be'. It is also a realistic model in its recognition that multiculturalism, and multicultural societies necessarily involve conflicts, tensions and difficult debates as part of an ongoing process of negotiation, interaction and integration.

References

Alibhai-Brown, Y. 2000. *After Multiculturalism*. London: The Foreign Policy Centre.

Ålund, A. and C. Schierup. 1991. *Paradoxes of Multiculturalism: Essays on Swedish Society*. Aldershot: Avebury.

Anthias, F., Yuval-Davis, N. and Cain, H. 1993. *Racialized Boundaries: Race, Nation, Gender, Colour and Class and the Anti-Racist Struggle*. London: Routledge.

Back, L., M. Keith, A. Khan, K. Shukra and J. Solomos. 2002. The Return of Assimilation: Race, Multiculturalism and New Labour. *Sociological Research Online* 7(2). Available at: http://www.socresonline.org.uk/7/2/back.html.

Benhabib, S. and D. Cornell. (eds) 1987. *Feminism as Critique*. Minneapolis: University of Minnesota Press.

Cabinet Office. 2007. *Fairness and Freedom. The Final Report of the Equalities Review*. Cabinet Office.

Cantle, T. 2001. *Community Cohesion: A Report of the Independent Review Team*. Chaired by Ted Cantle. London: Home Office.

Castles, S. 2000. *Ethnicity and Globalization: From Migrant Workers to Transnation Citizen*. London: Sage.

Castles, S., M. Korac, E. Vasta and S. Vertovec. 2002. *Integration: Mapping the Field*. Home Office online report 28/3. London: Home Office.

Commission for Integration and Cohesion. 2007. *Our Shared Future*. Commission for Integration and Cohesion.

Craig, G. 2003. Ethnicity, Racism and the Labour Market: a European Perspective. In *Citizenship, Welfare and the Labour Market*, eds. J.-G. Andersen and P. Jensen, 149–81. Bristol: Policy Press.

Dorling, D. 2005. Why Trevor is Wrong about Race Ghettos. *The Observer*. 25 September.

Erickson, T.H. 1997. Multiculturalism, Individualism and Human Rights: Romanticism, the Enlightenment and Lessons from Mauritius. In *Human Rights, Culture and Context*, ed. R. Wilson, 49–60. London: Pluto.

Faist, T. 2000. *The Volume and Dynamics of International Migration and Transnational Social Spaces*. Oxford: Oxford University Press.

Favell, A. 1998. *Philosophies of Integration: Immigration and the Idea of Citizenship in France and Britain*. Basingstoke: Macmillan Press.

Forst, R. 2007. A Critical Theory of Multicultural Toleration. In *Multiculturalism and Political Theory*, eds S. Laden and D. Owen, 292–312. Cambridge: Cambridge University Press.

Frazer, E. and N. Lacey. 1993. *The Politics of Community*. Toronto: University of Toronto Press.

Gasché, R. 1986. *The Tain of the Mirror*. London: Harvard University Press.

Gillborn, D. and H. Mirza. 2000. *Educational Inequality: Mapping Race, Class and Gender*. London: Institute of Education and Middlesex University.

Grillo, R. 1998. *Pluralism and the Politics of Difference: State, Culture and Ethnicity in Comparative Perspective*. Oxford: Clarendon.

Heath, A. and S.-Y. Cheung. 2007. *Unequal Chances: Ethnic Minorities in Western Labour Markets*. Oxford: Oxford University Press.

Kobayashi, A. 1993. Multiculturalism: Representing a Canadian Institution. In *Place/Culture/Representation*, ed. J. Duncan and D. Ley, 105–35. London: Routledge.

Kukathas, C. 1998. Liberalism and Multiculturalism: The Politics of Indifference. *Political Theory* 26(5): 686–99.

Kyambi, S. 2005. *Beyond Black and White. Mapping New Immigrant Communities*. Institute for Public Policy Research.

Kymlicka, W. 1995. *Multicultural Citizenship: A Theory of Liberal Rights*. Oxford: Clarendon.

Laden, S. and D. Owen. (eds) 2007. *Multiculturalism and Political Theory*. Cambridge: Cambridge University Press.

Lipsitz, G. 1998. *The Possessive Investment in Whiteness: How White People Profit from Identity Politics*. Philadelphia: Temple University Press.

Malik, K. 2006. Clashes and Conflicts. In *30. At the Turning of the Tide*. Commission for Racial Equality.

Modood, T., R. Berthoud et al. 1997. *Ethnic Minorities in Britain*. London: Policy Studies Institute.

Parekh, B. 1988. Integrating Minorities. In *Race in Britain: A Developing Agenda*, eds T. Blackstone, B. Parekh and P. Sanders, 1–21. London: Routledge.

Parekh, B. 2000. *The Future of Multi-ethnic Britain*. London: Runnymede Trust/ Profile Books.

Peach, C. 1996. Does Britain Have Ghettos? *Transactions of the Institute of British Geographers* 22(1): 216–35.

Piggott, G. 2006. *Simpson's Diversity Indices by Ward 1991 and 2001*. DMAG Briefing 2006/2, GLA.

Platt, L. 2003. *Parallel Lives?* London: Child Poverty Action Group.

Radtke, F.O. 1994. The Formation of Ethnic Minorities and the Transformation of Social into Ethnic Conflicts in a So-called Multi- Cultural Society – The Case of Germany. In *Ethnic Mobilization in a Multi-Cultural Europe*, ed. J. Rex and B. Drury, 30–38. Aldershot: Avebury.

Rai-Atkins, A. 2002. *Best Practice in Mental Health Advocacy for Black, Caribbean and South Asian Users*. York: Joseph Rowntree Foundation.

Rawls, J. 1971. *A Theory of Justice*. Cambridge: Belknap Press.
Rudiger, A. and S. Spencer. 2003. *Meeting the Challenge: Equality, Diversity and Cohesion in the European Union*. Joint European Commission/OECD Conference on the Economic Effects and Social Aspect of Migration, Brussels.
Sandel, M. 1998. *Liberalism and the Limits of Justice*. Cambridge: Cambridge University Press.
Scarman, Lord. 1982. *The Scarman Report: The Brixton Disorders, 10–12 April, 1981*. Pelican.
Solomos, J. and G. Singh. 1990. Race Equality, Housing and the Local State. In *Race and Local Politics*, eds W. Ball and J. Solomos, 95–114. London: Macmillan.
Somerville, W. 2007. *Immigration under New Labour*. Bristol: The Policy Press.
Taylor, C. 1994. The Politics of Recognition. In *Multiculturalism*, ed. A. Gutman, 25–74. Princeton: Princeton University Press.
Tully, J. 1995. *Strange Multiplicity: Constitutionalism in an Age of Diversity*. Cambridge: Cambridge University Press.
Turner, B. 1993. *Citizenship and Social Theory*. New York: Sage.
Turner, B. 1997. Citizenship Studies: A General Theory. *Citizenship Studies* 1(1): 5–18.
Vertovec, S. 2001. Transnational Challenges to the 'New' Multiculturalism'. Paper presented to the ASA Conference held at the University of Sussex, 30 March–2 April 2001.
Werbner, P. 1997. Afterword: Writing Multiculturalism and Politics in the New Europe. In *The Politics of Multiculturalism in the New Europe: Racism, Identity and Community*, ed. T. Modood and P. Werbner, 261–67. London: Zed Books.
Young, I.M. 1990. *Justice and the Politics of Difference*. Princeton, NJ: Princeton University Press.

Chapter 11

Squandered Opportunities: Explaining Austria's Reticence to Adopt Multicultural Policies

Barbara Herzog-Punzenberger and Govind Rao

Multiculturalism as an official policy has been adopted by a small number of nations. The policy has been put to use in Canada to facilitate and sustain high levels of immigration and to promote levels of 'social harmony' often in excess of 'social justice'. Notwithstanding, these limitations and this functionalist role, multiculturalism policy contributes to social mobility for a sizeable educated and professional elite of immigrants from racialized origins. Echoing the spirit of Adsett's chapter on Canada and France, for many Canadians the relative "openness" of Canadian society, as represented by multiculturalism policy, is preferable to the more closed society found in much of Europe.

We start from the assumption that the adoption of multiculturalism policy in Austria would bring about real improvement in the lived experiences of immigrant and racialized Austrians. Austria, located at the crossroads of Europe, appears as a likely candidate to adopt an official policy of multiculturalism. The country experienced significant and diverse streams of immigration in the late 1800s and into the early 1900s, which only added to its long-standing ethnic and cultural diversity. A conflicted Austrian identity related to its close historical and cultural ties to Germany would suggest the need for the state to distinguish and emphasize its unique ethnic and cultural heritage. And yet, as of 2008 Austria has made very few steps in that direction. What explains Austria's non-adoption of multiculturalism policy?[1]

A comparison of Austrian and Canadian citizenship policies would place them close to opposing poles on the spectrum of Western democracies. They do however share important parallels at the level of their national identity. We argue that a country's national identity is much more open to a struggle for definition than is usually accepted in academic and public debates. Bauböck (1996, 113) has argued that the adaptation of different societies to immigrants and national

---

1   For the purposes of this chapter, we define multiculturalism as a state policy which recognizes the ethnic heterogeneity of the national polity.

minorities is achieved in three different ways, by *segregation, assimilation,* or *accommodation.*[2]

We will demonstrate how Austria's citizenship regime[3] has consistently adapted to diversity and newcomers by emphasizing segregation and assimilation. In Canada, by contrast, the citizenship regime was adapted to diversity by emphasizing assimilation and accommodation. The choice of adaptation model is tied to the nature of a country's national identity and social struggles. Austrian and Canadian citizenship regimes were largely influenced by a fissure in their national identities, which runs along cultural-ideological lines in the former and cultural-linguistic lines in the latter. This fissure in national identity is reflected in social struggles to reshape the core institutions of civil society to accommodate diversity.

Multiculturalism may be a significant marketing strategy in Canada, but it would not have become entrenched in society without real changes to the national identity, accommodation towards minorities, and in the relative openness of Canadian society for immigrants. The continued official rejection of multiculturalism in Austria rests on and reinforces the anti-immigrant rhetoric of almost all Austrian political parties (SPÖ, ÖVP, BZÖ, FPÖ), the social partners (labour-unions and chamber of commerce) and tabloids, and a continuing anti-pluralist stance of the majority of the population consistent with an emphasis on segregation and assimilation. Multiculturalism's adoption in Austria would therefore be an important step forward in breaking the imagined homogeneity of Austrian society and weaken xenophobic currents.

Fighting Incorporation into a Larger Neighbour

Austria and Canada are surprisingly well-suited to comparison.[4] Economically, they were late followers to capitalist development in the 1870s and had to deal

2   Bauböck (1996, 114) describes *segregation* as preserving the existing social structure by confining individuals and groups to clearly demarked segments of society. *Assimilation* emphasizes change in new elements to make them indistinguishable from already-existing ones. He describes *accommodation* as the adaptation of both the new elements and the larger structure of society. Whereas *accommodation* stresses the *internalization of difference*, *segregation* emphasizes the *externalization of difference*.

3   We define the term "citizenship regime" not only as those regulations targeting nationality, i.e. naturalization but all policies and politics that have an impact on the specific understanding of being a citizen in a specific polity.

4   This comparison has been presented previously by a number of authors. In the volume *Unequal Partners: A Comparative Analysis of Relations Between Austria and the Federal Republic of Germany and Between Canada and the United States* (1993) edited by Harald von Riekhoff and Hanspeter Neuhold authors examined relationships in the cultural, economic and political spheres. Helmut Konrad (2002, 35–43) in his article "Identität durch Negation. Kanada und Österreich im Vergleich" ("Identity Through Negation. A

with the societal challenges posed by the industrialization process without recourse to the power of a unified nationalist ideology. Both countries face a fundamental fissure at the heart of their national identities. Austria before the fall of the Habsburg Monarchy was a multi-ethnic and multi-lingual entity. Among the residents of the Western half of the Monarchy, numerous identities competed for the loyalty of the citizenry: Pan-Germans, Habsburg loyalists, German-Austrian nationalists, as well as constituent nationalities and nationalisms of the Monarchy. In Canada, the loyalties of the population were split between the British Empire and French Canada along linguistic lines, but even among English-speakers there was not unanimity. As early as the 1880s the 'Canada First' movement identified themselves as only Canadians, while others strongly identified a British connection and still others preferred annexation to the United States.

These challenges for national identity and multiple competing loyalties were not significantly overcome in either country until the mid-1970s. A popular pan-Canadian nationalism emerged for the first time in the 1960s that articulated itself as independent of Britain and the United States. The state responded to, and at times led, this upsurge in popular sentiment with policies aimed at wresting greater control of the economy to Canadian business and governments. Policies which arose out of the historical inability of the state to subsume difference became two of the touchstones of modern Canadian nationalism – bilingualism and multiculturalism. Although pan-Canadianism had stronger adherents in some regions of Canada over others, it still had enough currency to win 59.6 percent of the Quebec electorate in the 1980 referendum. Austria enjoyed steady growth from the late 1950s through the 1970s, when other countries around the world ran into the wall of stagflation. More than any other factor, the ability of the Austrian state to demonstrate that it was economically viable led to rising support for the idea of an Austrian nation. By 1980, 86 percent of Austrians agreed with either the statement that 'Austria is a nation' or 'Austria is becoming a nation'. This was a change from 1956 when Austrians were evenly split between 'Austria is a nation' and 'Austria is not a nation' (Kreissler 1984, 496–7).

Another clear similarity between Austria and Canada is that their cultural, political and economic realities have been significantly shaped in the last one hundred years by Germany and the United States, respectively. The disastrous twenty-years of depression that followed the First World War in Austria, and the increased German influence in economic, political, and social spheres, contributed to the 1938 'Anschluss'. The lack of a popular resistance to Nazi annexation was only partly due to sympathy for Nazi ideology among sections of Austrian society. Significant as well, was the lack of a unified Austrian national identity

---

Comparison of Canada and Austria") he notes the areas of language, cultural tradition, welfare state, irony, tolerance and media as fields where the relationship of Canada and Austria to their larger neighbours showed substantial similarity. On the other hand, Konrad proposes that boundary between the "partners" was more distinct in the fields of sports, the metric system, the educational system, as well as national symbols.

as the country was split along cultural-ideological lines (socialist vs. Christian-democratic) which hampered calls for continued Austrian independence. Thirty years later, Canada faced a similar threat to its political independence in the overwhelming wave of American foreign ownership and cultural influence in the country during the 1950s and 1960s. The popular nationalist response in English-speaking Canada was rooted in a fear that the country was close to annexation, a fear that was taken seriously by many Canadian-based businesses and sections of the federal state. For both Austrians and Canadians, nation-building activities are carried out on the backdrop of the need to distance and distinguish their country from an overbearing "bigger brother".

Austrian National Identity and History of Migration

Austrian Kabaretist Georg Kreisler in his song *Telefonbuchpolka* pokes fun at the legacy of migration created by the Austro-Hungarian Empire, manifested in the surnames of the Vienna telephone book. Throughout the centuries, not least since the mercantilistic economy in the eighteenth century, migration and recruitment of foreign workers was a central part of economic development of the Empire. In the second half of the nineteenth century foreigners accounted for more than half of the inhabitants of many towns and cities in what is now Austria (Hahn 2002, 90). In fact, several languages, especially Slavic, German and Hungarian mixed with less common Yiddish and Romani languages, were present, the first ones in the public the latter two more or less reduced to the private sphere.

Although the mixed heritage and legacy of migration from central and south-eastern Europe is a historical fact, it has been a repressed part of the Austrian national identity, the legacy of Nazi propaganda and policies during the first half of the twentieth century. The fact that many Austrians have some Slavic or Hungarian ancestry did not mean that this heritage was a matter of pride. While Austrian national identity remains tied to an imaginary past rooted in Habsburg folklore the tacit Germanness of Austrian self-perception was a fact throughout history. This explains a complicated relationship between Austria and Germany in terms of national identity. Apart from that the post-war emphasis on official neutrality and being a small prosperous country serve as markers in the boundary-drawing between Austrian and German identity, the former much more occupied with it than the latter.

We begin our analysis of Austria's non-adoption of multiculturalism with an examination of the nature of its national identity. Austrian identity and nationalism has a German-Austrian ethnic basis, which is complicated by Germany sharing a common language and cultural/artistic touchstones as a basis for German national identity.[5] During the post-World War Two period, Austria went through the

---

5   For example, the national hymn Germany adopted in 1922 was the same tune composed by Joseph Haydn for the Austrian Emperor in 1797 and served as the unofficial

process of identity-formation and nation-building. Separated from Germany by defeat in war, and with the Pan-German nationalist option delegitimized by broad devastation and dehumanizing racism culminating in the concentration camps, an Austrian identity grew steadily alongside official neutrality and Austrocorporatism between the 1950s and 1970s. Also, the reinterpretation of Austria as the first victim of Nazi-Germany made it easier to distance itself from Germany and not to look to closely into the near past.[6] The "realpolitik" of the Cold War determined official neutrality for Austria after 1955, and became an important part of the new Austrian identity. Much of the development in Austrian national attachment drew sustenance from the first period of sustained economic growth the country had experienced since 1913. The overwhelming emphasis for identity formation in the post-war period was to establish a vibrant Austrian identity that could be distinct and separate from Germany.

The history and culture of discrimination that was commonplace in Austria prior to and during the Nazi period left their mark on post-war Austria. At the level of the family unit, overwhelming societal pressure to assimilate, to speak unaccented German, to Germanize one's name continued. The result was the reinforcement of strong assimilatory pressures that quickly imbued immigrant children with Austrian attitudes towards immigrants. In effect, each new generation of newcomers to Austria had to begin the struggle for acceptance and integration. This, in contrast, to a popular and school culture in Canada where personal migration history is a matter of course and much more alive, that history is quickly expunged in Austria.

Canada had by the 1960s developed a coherent territorial nationalism, and the dominant Anglo-ethnic nationalism which defined Canada at the national level lost ground not only to French Canadian demands, but also those of a 'third-force' of Canadians of Ukrainian, Italian, and German heritage (among others). In fact, multiculturalism was needed to get minority ethnic groups to support bilingualism at a time when Quebecois secessionism was one of the biggest threats perceived by Canadians. The differing histories of assimilation and incorporation of immigrants in Austria and Canada were to affect the pressures brought to bear on redefining the nation. Many second and third generation Canadians of the 'third-force' group were at the forefront of pushing for multiculturalism policy and the recognition of non-British and non-French heritage. Second and third generation Austrians historically have been more likely to acquiesce to assimilation pressures and put distance between their family past as immigrants. Austrian society was less open to ethnic difference in the 1960s, not least because foreign workers were conceptualized as short-term makeshift and not as (future) citizens. While both countries subjected migrants to strong assimilatory pressures, they were stronger

---

national anthem until 1918.

6   The first serious public discussions about Austria's role between 1938 and 1945 started with protests against the election of Kurt Waldheim as federal president of Austria in 1986.

in Austria. Ironically, the resistance of Austria's citizenship regime to official recognition of diversity is partly a result of the 'success' experienced at the turn of the last century and in the early post-war period in assimilating immigrants, especially those from Czech, Slovak, Hungarian and Jewish descent. Not enough Austrians remember and identify with their personal migration histories.

In terms of the struggle over national identity definition at the level of the state, the identity fissures that ran through Austrian society along Pan-German/German-Austrian/Habsburg-loyalist/minority nationalist lines pre-World War One, were replaced by a fissure along ideological lines in the 1920s and 1930s. The Civil War and the period of Austro-fascism (1934–1938) left deep societal wounds which became the focus of post-war healing. The citizenship regime hinged on the consensus position of the Christian-Democrat and Socialist parties. The former, except for a very weak liberal wing of mainly industrialists, were not much interested in building an Austrian identity that diverged from a traditional self-understanding rooted in Catholicism and the countryside, while the socialists blamed failures in their political struggles on the lack of unity of a labour movement divided along linguistic and ethnic lines. In the context of Austro-Corporatism then, neither Christian-Democrats nor Socialists were much interested in moving away from the pursuit of a monistic Austrian identity.[7] Nor was there a way for newcomers to break into this institutionalized structure of power.

The Canadian identity fissure in the post-war period ran most deeply along cultural-linguistic lines (English/French). It is in this context that the nation-building initiatives of the late 1960s and 1970s need to be placed, as outlined by the Adsett, Reiss and Hasmath chapters. It was becoming increasingly untenable to assert a homogeneous ethnic picture of Canada, or one that lent asymmetrical power to British-Canadians in the face of French-Canadian nationalism. In fact, it was this historical failure of the Canadian state and the dominant British ethnic group to assimilate immigrants and French-Canadians which paved the way for some sort of Bi- or Multi-culturalism. One aspect of the Canadian experience that bolstered claims for recognition for immigrants to Canada was the fact that many shared in the status of being 'settlers'. From Italians and Chinese who worked to build the country's railways in the late 1800s, to Ukrainians who settled with other immigrants on the prairies, immigrants were clearly present at an early stage in the country's history. In a new settler society where legitimacy was derived from being a 'nation-builder' this fact strengthened the case of immigrant communities in the debate that took place in the run-up to the adoption of multiculturalism in Canada.

In Austria, immigrants could not as easily claim to have made early contributions to the Austrian nation. Ideological hegemony in Austria rested firmly with Catholic German-speakers. Also members of autochthonous

---

7   On the contrary, foreign labour was seen as an instrument for short-term economic ends. Those workers should not be considered part of the Austrian citizenry.

minorities who dominated certain regions as was the case with Slovenes in parts of Southern Styria and Carinthia conformed to the strong assimilation pressure of the German-speaking urban elites in growing numbers so that today only a small fraction of the population would identify with and speak the Slovenian language. Relentless assimilation pressures working at the levels of family and the state have kept German-speaking Austrians in control of the definition of Austrian national identity as ethnically German. Ideas about national identity set boundaries on the type of citizenship regime a country can adopt.

Citizenship Regimes in Austria and Canada

We define the term "citizenship regime" not only as those regulations targeting nationality, i.e. naturalization, but all policies and politics that have an impact on the understanding of being a citizen in a specific polity, i.e. the role a citizen plays in its society. As citizenship understood in this wide sense is a basic mechanism of societal cohesion in every modern society, we argue that citizenship regimes and the specific shape and form of civil society are crucial to understand the existence of multiculturalism in Austria and Canada.

State policies and the popular conception of the nation are key areas in which a heterogeneous view of the polity must win out if multiculturalism is to be adopted. The most common claims made by opponents of official multiculturalism in Austria is that the country is not one of immigration, nor is it as predisposed to the acceptance of ethnic pluralism as a country such as Canada. However, this argument overlooks Canada's long history of overt discriminatory practices. From the creation of the reservation system for the First Nations peoples, the Chinese Exclusion Act of 1923–1947, the internment of Canadians of Japanese origin, the blocking of American blacks from settlement on the prairies, the shutdown of Ukrainian language schools, and quotas on Jewish students at universities until the 1960s, Canada's history contains as much or more racial and ethnic antagonism as found in Austria and other European societies. The turn to a policy of official non-discrimination was a shocking break from such discriminatory policies. What prompted such a break in Canada and why has it not yet fully come about in Austria?

We argue that the struggles for recognition in civil society, hence the specific understanding of the role of citizens, are crucially important in determining why Austria remained closed to multiculturalism. In Bauböck's (1996, 76) conception of civil society, it maintains a balance and boundary between the three core institutions of state, market and family. He writes that "civil society [is] in a narrower sense … the intermediate sphere different from all three institutional cornerstones of modern society". In the social space between these institutions, diverse associations engage in dialogue and struggle. In the remaining portions of the chapter we look at how citizenship is constructed in relation to state, market and family as well as in civil society proper. Our understanding of citizenship regimes includes not only legal regulations pertaining to naturalization and the targeting of non-nationals, but also encompasses ideals of individual autonomy, equality and civil society that prevail in a country. We examine four factors in Austria to make our case: reactions to cultural diversity, the organization of labour migration, approaches to education and training, and migrants' legal status and recognition.

Responses to Cultural Diversity

Cultural diversity has long been a reality in most of the provinces of the present-day Austrian republic. Certainly, cultural and linguistic diversity has been regionally concentrated in Vienna, but small minority communities continue to exist in today's provinces: Burgenland in the east (Hungarian, Croatian), Carinthia and Styria in the south (Slovene), Upper and Lower Austria in the north (Czech and Slovak) in Tyrol (see Fait chapter for an Italian perspective on Tyrol) and Vorarlberg in the west (Italian, Ladin), as well Austrian Jews and Roma citizens. Many cities throughout the whole country depend on a diverse migrant population economically.

These historical immigrant streams and minority communities would seem to provide a fertile ground on which to build a multicultural interpretation of Austria's history, but until today the implementation of minority rights, even those enshrined in the State Treaty of 1955, stir a lot of resentment. The fulfilment of Article 7 of Austria's State Treaty[8] has resulted in violent clashes in past decades. In 1972 Austria's popular chancellor Bruno Kreisky was physically attacked over the issue of bilingual town signs by German-speaking Austrian nationalists in Carinthia. The police force whose responsibility it was to guard the signs did not dare to intervene, as participants in the fighting threatened it would provoke another civil war (Gstettner 2004, 247–72). The reaction of Anglo-Canadians was similarly visceral in response to official bilingualism and the French-language sharing space with English on cereal boxes. The difference in Canada was the compromised status of Canadians of British backgrounds, who were outnumbered by their compatriots. In battle after battle over the symbols of the Canadian identity, such as the Canadian Flag debate in 1965, supporters with ethnic ties to Britain were defeated. In Austria, German ethnic dominance was not similarly challenged and subsequently, this lead to national minorities' defeats in conflicts of this sort. Unless national minorities can win battles for accommodation first, there is much less of a chance for migrant groups to increase accommodation and recognition of new diversity in Austrian society.

---

8   The 1955 Austrian State Treaty was the document which reestablished Austria as a sovereign state. Article 7 laid out recognition of national minorities and rights to minority language protection.

In Austria today, the stalemate is between the rule of law and the rights of minorities versus a populist governor of the province of Carinthia, Jörg Haider, who has decided to ignore the ruling of the constitutional court in the dispute over bilingual town signs. The overwhelming majority of the provincial population supports an anti-minority, anti-pluralist position. In Haider's words, a democracy is about the rule of the majority, not the judges of the constitutional court nor any other authority. Although the situation in Carinthia is in some ways the extreme end of a continuum in Austria – also in the most eastern province of Burgenland with a social-democratic governor the full number of bilingual signs was only installed in the year 2000 – it shows quite well how difficult it is until today for a substantial part of the Austrian population to accept that Austria is not a monolingual (German), monoreligious (Catholicism), monocultural country. Even foundational institutions at the heart of the polity such as the constitution and state treaties are not functional if an elite consensus for accommodation, not to speak about the population as a whole, is lacking.

The institutional structures of parliamentary democracy in Austria work to sustain the 50-year-old stalemate between the federal government and the province of Carinthia. In a proportional representation system, the extremes of the political spectrum benefit from being able to pitch to their constituency without much need to moderate their position to attract voters in the middle of the spectrum.[9] The approximately 20–25 percent of the Austrian population that holds strong anti-immigrant views ensure an anti-immigrant block in parliament, but more than this, influence the parties of the centre – Christian-Democrat and Social-Democrat – to attempt to win votes from this constituency by articulating an anti-immigrant platform. When this dynamic is combined with conservative citizenship laws which limit the political enfranchisement of immigrants, there is little gain from a federal defence of minority rights, but much potential political harm in the action. Also, the two big parties – Social-Democrats and Christian-Democrats – each have a strong wing which in its self-understanding is anti-immigrant and culturally monistic, aiming to protect in the former case the native workers and in the latter the traditional culture including language and religion.

In comparison, as early as 1959 the political dynamic in Canada started to shift from segregation to accommodation. The Diefenbaker government wanted to limit provisions for family reunification because of a worry about the number of southern and eastern Europeans who were taking advantage of these to bring in relatives. The response from immigrant communities was strong. Through political pressure within parliament using the Liberal Party and in newspapers, letters to Members of Parliaments, and other forums, they were able to force the Conservatives to drop the idea. In the 1960 election, an Italian-Canadian candidate

---

9   It should be mentioned, however, that the xenophobic discourse goes together with an anti-elite discourse which was fuelled by the all encompassing power position of the two major parties, building on frequent coalition governments between them and social partnership as a non-parliamentarian and mostly inofficial way of decision-making.

defeated the Minister of Immigration, Ellen Fairclough in her riding. The success had important outcomes for winning immigrant communities a say in issue over questions of residence and citizenship in Canada. The ability to expand the definition of who had a right to determine immigration policy rested on both the fact that most immigrants could vote, and that the clumping of ethnic communities facilitated the election of immigrant representatives to parliament under the British Parliamentary model.

Thus, the British Westminister system brings about two outcomes for immigrants (1) ridings that match ethnic neighbourhoods make it possible for ethnic minorities to win election by relying on their community votes, and (2) the 'first past the post' system of plurality voting means that parties must try to win the vote of the political centre, where the most votes reside. This reduces extremism in the political system and forces parties to moderate their platforms *vis-à-vis* immigrants. This dynamic helped bring about changes in support of accommodation in the 1960s and 1970s.

The 1968 Canadian Bilingualism and Biculturalism Committee Report noted a 'Quiet Crisis' brewing that threatened the future of the country (Igartua 2006). The key challenge was to re-establish the basis of Canadians' allegiance to the federal state. The trifecta of policies adopted to this purpose was bilingualism, multiculturalism and patriation of the Canadian Constitution. These policies aimed not only to modernize the Canadian identity, but had as a central goal the distancing of Canada from the United States in the realm of identity. Lacking the post World War Two popular opposition and international restrictions to annexation which were present in Austria *vis-à-vis* Germany, Canada faced a real threat to its independence in the mid-1960s.

In Canada, the shift to multiculturalism mirrored changes in the demographic make-up of political and economic power in 1960s Canadian society. The non-British, non-French component of the population, as a result of strong post-war immigration, became the plurality of the population by 1966. That plurality was not matched by economic or political power, as John Porter's original 1965 study *The Vertical Mosaic* found that 92.3 percent of the corporate elite were from British backgrounds. This figure had fallen to below 60 percent by the early eighties, and even further since (Breton and Jenson 1991, 159). A relative diversification in the ethnic background of the Canadian elite does not, however, erase the significant ethnic penalty in the labour market which persists for ethnic minority and racialized groups, even when controlling for generation, immigrant status and crucially, education.

The shift in Canadian immigrant-sourcing to Asia and the developing world in the 1960s and 1970s was a response to the drying up of European sources of immigration due to rebuilding of the Western European economy. With much of Eastern Europe closed by the Soviet-Bloc's restrictions on emigration, Canada turned by default to new sources of skilled and professional immigrants in Asia (east and west) and Latin America (although there remain institutional barriers to immigration from Black Africa). In the tumult of the era, society was called to fulfil the promises of liberalism. Canadians who had been long shut out of full participation in the economic and political life of the country wanted their newly acquired respectability to be reflected in the nation's image.

Thus, the ethnic associations making representations to the government for the fourth book of the Royal Commission on Bilingualism and Biculturalism were representative of immigrant communities' intelligentsia and professional strata. Processes of assimilation which did not erase diversity at the level of the family and the individual were relevant. Community representatives who argued for the recognition of diversity had the benefit of being part of the 'in-group' of Canadian society, and made their arguments on the basis of their being Canadians of non-British and non-French backgrounds. Multiculturalism arose alongside the expansion of state employment, the professions, and opening up of white-collar service sector jobs to these immigrant communities. The success immigrant communities enjoyed, especially those of the second generation, of expanding into areas of the market economy, such as insurance and real estate diversified their incorporation into the Canadian economy. Having fought the vertical mosaic to establish themselves as petty-bourgeois, ethnic and racialized minorities sought to have this new status reflected in state policy. Therefore, there is certainly merit to the argument that multiculturalism's role was to "buy off the compliance of a potential third force of immigrants, while bilingualism was intended to appease a revitalized Quebec and to contain its claims to political power" (Kallen 1982, 55).

Labour Migration

Labour migration has been at the heart of the Austrian and Canadian state accumulation strategies and management of the labour market in the post-war period. However, the history of labour importation goes back much further. In the Austrian half of the Monarchy, workers were drawn from peripheral provinces of both halves of the Monarchy to the growing centres of industrialization in and around Vienna, Bohemia and other regions. Most workers did not have resident permits in their new homes (*'Heimatrecht'*), the significance of which will be discussed below. In the post-war period, after the initial rebuilding stage lasting to 1960, the Austrian economy began to experience a lack of workers, not least because Austrians preferred to work in neighbouring countries such as Switzerland and Germany where the wage levels were considerably higher. In 1961 the social partners agreed to recruit foreign workers and in 1962, 1964 and 1966 Austria signed recruitment contracts with Spain, Turkey and Yugoslavia respectively. Since then the number of foreign workers has steadily grown with a low of 147,000 in 1984. In 2006 more than 430,000 employees or employment-seeking persons with a non-Austrian citizenship were registered which is around 10 percent of the total workforce. Additionally, we estimate around the same number of naturalized persons with migration background is part of the Austrian workforce today.

Overwhelmingly, immigrants to Austria were stratified by ethnicity. The large numbers of Sudeten Germans and other ethnic Germans displaced by World War Two found themselves farther up the Austrian social and economic hierarchy than recruited labour migrants. Ethnic German immigrants, all naturalized until 1955, could also climb the social ladder together with the natives as they were already incorporated into Austrian society when the labour migrants came and the entire labour-market expanded. The dominance of German-speaking Austrians reinforced segregation on the basis of ethnicity. The 'cheap labour' imported from Yugoslavia and Turkey was planned as a temporary workforce, in contrast to the 500,000 ethnic German refugees and displaced persons granted permanent residence after 1945. The foreign labour force was conceived of as a mobile mass that would leave once the national economy no longer depended on it or when native unemployment rates rose.

Austrian decisions about the numbers of labour migrants to be imported to manage the labour market shortage that began in the 1960s were taken in a consociational manner. In fact, the acceptance of a yearly allotment of foreign workers by the trade-unions enabled them to get a strong position in the commission on the agreed minimum wages. So, the "bargaining chip" of foreign workers was one of the most important issues in the establishment of Austrian social partnership which makes it more comprehensible why foreign workers were not seen as equals at any time (Wollner 1996). The particular segregation of decision-making between the parties representing the two dominant ideological camps to the exclusion of outgroups has drawbacks for migrant groups looking to influence the political process. When combined with the lack of voting rights, a proportional and party list system, the opportunity and support for new groups to break into the system and be heard is very limited. Furthermore, many workers were not able to legally join unions or stand for election as union representatives. The structures of Austro-corporatism took on preeminent importance while immigrant organizations and migrant NGOs were forced to the wayside. In a paper from the Institute for Economic Research (WIFO 1962: 232) on labour recruitment, the expected benefits for the Austrian economy and native workers were explained as follows:

- Austria will be able to export a substantial share of seasonal unemployment by limiting the workers' permits (Switzerland is described as the model in this respect)
- Native workers will move up the social ladder, moving to better paid jobs or sectors with higher wage levels because foreign workers are satisfied in the worst positions
- In the collective wage negotiations (social partnership) wage demands will be moderated
- Price stabilization through higher number of goods, while at the same time demand will not grow because foreign workers do not spend but save their money.

As the guestworker scheme was built on the rotation of the recruited workers, the children of these workers were meant to return home after a short while. For a large part this was only theoretical even though migrants themselves oftentimes were not entirely clear how to deal with being in a situation of 'unwelcome settlers'. Many of them had some non-specific aspiration to return to their home country. Rather than emphasize assimilation to Austrian culture and language, families left in this sort of limbo fell back on their native culture, with the children somewhere in between. In the recruitment contract between Austria and Turkey as well as Yugoslavia, the source countries had negotiated the right to send teachers to prepare children to return to Turkey or Yugoslavia. Children could take voluntary mother tongue language courses once a week with some additional course material on the source country itself. These teachers were sent by the source country and oftentimes were not very well integrated in the regular school staff. Many had not lived for a long time in Austria.[10] Accommodation, in this case to minority language and culture, was done on the assumption that it would make repatriation of the foreign workers easier.

The rigid class structure largely building on the concept of a workforce, not meant to become part of the society, distinguishes European immigration and incorporation from the North American variant. The general mechanisms of societal cohesion in a given nation-state will determine to a large degree the incorporation of immigrants. It makes some difference if, as in the case of Austria, societal subgroups understand their position in reference to a century old hierarchical structure, or to a dictatorship (as in national socialism), or an indisputable authority (as in Catholicism). In the case of Canada, as the Adsett chapter points out, liberal ideals such as individual autonomy, equality and democracy are much more deeply entrenched in the collective self-understanding.[11] While Canadian immigrants from Southern and Eastern Europe were also slotted into working class professions, the myth of classlessness of a liberal society provided a different frame for expectations of a common future society. It also mitigated against some of the discrimination faced by immigrants to Canada, and opened up opportunities for success to a sizeable minority of the immigrant population.

---

10   Austria did not go as far down the path of segregation as the German province of Bavaria where entire classes were created with homogenous student populations from a specific source country. The Austrian Ministry of Education held that children with migration background should participate in regular classes from the beginning, so that they experienced a mixed learning environment in terms of migration background.

11   In our view, every liberal democracy has to constantly work on the balance between the internal differentiation of society which on the one side allows for a great deal of inequality – a function of individual autonomy and on the other hand to safeguard equal opportunities to increase (the realistic chance to exercise) individual autonomy for everybody. The question in a country comparative view is not either or but rather on the differences in degree.

Differing Approaches to Education and Training

Canada and Austria have different approaches towards the role of education in society as well as the import of education through immigrants. The Canadian state has always made up for shortcomings in domestic education and training infrastructure by 'poaching' sources of skilled immigrants from sending countries, and received a significant benefit from human capital inflows in the process, estimated by R.G. Coulson and D.J. DeVoretz (1993, 359) at CA$12.8 billion (~US$12.8 billion) in the period from 1967–1987[12]. Contrary to that, Austria never perceived immigrants as a possibility to make up for shortcomings in domestic education. Until the Organization for Economic Co-operation and Development OECD ignited recent discussions about school-systems based on quantified analyses such as the Program for International Student Assessment (PISA) the approach to the educational system in Austria simply was that there were no shortcomings. Not only that. The school-system in the German-speaking countries aims at separating the academically talented from the less talented students, from age 10 onwards.

This structure is deeply rooted in history. The belief is not only engrained in Austria as a non-liberal 'rank' society but reflects the reconstitution of the social structure in the interwar period in Austria[13] around the professions. Professional positions are remarkably often 'inherited' in the family rather than being an outcome of individual choice and educational achievement. When asked which professional position 15-year-old students think they will most likely take up when they are 30 years old, Austrian students respond much more often the professional position their father has than Canadian students who are inclined to think that they can take up a different position (data from PISA 2003). In the logic of strongly hierarchical understandings rooted in a biological pre-determination of individuals, immigrants coming from low social background are not seen fit to become part of the citizenry proper. A case in point is the legal provision that a student (from age 10 onwards) with a negative mark (equals too few points to pass) in the subject "German" is not eligible for naturalization.

Whereas relatively speaking, in Canada a more deeply rooted liberalism in terms of educational meritocracy based on individual achievement provides a different

---

12   Anti-foreigner elements pose a real threat to the central place of immigration in the state's accumulation strategy. According to polls between 1975 and 1987, the portion of the population which supported increased immigration varied between only 8–17 percent of the population while between 35–48 percent wanted it decreased (Campbell 2000, 144).

13   Between 1933 and the annexation by Germany in 1938, Austria was defined as a (non-democratic) corporate rank state (Ständestaat) by the leaders of the clerico-conservative camp who installed an authoritarian regime. In a certain way the societal institution of "Sozialpartnerschaft", including representatives of employers, employees and agriculture can be seen as a continuation of that tradition. Since the 1960s it is the social partnership which effectively prepares the decision-making on laws in Austria.

frame. The commitment to immigration, the full inclusion at an early point in time through naturalization and the prior selection of the immigrants based on a more objective scheme than Austria, using points which reward real and potential human capital, both social, cultural and economic, makes for a radically different view. Especially, the changing composition of the immigration stream in the 1960s from Europe towards Asia made it clear to contemporary Canadian policy-makers that continuing past reliance on labour migration would mean a much more racially diverse immigrant population. In the context of laws for permanent settlement, as explored below, multiculturalism was seen to have an important role in supporting and legitimating the intake of new workers from all kinds of regional and cultural background.

Legal Status and Naturalization Regulations

Foreign workers in Austria, as long as they are not naturalized, are treated as second class citizens instrumentalized according to the needs of the national economy. The logic states that as soon as they are not useful for the economy anymore they are to be sent home – unemployment should be avoided for natives and be exportable. Actually, in Austria the belief in the feasibility of this approach towards all foreigners including recruited guestworkers was very strong until the end of the 1990s and continues to be a major approach. Mainly the legal provisions on equal treatment of long-term resident third country nationals within the European Union brought about a slow change.

While in Sweden[14] and some other European countries it was accepted at the end of the 1970s that people who were working for years in the country are likely to stay forever and therefore incorporation policies have to be developed accordingly, Austrian policy was based on the idea that population movement could be regulated in a bureaucratic manner. In response to this rather hostile context migrants oftentimes did not become immigrants in their own view either.

In stark contrast to Canadian policy, naturalization was not encouraged in Austria whatsoever. A more liberal naturalization policy in Austria is derailed by the close relationship of ethnicity and citizenship for most Austrians. The dominance of territorial nationalism in Canada leads to a view of citizenship which is much looser: recognition of membership in a territorial community. In 2003 when there was a high of 44,694 (0,55 percent of the total population of 8,1 million inhabitants) naturalizations in Austria, the headlines of the newspapers were inflamatory – 'Foreign Infiltration Lurking' (*Die Überfremdung droht*). To become an Austrian national is meant to be, as stated explicitly by administration and politicians, the reward at the end of a successful (one-sided) integration process. A selective process, which in the Canadian case is the creaming-off of the

---

14   For an insightful analysis of the processes in Swedish policy development at that time from a researcher who was part of the scientific support structure see Hammar 2004.

sending-countries' educated elite, which takes place in the Canadian case through the point system, is conducted in the Austrian case through the instrument of a selective naturalization process. The Canadian territorial border is meant to be identical with the boundary of the polity, so that the coherence of the civil society is protected through providing landed immigrants with almost the same legal status as natives and encouraging early naturalization. In contrast, in the Austrian case, borders are transferred into the territory, the *Fremdenpolizei* (foreigners' police) signifying the mobile border. The internal boundaries between the majority and migrant communities are enforced through strict rules about significantly different legal statuses which determine the access to social goods such as welfare, subsidized housing, retirement homes, etc.

As Klaus J. Bade and Michael Bommes (2004) describe the case regarding the official rhetoric on migrants in Germany, Austrian government statements were at times much worse than what existed in actual practice. There was some discretionary room for Austrian naturalization officers and the application of the legal regulations differs by province, so that an increasing number of migrants succeeded in naturalizing earlier than the general law would aim at. Since new policy amendments recently passed, naturalization is more restrictive again. Nevertheless, the hostile rhetoric made clear that there is little interest in new citizens who represent cultural plurality and no interest in enforcing anti-discrimination which is part and parcel of effective multiculturalism. The lack of political pressure to enforce anti-discrimination laws is itself related to restrictive naturalization laws, and the small number of immigrant voters. As Austrian politicians and especially Ministers of the Interior are fond of saying, "those who don't like it here can leave at any time". In contrast, Canada has long encouraged permanent settlement for the bulk of its migrant population. One outcome is the right to vote, and also the creation of large immigrant enclaves, schools, churches, newspapers, and other institutions which give immigrants power and confidence in the society.

Conclusion

In this chapter we have argued that Austria's citizenship regime was distinguished by segregation and assimilation tendencies. These tendencies are a result of struggles in civil society and within the core institutions of the state, market, and family. Both Austria and Canada evidenced significant cultural diversity and labour migration. The difference in Canada was the emphasis placed on accommodation together with assimilation.

The bases of the modern Austrian identity – music, geography, and an Habsburg imperial past – have not yet run out of steam, especially because it covers up so nicely the more problematic strands of the anti-liberal, hierarchical and authoritarian history in between. The tradition of strong assimilation pressures had successfully Austrianized a large portion of the non-German immigrants of the Habsburg Empire to the extent that they identified with the dominant culture. This historical legacy can be seen as one of the underlying currents in the national discourse and legislation around immigration and settlement in Austria.[15] The American threat to Canada's continued independence and the state's requirement that a new identity be invented to replace the quickly fading and increasingly improbable imperial tie to Britain, meant that the very challenge the state faced as a hurdle to unity – multiple cultural communities – was drawn upon to refound a modern Canadian identity.

Secondly, the citizenship regimes of Austria and Canada reflect the respective emphases on segregation versus accommodation. The countries were generally similar in their cultural diversity and reliance on labour migration, but the most important difference was in terms of citizenship and naturalization policies. Whereas in Canada naturalization was encouraged, this has not been the case in Austria due to the belief that the foreign labour force was a relocatable mass rather than human beings with families who would become a future part of the Austrian society. Segregation of immigrant communities was reinforced in the nature of ethnic politics and the dynamics of vote-getting in Austria. Whereas in Canada parties are forced to the centre of the political spectrum by the need to win immigrant votes and the nature of the 'first past the post' electoral system, in Austria proportional representation provided a guaranteed minimum vote for anti-immigrant parties.

Multiculturalism as a policy is not a solution to all the challenges regarding migrant incorporation facing Austrian society. In the case of Austria, multiculturalism would be less a marketing strategy than a way to measure the distance the society has moved towards accommodation of difference and recognition of the heterogeneous character of Austrian culture and its population.

References

Bade, K.J. and M. Bommes. (eds) 2004. *Migration – Integration – Bildung. Grundfragen und Problembereiche*. Universität Osnabrück.

Bauböck, R. 1996. Social and Cultural Integration in a Civil Society. In *The Challenge of Diversity: Integration and Pluralism in Societies of Immigration*, eds R. Bauböck et. al., 67–131. Aldershot: Avebury.

Biffl, G. 1986. Der Strukturwandel der Ausländerbeschäftigung in Österreich. In *Ausländische Arbeitskräfte in Österreich*, ed. H. Wimmer, 33–88. Frankfurt/ Main; New York: Campus Verlag.

Breton, G. and J. Jenson. 1991. After Free Trade and Meech Lake: Quo de Neuf? *Studies in Political Economy* 34: 199–218.

---

15   There are certainly counteracting strands and ideals inherent in liberal democracy which are based on the equal moral worth of each person and equal status of each citizen.

Campbell, C.M. 2000. *Betrayal and Deceit: The Politics of Canadian Immigration.* Vancouver: Jasmine Books.

Coulson, R. G. and D. J. DeVoretz. 1993. *Human Capital Content of Canadian Immigrants*, 1967–1987. Canadian Public Policy / Analyse de Politiques 19: 357–66.

Gstettner, P. 2004. "... wo alle Macht vom Volk ausgeht". Eine nachhaltige Verhinderung. Zur Mikropolitik rund um den „Ortstafelsturm" in Kärnten. In *Österreichische Zeitschrift für Politikwissenschaft* 33: 81–94.

Hahn, S., I. Bauer and J. Ehmer. (eds) 2002. *Walz – Migration – Besatzung. Historische Szenarien des Eigenen und des Fremden.* Klagenfurt: Drava Verlag.

Hammar, T. 2004. Research and Politics in Swedish Immigration Management 1965–1984. In *Towards A Multilateral Migration Regime. Special Anniversary Edition Dedicated to Jonas Widgren*, eds J, Michael and I. Stacher, International Centre for Migration Policy Development. Vienna: ICMPD, 2004, 11–34.

Igartua, J. 2006. *The Other Quiet Rrevolution National Identities in English Canada, 1945–71.* Vancouver: University of British Columbia Press.

Jandl, M. and A. Kraler. 2003. *Austria: A Country of Immigration?* International Centre for Migration Policy Development. Available at: http://www. migrationinformation.org/Profiles/display.cfm?ID=105.

Kallen, E. 1982. Multiculturalism: Ideology, Policy and Reality. *Journal of Canadian Studies* 17(1): 51–63.

Konrad, H. 2002. Identität durch Negation. Kanada und Österreich im Vergleich. In *Gestörte Identitäten?* eds L. Musner et al., Innsbruck, Wien, München, Bozen: Studienverlag.

Kreissler, F. 1984. *Der Österreicher und seine Nation: ein Lernprozeß mit Hindernissen.* Wien: Böhlau.

Nowotny, I. 2007. Das Ausländerbeschäftigungsgesetz: Die Regelung des Zugangs von AusländerInnen zum österreichischen Arbeitsmarkt. In *2. Österreichischer Migrations- und Integrationsbericht.Rechtliche Rahmenbedingungen, demographische Entwicklungen, sozioökonomische Strukturen*, 47–73. Klagenfurt/Celovec: Drava Verlag.

Parekh, B. 2000. *Rethinking Multiculturalism.* Houndmills: Macmillan Press Ltd.

von Riekhoff, H and H. Neuhold. (eds) 1993. *Unequal Partners: A Comparative Analysis of Relations between Austria and the Federal Republic of Germany and between Canada and the United States.* Boulder: Westview Press.

WIFO-Monatsbericht 5/1962. Wien: Österreichisches Wirtschaftsforschungsinstitut. (Cited in Wimmer, Hannes. Zur Ausländerbeschäftigungspolitik in Österreich. In Wimmer, Hannes ed. *Ausländische Arbeitskräfte in Österreich*, 5–32. Frankfurt/ New York: Campus).

Wollner, E. 1996. *Auf dem Weg zur sozialpartnerschaftlich regulierten Ausländerbeschäftigung in Österreich. Die Reform der Ausländerbeschäftigung und der Anwerbung bis Ende der 1960er Jahre.* Universität Wien, unveröffentlichte Diplomarbeit.

Chapter 12

Whereto for Multiculturalism?
The German Debate on *Leitkultur* and the
Promise of Cultural Studies[1]

Ming-Bao Yue

In the long run, immigration and integration will only be successful if wide support is forthcoming from the population. This means that integration is a two-way street: The host country must be tolerant and open, and immigrants who wish to remain long-term in this country and live amongst us, must, for their part, be willing to respect the rules for coexistence in Germany. I have called these rules our core cultural values.

– Friedrich Merz "Einwanderung und Identität"

On October 25, 2000, a major German daily newspaper, *Die Welt*, published the article "Immigration and Identity" from which the above quote is taken.[2] The author, Friedrich Merz, was at the time chairman of the conservative block CDU/CSU [Christian Democratic Union/Christian Social Union] in the *Bundestag* [German Parliament]. By his own admission, Merz never anticipated the extent of the debate on *Deutsche Leitkultur* that his article provoked in the following months.[3] Media attention was so intense that *Leitkultur* made it to eighth place in the category "Word of the Year" for 2000, although first prize for "*Unwort* [Non-Word] of

---

1   Unless referenced, all translations are mine. I would like to thank Richard Nettell for stimulating discussion of this subject and for offering suggestions on earlier drafts of this paper. I would also like to express my gratitude to Boreth Ly for being such a patient listener and discussant and for helping me to obtain research material.

2   Friedrich Merz, "Einwanderung und Identität", *Die Welt*, October 25, 2000, 3. According to one source, the article could be found on Friedrich Merz's webpage for two and a half months after the date of publication, but it was subsequently removed in January 2001 (see Joanne Moar, http:// www.becoming-german.de). Attempts to "google" the infamous article are therefore fruitless, and I was only able to obtain a copy of it through a library microfilm collection of the German newspaper. Friedrich Merz was the Chairman of the CDU/CSU coalition from 2000–2002 and Vice-Chairman from 2002–2004. Earlier this year, Friedrich Merz announced that he intends to resign from politics in 2009. http://www.zeit.de/online/2007/07/Merz-Geruecht.

3   Interview with Friedrich Merz, *Bild Am Sonntag*, December 3, 2000. http://www.muslim-markt.de/Aktion/Leitkultur/interviewmerz.htm.

the Year" went to *Deutsche Leitkultur*.[4] Literally, the term translates as "guiding culture" and implies, as in the quote by Merz, a need for a set of "core" values as a basis for a culturally pluralistic society, setting the foundations of Robinson's 'meaningful life' in a multi-ethnic environment. While conservatives quickly mobilized around the concept to reinforce their notion of *Deutschtum* [German-ness], liberals and those on the left expressed strong opposition, admonishing the German public not to repeat "historical mistakes", by giving in to cultural chauvinism, xenophobia, and the rhetoric of assimilation.[5] Almost immediately, *Leitkultur* became a euphemism in public discourse for the country's ambivalent attitude towards immigration, with Germany's revised citizenship law (2000) based no longer on blood, but on residency and birth; and recognizing finally, that the country had become de facto a multicultural society. Nevertheless, after a couple of months of polemical if unresolved discussion of the term's meaning, origin, and usefulness, the initial media attention gradually subsided although the word never disappeared from public discourse. Then, in 2005, *Leitkultur* made an unexpected come-back when Norbert Lammert became President of the *Bundestag* and called for a "revival of the *Leitkultur* debate."[6] This time around, however, the culture in question was referred to as "European" rather than "German," and his efforts resulted in a collection of essays, which he edited and published in 2006, under the title "Constitution, Patriotism, Core Cultural Values: What Holds our Society Together." The solicited contributions certainly represent a wide spectrum of opinions on the subject by leading German intellectuals and politicians from the left as well as the right (Lammert 2006). Since then, however, a less impassioned and more substantive debate focusing on "integration" and "cultural plurality" has emerged, this time with noticeable participation from so-called *deutsche Ausländer* [German foreigners] or *Deutschländer* [Germaners], the second and third generations.[7]

This chapter will attempt to engage the debate on multiculturalism in Germany not from conventional sociological or political science perspectives, but rather from the vantage point of Cultural Studies understandings of discourse and ideology. The typical objection that Cultural Studies approaches focus on peripheral actors and voices ignores the fact that, in order to unravel the larger discursive context and connections that constitute any given field of knowledge, it is not only necessary but also highly beneficial to cast our critical sight away

---

4   For *Leitkultur* as "the word of the year" see http://www.gfds.de/woerter.html. And for the *Deutsche Leitkultur* as "the non-word of the year" see http://archiv.tagesspeigel. de/archiv/15.11.2000/ak-po-in-16356.html.

5   For a brief chronological outline of the debate in 2000, which covers the major issues, see http://www.3sat.de/kulturzeit/themem/11772/index/html.

6   See http://www.dradio.de/dif/sendungen/kulturheute/430815/.

7   These expressions circulate widely in popular German discourse. See, for instance, Bassam Tibi *Europa Ohne Identität? Leitkultur Oder Wertebeliebigkeit* (Aalen: Bertelsman Verlag, 2000), 20.

from mainstream action and players to "look awry." As Zizek explains, "this way of looking awry" can be considered an intellectual positioning that "makes it possible to discern features that usually escape a 'straightforward' academic look" (Zizek 1991, viii). With that in mind, this chapter begins with a discussion of the transnational discursive formation underlying the *Leitkultur* debate, which could be considered Germany's first sustained public attempt to come to terms with the idea of a multicultural society. Undeniably, the *Leitkultur* debate unfolded at the national level, as the culmination of political and intellectual efforts throughout the 1990s, to acknowledge and discuss the long-overdue issue of immigration in contemporary Germany. But unlike the United State, Canada or Australia, which consider themselves immigrant nations, Germany has traditionally been an emigrant country with no "native" or homegrown models to help deal with a multicultural society. Thus, the trials and tribulations of US multiculturalism – the neo-conservative attacks beginning in the late 1980s and renewed intellectual interest in "cultural plurality" in the 1990s – have crucially shaped the conceptual trajectory of the *Leitkultur* debate and dampened the prospect of movement towards a truly democratic, multicultural society. Arguably, in the wake of globalization, the hard won victories of a multiculturalism, which sought more social justice and equality, have been compromised by the rise of neo-liberalism and its recognition of economic benefits that could be gained from a multicultural environment. Yet part of the problem that enables such type of symbolic endorsement of multiculturalism lies with the concept itself or, more precisely, with the ambiguity-cum-complexity surrounding the meaning of "culture" and its notable discursive popularity in the second half of the twentieth century commonly referenced as "the cultural turn" (Hall 1997, 210). Commenting on this continuing preoccupation with "the idea of culture," Terry Eagleton rightly observes that culture's meaning is "both too broad and too narrow to be greatly useful" (Eagleton 2000, 32). This dilemma is further compounded by the bleak reality that today's intellectuals and cultural critics are facing "a world subjected to the automatization of minds by technology and to wars of religion that encourage archaism and terrorism" (Kristeva 2006, 13–21). Arguably, such "dark times" are extremely challenging for intellectuals who aim to "reconstruct the new humanism we need" (Kristeva 2006, 14) or, in other words, to have an impact on politics and social life.

Cultural Studies, according to Henry Giroux, must step up to meet this challenge, via the work of Antonio Gramsci, by reaffirming one of its central goals: to create "resisting intellectuals" rather than "professional academics" and to forge "oppositional public spheres" instead of "complicit disciplines and cultures" (Giroux et al. 2006). Taking the lead from Stuart Hall, he suggests that one way to do this would be to reject a "celebratory response to cultural globalization" and instead claim a theoretical/pedagogical space for "the centrality of culture." As Giroux remarks elsewhere, "for Hall, culture provides the constitutive framework for making the pedagogical political – recognizing that how we learn and what we learn is imminently tied to strategies of understanding, representation, and disruption" (Giroux 2000, 352). Culture, in this sense, is much more than just a canonical text or a postmodern commodity, and, to quote Lawrence Grossberg, it is essentially the site of "production and struggle for power" (Grossberg 1997, 248) and analysis of ethno-cultural economic and political stratification. With these considerations in mind, this chapter will conclude with a discussion of two discursive responses to the *Leitkultur* debate which have gone largely unnoticed by the German public: 1) the concept of *Kulturarbeit* [culture work], and 2) the case of writer Yoko Tawada. I will also argue, following Kristeva, that literature and writing constitute "a decisive element in the reconstruction of the humanism we need [today]" (Kristeva 2006, 17), and following Giroux and Hall, I hope to suggest that the relevance of Cultural Studies today lies in its – as yet under-explored – potential to furnish this important project with the necessary conceptual tools.

"Immigration Yes, Ghettos No": Bassam Tibi's Concept of *Leitkultur*

At the height of the *Leitkultur* debate in 2000, with mounting public outrage and virulent attacks from liberal SPD [German Socialist Party] and Green Party politicians – who accused conservatives of promoting *Ausländerfeindlichkeit* [xenophobia] in the name of tolerance, Friedrich Merz defended himself by implicating Theo Sommer, editor of the centrist newspaper *Die Zeit*, as the originator of the concept *deutsche Leitkultur* (Benda 2000). Sommer had in fact published an editorial in 1998 on immigration in which he introduced the concept in his concluding sentence: "Integration necessarily requires a great deal of assimilation into German culture and its core values" (Sommer 2000). However, Sommer immediately wrote a rebuttal to clarify his position, summed up in his title "Immigration Yes, Ghettos No," claiming that the concept in dispute had actually been coined by Bassam Tibi, whom he had encountered at a number of public forums on immigration (Sommer 2000).

Although Bassam Tibi's participation remained peripheral throughout the national debate on *Leitkultur*, he did indeed introduce the concept as early as 1996 – but not with the emphasis on "German-ness" that the term later acquired. This is evident from his provocative book "Europe without an Identity? Core Culture or Laissez-Faire Values" published in 1998.[8] As a 400–page passionately written narrative oscillating between the "personal" and the "factual," the book was intended to kickstart a *rational* debate on the sensitive issue of immigration in Germany. However, by the author's own admission, the immediate reaction was "hitting a wall and a taboo" (Tibi 2000, XV). Ironically, while Tibi's overall attitude towards the debate was one of condemnation and bitterness at its having been

---

8   See "Des einen Freund, des anderen Leid: Die mediale Karriere eines Begriffs" [Friend to some, burden to others: One concept's career in the media] for a chronological account of the debate in http://www.3sat.de/kulturzeit/themen/11772/index.html. See also Bassam Tibi, footnote 6.

"exploited for political purposes," the level of public discussion in 2000 propelled his relatively unknown book to national attention, and sales have risen accordingly. The book is now in its third edition and includes two prefaces, in the second of which (2000) Tibi emphatically defends his "good reputation and intentions" (Tibi 2000, XIV). He basically accuses Merz for deliberately conflating *Leitkultur* with "German-ness" as a tactics to valorize the Christian-occidental tradition as the religious stronghold in Europe. However, doing so, he argues, blatantly ignores the fact that there are 3.5 million Muslims living in Germany and the reality of Islam secularism in Europe. Secondly, Tibi vehemently opposes the notion that he intended to "fraternize with the CDU" and propagate an "anti-immigrant" position. Being a so-called "foreigner" himself, he favors immigration but rejects closed societies in any form, be it ethnical, religious, cultural or political. Thirdly, as the title of his book indicates, his notion of *Leitkultur* affirms what he considers "European values." From the very beginning, Tibi closely links his concept to the Habermasian project of cultural modernity, which draws on the values of European enlightenment thinking, particularly the French idea of a secular state, *laïcité*, as discussed in the Adsett chapter of this book; and citizen member of a political – rather than ethnic or religious – community (Tibi 2000, 18). That is to say, as Tibi repeatedly asserts throughout his book, his concept of *Leitkultur* "is meant as an orientation or 'value consensus' with regard to European values of civilization, such as secular democracy, individual (not collective) human rights, civil society, tolerance, religious and cultural pluralism" (Tibi 2000, 18). His book, he further maintains, also aims to defend Islam against fundamentalism and forge a much-needed dialogue between the Islamic world and Europe. This is to be based on the concept of *Euro-Islam*, a "strategy for Muslims living in Europe," which Tibi places within the framework of Islamic rationalism and therefore considers it compatible with 1) *laïcité*, (division between religion and politics), 2) secular tolerance (freedom of belief), and 3) pluralism (Tibi 2000, 257). Nevertheless, unlike Britain (discussed in Chapter Ten), neither the issue of Islam in Europe nor the concept of *Euro-Islam* figured prominently during the *Leitkultur* debate in Germany and, more often than not, no distinction was made between Islamic fundamentalism and Islam as a religion.

In an interesting way, Tibi's own life can be seen as an embodiment of the whole debate, which was less about the "politics of culture" and more about "cultural politics." While these two concepts are often considered interchangeable,there is a crucial difference between them that matters to Cultural Studies and is also shared by Marxist critics. Maintaining that "identity politics" today is very much an expression of "cultural politics," Terry Eagleton explains that the term incorrectly implies that there is a certain form of politics that might be considered "specifically cultural" (Eagleton 2000, 122). But although culture is the product of conditions of politics, there is nothing inherently political in culture itself, and it only becomes so "under specific historical conditions" and when cultural practices are "caught up with the process of domination and resistance" (Eagleton 2000, 122). Thus, what mattered to Raymond Williams and his brand of Cultural Studies is a "politics of culture" which is "to restore to them [*sic:* cultural practices] their innocuousness, so that one can sing, paint, or make love without the bothersome distraction of political strife" (Eagleton 2000, 123). The point here, it would appear, is not so much to assert that this goal is attainable but rather, I would argue, to emphasize that cultural forms are "terrains of struggle" because they are enmeshed with social relationships embedded within a power structure that render their "innocuous" practice possible for some, but simultaneously impossible for others. As regards the current xenophobic atmopshere in Europe, what is at stake here is clearly not the will to defend the "innocuous" practice of religion per se, but rather the fear that Islam, secular or not, will undermine the Christian hegemony of Western Europe.

Born in 1944 and raised in Damascus as a member of the old Banu al-Tibi family in Syria, he arrived in Germany in 1963, at the age of eighteen, to study sociology, philosophy, and history under Adorno, Horkheimer, Mitscherlich and Fetscher at the University of Frankfurt. Oppositional politics – he was active in the 1960s student movement – prevented him from returning to his native Syria, and he became, in his own words, an "unwilling migrant" who nevertheless decided to adopt German citizenship in 1979 (Tibi 2000,18). After receiving his Ph.D. degree in 1971, he joined the faculty of sociology at the University of Göttingen, where he founded a new discipline, International Relations, with a focus on developing countries. Within this track, he also devoted his intellectual energy to the study of secular Islam, particularly Islam in Europe, and was an active member in various international Islamic organizations and political commissions. Partially in response to the "demonization" and "defamation" he was subjected to during the *Leitkultur* debate, Tibi announced in 2006 that he would emigrate to the US upon reaching mandatory retirement age in 2009 to join the permanent staff of Cornell University, where he has been the A.D. White Professor-at-Large since 2004 (Lau 2006). Immediately following Tibi's announcement, the president of the University of Göttingen decided that the program on secular Islam, which Tibi had founded, would be shut down due to its "lack of profitability" (Lau 2006).

Since then, in a number of interviews and newspaper reports, Bassam Tibi has openly expressed his resentment, not to say anger, at Germany for treating him little better than "a guest-worker."[9] Despite the fact that he is an internationally acclaimed scholar, neither Göttingen University nor Germany itself has been willing to grant him the recognition he rightly deserves. As one newspaper has provocatively commented, "the prophet is not recognized in his own country."[10] Although Tibi is married to a German, speaks fluent German, and considers himself an "integrated foreigner," he has never felt really accepted in Germany where, even after 45 years of residence, he is still referred to as an outsider, a "Syrian with a German

---

9   See http://wwwuser.gwdg.de/~uspw/iib/Bericht_leben.htm.

10   Interview "Der Prophet gilt nichts im eigenen Land," [The prophet is not recognized in his own country], in *Heilbronner Stimme*, January 31, 2007, 7. See http://wwwuser.gwdg. de/~uspw/iib/interview_heilbronner_stimme.pd.

passport."[11] In other words, obtaining a German passport does not, in the minds of many native Germans, override a person's status as foreigner, and to become an *Inländer* [native citizen] requires more of migrants than mere naturalization.[12] For proponents of the *Deutsche Leitkultur* concept, this "more" apparently consists of a broad acceptance of German culture or, more precisely, the principles of a Christian-occidental tradition.[13] This, however, further sanctions the *ethnicizing* of the German concept of culture, which is strongly tied to the idea of a "people". This is the reason why Tibi maintains that successful integration of immigrants in Germany can only be accomplished within a European identity based on Enlightenment values. For Tibi, an Arab-Muslim who clearly believes that a form of secular Islam is compatible with the Enlightenment values he espouses, cultural plurality in conjunction with Habermas' notion of "constitutional patriotism" is the cornerstone of a new European identity, which "immigrants can share with Germans if they do not wish to end up in parallel societies" (Tibi 2000, XIV). Tibi, of course, is not advocating Euro-centrism, and he devotes a whole chapter to a set of prescriptive tools to overcome this structure of feeling: 1) de-romanticizing European cultural hegemony, 2) deconstructing Euro-arrogance (and its flipside Euro-bashing), and 3) de-westernizing European values without "giving up on Europe" (Tibi 2000, 63–5).

In many ways, Tibi sees the *Leitkultur* debate as symptomatic of Europe's identity crisis, i.e. the challenge to the "universality" of Enlightenment values and democratic ideals represented by globalization and global migration. So far, Europe has responded to this crisis in a typical fashion: with either "neo-absolutism," i.e. Euro-arrogance, or its flipside, "cultural relativity," i.e. Euro-denial or what Ien Ang has termed "reluctant Eurocentrism" (Ang 1998, 87–108). However, according to Tibi, European consciousness now needs a "second enlightenment" which is not ethnically exclusive. To accomplish this, Europe needs to define her relationship with the non-European rest of the world not through a discourse of multiculturalism, which for Tibi represents a dangerous form of "cultural relativity", but through an "intercultural dialogue" (Parekh 2005,19), which aims to forge what Anthony Giddens has termed a "dialogical democracy" by which he means a new form of self-management and interpersonal interaction that fosters social solidarity and encourages ethical responsibility (Giddens 1992, 1994).

While Tibi doubts that even the US has come this far, he is quick to praise the US model of an immigrant nation based not on ethnicity but on value consensus, i.e. the principles of constitutional democracy. But he also faults the liberal rhetoric of multiculturalism for advocating what he calls the "laissez-faire values" which sanction ethnic ghettos and privilege communitarianism over individual identity. As he explains, "communitarianism comes from the English 'community' and

---

11   Ibid.

12   Ibid.

13   "Was ist Leitkultur?" [What is *Leitkultur*?], *Biblekritiker*, 3. http://www.was-ist-leitkultur.de/wasistleitkultur.htm.

206 Managing Ethnic Diversity

encourages the formation of 'parallel societies,' and subcultures in the name of 'tolerance'" (Tibi 2000, 161). Such an ideology, in Tibi's opinion, can only lead to "the end of individualism," and he explicitly cites the work of US scholar Amitai Etzoni, widely regarded as the founder of communitarianism (Tibi 2000, 163). To further lend authority to his argument, Tibi then references the debate on cultural relativity (1994) between Ernest Gellner and Cliffort Geertz and, not surprisingly, repeatedly cites Arthur Schlesinger's *The Disuniting of America: Reflections on a Multicultural Society* (1998) as well as Samuel Huntington's *The Clash of Civilizations* (1997), although he cautions against the German mistranslation of the title as "The War of Cultures" (Tibi 2000, 249). Tibi therefore opposes multiculturalism as a discourse that 1) legitimizes the formation of ethnic enclaves but does not offer binding values to a culturally pluralistic collectivity, 2) forms "we groups" to exclude others, and 3) conflates "democratic integration" with "cultural assimilation" (Tibi 2000, 83 and 103). This, in his opinion, effectively renders multiculturalism incompatible with democracy, which requires, in the form of a constitution, a set of binding core values that reinforces social trust among inter-ethnic groups and guarantees a measure of coherence in a culturally pluralistic society. As Tibi emphatically states, the concept of cultural plurality means that cultures maintain their particularity *but only within* a larger frame of basic common values, which, in case of Europe, must be drawn from "cultural modernity" (Tibi 2000, 50).

The Neo-Liberal Turn: From Multiculturalism to Cultural Plurality

Since the US provides a frame of reference for Tibi's work, it is no coincidence that many of the conceptual arguments for immigration, but against the notion of multiculturalism in Germany – crystallized in Tibi's book and echoed during the *Leitkultur* debate – run parallel to 1990s discussions in the US on Affirmative Action and Proposition 187. We hardly need reminding of a string of "anti-multiculturalism" publications led by Allan Bloom's contentious book *The Closing of the American Mind* (1987).[14] On the one hand, the desire to absorb lessons from the US experience is understandable, an "immigrant nation" that, after all, prides itself on its celebration of diversity. On the other, the transatlantic borrowing in this particular case has not always been to Europe's advantage, and comparisons with earlier US models of assimilation have been detrimental for the project of multiculturalism in Europe (Klopp 2002, 8). To begin with, unlike in the US, the majority of the immigrants in Europe come from Muslim societies, primarily from Turkey, Bosnia, Algeria, and Morocco. Thus the debate on multiculturalism in Europe, from the 1990s onwards, has been explicitly focused on Islam and its

---

14   See also Dinesh D'Souza's *Illiberal Education* (1991), Francis Fukuyama's *The End of History* (1992), and last, but not least, Samuel Huntington's *Clash of Civilizations* (1997) and Arthur Schlesinger's *The Disuniting of America* (1998).

status in the Western world. The 9/11 and 7/7 attacks have predictably increased tension concerning Muslim integration – particularly in conjunction with a series of "honor-killings," the headscarf debate, and the 2004 murder of Dutch filmmaker Theo Van Gogh – and strengthened opposition to Turkey's entry into the EU (Wikan 2006). In this climate and post *Leitkultur* debate, the concept of multiculturalism in Germany, usually negatively reduced to *multikulti*, has been declared "politically useless" or even "dead" in many quarters, including many of the SPD and Green Party politicians and intellectuals who were once amongst its strongest advocates (Malzahn 2006).

Although Germany has never had an official policy on multiculturalism, the concept has been a salient political issue at local, state and federal levels at least since the 1980s, when many cities established "foreigner affairs" bureaus to deal primarily with the Turkish diaspora (Görtürk 2007, 12). In an unprecedented move in 1989, for example, the Frankfurt city council created the Office of Multicultural Affairs to deal with an exploding immigrant population and appointed Daniel Cohn-Bendit as its Honorary Director, a position he held until 1997. A French-German Jew whose life and work has been likened to that of US sociologist Horace Kallen, Cohn-Bendit argues that "Germany is an immigrant country, and therefore multicultural" (Cohn-Bendit and Schmidt 1992, 11).[15] It should be noted, however, that Cohn-Bendit's definition of multiculturalism does not reflect the concept's current postmodern usage in US discussions, which Bassam Tibi has condemned as "cultural relativity." Instead, it actually validates Kallen's notion of cultural plurality, "'a multiplicity in a unity, an orchestration of mankind' whose main goal is not the oneness of union but the harmony of the many" (Kallen 1924, 61). In his much-quoted collection of essays *Cultural Pluralism and the American Idea*, Kallen makes it clear that cultural plurality cannot exist in a vacuum but needs a unifying bond of liberal-democratic ideals: "Americanization seeking a cultural monism was challenged and is slowly and unevenly being displaced by Americanization, supporting, cultivating, a cultural pluralism, grounded on and consummated in the American idea" (Kallen 1956, 56). This view is echoed by Cohen-Bendit: "Democracy does not develop naturally from a multicultural reality. Democracy needs a common understanding about binding values, about a unity that must be founded" (Hornung 1998, 226). Cohn-Bendit specifically proposes three concrete steps in that direction: 1) to recognize Germany as a country of immigration, 2) to separate immigration from political asylum, and 3) to grant citizenship based on the American *jus soli* [right of soil], instead of *jus sanguinis*, [right by blood], which grants nationality or citizenship based on ancestry (Hornung 1998, 225).

---

15   For the connection between Cohn-Bendit and Kallen, see Alfred Hornung, "The Transatlantic Ties of Cultural Pluralism – Germany and the United States: Horace M. Kallen and Daniel Cohn-Bendit," in *Multiculturalism in Transit: A German-American Exchange*, ed. Klaus Milich, (New York: Berghahn Books, 1998), 213–28.

On the whole in Germany, however, there is a surprising silence on the history of the discourse, with some commentators claiming that the concept of multiculturalism was first introduced in a statement issued by the Protestant, Catholic, and Greek Orthodox churches to celebrate "foreign fellow-citizen day" (Hornung 1998, 224). Despite its basic sincerity, this type of mandated xenophilia serves primarily to retain the category "foreigners" in their "particularity" and cannot be seen as evidence of a will to integrate. No wonder, then, that multiculturalism is often depicted as more of a "life-style," what is sometimes referred to as "the *Döner* principle" (a Turkish alternative to the Big-Mac), rather than genuine political commitment to a program for social transformation (Amir-Moazami 2006, 22). Unfortunately, this perception has recently been re-affirmed in media commentaries after a series of German court verdicts, in the name of multiculturalism and "tolerating difference," failed to grant either divorce or legal protection to Muslim women victims of violent domestic abuse (Hari 2007). This has led to the view, amongst some Turkish sociologists, that supporters of multiculturalism in Germany are "worse than the conservatives because the multicultural ideology does not allow foreigners to integrate" (Tibi 2000, 106). For Seyran Ates, a Turkish-German lawyer and feminist activist from Berlin, "*Multikulti* is tantamount to organized irresponsibility."[16] Thus, in contemporary German public discourse, mulitkulti has become a pejorative label for nothing more than a form of "philo-othering," superficially celebrating folklore festivals as well as tolerating the often oppressive traditions of other cultural groups.[17]

Multiculturalism also fell into disrepute during the *Leitkultur* debate in 2000, when, two years before the national elections, the conservative opposition needed to articulate a popular campaign platform to rally voter support.[18] Even in 1982, recently elected Chancellor and CDU politician Helmut Kohl was moved to call for a "change in the foreigner policies" which resulted in his landslide re-election in 1986. What Kohl meant by "change," however, was a reduction in the number of "guest-workers," and despite the fact that immigrants at that time made up 7.5 percent of the total population, the Chancellor stubbornly maintained that "Germany is not an immigration country" (Görtürk 2007, XVI and 17). With the fall of the Berlin Wall in 1989 and the official onset of globalization, however, the immigration question moved effectively from the political wings to the economic center-stage. The mass migration to the West of East Germans and German-heritage re-settlers from Eastern Europe was beginning to unsettle both the economy and

---

16   Heinrich Wefing, "Seyran Ates: Ätsch, ich darf stolz sein" [Seyran Ates: Whatever, I am allowed to be proud] in *Frankfurter Allgemeine Zeitung*, FAZ.net see: http://www.faz.net/s/Rub117C535CDF414415BB243B181B8B60AE/Doc~EE18C49A9383E4692A0BF F5F4F4745894~ATpl~Ecommon~Scontent.html.

17   Ibid.

18   See "Meyer kritisiert den Begriff 'Leitkultur': Union will Zuwanderungsfrage vor der Bundestagswahl mit der SPD-Regierung lösen," *Die Welt*, Oktober 28, 2000; and Martin Klingst "Ende einer Lebenslüge" in *Die Zeit*, 43/2000.

an *Ausländerpolitk* that, up until the late 1990s, was marked by liberal asylum law and no explicit immigration policy. After reunification, however, debates on asylum dominated the national media and fueled a xenophobic backlash which characterized all foreigners as "free-loaders" who abused the social welfare system and therefore represented an unacceptable burden on German tax payers. At the center of this issue was the 1995 media exposure of seven Sudanese people who had provided false identification and incorrect information in order to claim "political asylum" (Tibi 2000, 280). This resulted in the 1997 constitutional amendment implementing stricter guidelines. Yet, with the opening of borders in Eastern Europe, illegal immigration increased dramatically in the mid-1990s, further complicating the concept of "foreigner" by adding "refugee" to the pre-existing categories of "guest-worker," "asylum seeker," as well as *Aussiedler* and *Übersiedler*. It wasn't until the *Leitkultur* debate in 2000 that the German public began to realize that the host of distinctive labels they attached to their "foreign others" actually impaired their recognition of their country as a multicultural society.

What also proved particularly influential in shifting the immigration debate from a political to an economic discourse was Ulrich Beck's book "What is Globalization?" published in 1997. Beck advanced the now widely-accepted thesis that Germany's post-war image of an industrial export country is no longer appropriate for the twenty-first century. (Beck 1997).[19] In other words, in order for Germany to stay competitive and maintain its high standard of living, increased immigration will be necessary. Accordingly, in February 2000, then Chancellor and SPD politician Gerhard Schröder announced his "Green Card Initiative" at a computer trade show in Hannover, thereby overturning the previous restriction of no more than 20,000 foreign computer specialists to fill the gap in domestic expertise (Görtürk 2007, 508). Later, in September that year, Schröder's Minister of the Interior, Otto Schilly (CDU), appointed a 21-member independent commission on immigration, headed by Rita Süssmuth (CDU), President of the German *Bundestag* from 1988–1998. The commission's report unambiguously concluded that immigration must be recognized as a structural feature of the German economy. Overall, however, the report espouses many of the same goals which later influenced the writing of the 2004 Immigration Act: the full linguistic and cultural integration of the current immigrant population as well as the strategic recruitment of highly qualified immigrants in order to counteract Germany's low birthrate and aging population (Görtürk 2007, 182–4).[20]

By all accounts, the commission's report marked a pivotal moment in the history of citizenship and immigration law and effectively ended the tumultuous

---

19   Also quoted in Denis Görtürk et al. eds *Germany in Transit: Nation and Migration, 1955–2005*, (Berkeley: University of California Press, 2007), 449–81.

20   For the full report see *"Zuwanderung Gestalten, Integration Fördern"* [Shaping Immigration, Facilitating Integration], http://www.bmi.bund.de/Internet/Content/Common/Anlagen/Broschueren/2001/Zuwanderung-gestalten-Integration.Id.7647.de.pdf.

20-year-old debate on whether Germany is an immigrant country. According to statistics for 2005, of the 82.5 million people living in Germany, 7.3 percent are immigrants. Although 1 million have become German citizens since the passing of the new Citizenship Law in 2000, there are still an estimated 1.4 million undocumented immigrants living in Germany today (Görtürk 2007, 510). Furthermore, within the European Union, member states are now under even more pressure to increase, rather than decrease, their immigrant populations. As part of the EU's stated goal to remain globally competitive and have each EU country invest 3 percent of the GNP in science and technology, roughly 70,000 scientists will be needed by the end of 2010. That this number cannot be generated from within the EU has already been established (Rötzer 2004). The specific implications of this mandate for Germany were spelled out in a 2000 study sponsored by the UN: If Germany wishes to maintain the current ratio of 4:1 between working to non-working people, the country needs to admit 3.6 million immigrants a year until 2050. By the middle of the twenty-first century, 80 percent of the German population would then be immigrants or their descendants. If Germany wants to avoid this scenario, the mandatory retirement age, currently at 65, would have to be raised to 75 effective immediately (Sommer 2000). In light of this daunting picture, Germany's new catchword is "integration," a euphemism for the officially sanctioned controlled immigration, and a number of integration measures have been implemented. In addition to Schröder's Green Card Initiative, which was modeled after the US type H-1 visa for professionals, the revised Citizenship Law (2000) now grants German citizenship to immigrants after 8 years of [continued?] residence. Immigrant children born in Germany are permitted to keep dual citizenship until age 23, when they have to decide on one. The implicit assumption here is that "integrated foreigners" will want to acquire German citizenship, for which a certain level of language proficiency is required. Thus, the new Immigration Law, passed on January 1, 2005, mandates "integration courses" consisting of 600 hours language instruction, plus 30 hours "orientation," for all new immigrants (Hentges 2006). Needless to say, critics of this "top-down" integration approach have questioned the efficacy of the government mandate at various levels, in particular the idealistic assumption that language and cultural proficiency will actually foster a will to integrate or loyalty to the nation-state (Hentges 2006). Similar doubts surfaced in 2001 when the media reported that three of the four 9/11 pilots spoke fluent German and that two of their accomplices held German citizenship (Tibi 2000, 395).

Rethinking Multiculturalism: *Kulturarbeit*, Common Culture, and Yoko Tawada

Despite the fact that the German government's new approach to immigration has encountered strong criticism, neither the focus on citizenship nor the idea of integration is incompatible with a multicultural project. In fact, both reflect an ongoing critical trend within this discourse to resolve ethnic tension in the age of globalization. Beginning with Charles Taylor's "politics of recognition," a number of noted multicultural theorists, such as Will Kymlicka, Arjun Appadurai, Bikuh Parehk, have convincingly argued for a greater need to allow ethnic group affiliations in pluralist democracies to attain citizenship. Much here obviously depends on a climate of tolerance to guard against discrimination, and it is, of course, for the state to ensure that such conditions prevail. In the study of ethnic theory, this new emphasis has been welcomed as a theoretical shift away from "cultural assimilation" to "civic incorporation," i.e. the idea that the state and hegemonic groups play an important role in determining whether minority groups are "allowed" to participate at the sociopolitical level (Krivisto 2002, 35). In his *Rethinking Multiculturalism*, Bhikhu Parekh therefore maintains that no multicultural society can be stable and vibrant unless it ensures that its constituent communities receive both just recognition and a just share of economic and political power. It requires a robust form of social, economic and political democracy to underpin its commitment to multiculturalism (Parekh 2000, 341). In the absence of both components, the ability of constituent communities to participate as full-citizens will be severely reduced.

While such conditions of "tolerance" are to some extent being created by Germany's post-*Leitkultur* fixation on "integration," the problem with such an emphasis on "civic incorporation," as the quote from Parekh shows, is that it actually eschews rather than confronts what Stuart Hall has called "the centrality of culture" (Hall 1997). This is not to be confused with "the cultural turn" we have seen in the social and human sciences, which is merely a "reconfiguration of elements" rather than a "total rupture." The latter would give culture "either the substantive centrality or the epistemological weight it deserves" (Hall 1997, 208). More often than not during the *Leitkultur* debate, the concept of culture was either taken for granted or, in case of Tibi's "European values," simply equated with the idea of civilization. Instead of calling such concepts into question, the notion of "civic incorporation" leaves intact the idea of culture as autonomous realm and thus distinct from the socio-political sphere. Culture, in this understanding is typically equated with folklore tradition and the idea of civilization that exists remains largely "untouched" by politics. This, for Mark Terkessidis, is precisely the problem with Germany's current "top-down" approach to immigration: the whole concept of *Leitkultur*, even in its pan-European version, reflects a hegemonic understanding of culture which either limits it to the realm of arts and civilization or, as evidenced by the *Leitkultur* debate, problematically attaches it to notions of nationality, race, and ethnicity (Terkessidis 2001). So, instead of trying to salvage the hierarchical notion of *Leitkultur*, as did Norbert Lammert in his 2005 call for a revival of the debate, Terkessidis suggests that we need to think in a more egalitarian fashion in terms of "citizenship education" or "civic culture work", both of which reinforce the broader concept of "culture work in an immigrant society". Unlike the new buzzword "integration," of course, these concepts resist uni-directionality and the simplistic division of Germans and foreigners into "us" and "them." Instead, they postulate a common ground, based either on shared experiences of an immigrant society or a shared status as citizens. But most importantly, and contrary to Habermas' "constitutional patriotism", which many contributors to the Lammert volume preferred over *Leitkultur*, the idea of "culture work in immigrant societies" avoids nationalistic overtones. Indeed, the concept positions the immigrant as a subject who, caught between "home" and "host" country, is negotiating a "space between states".

As a psychologist and freelance journalist working with migrant communities in Germany, Terkessidis draws for his understanding of "culture work" on personal observations of immigrant networks and social practices formed initially through so-called "folklore groups". The format itself is not so much a preference on the part of Germany's immigrants, but a reflection of structural limitations due to the country's citizenship laws, which considerably restrict meaningful socio-political participation by immigrants in the public sphere. Nonetheless, these "folklore groups" frequently move beyond support for their native religion, country, and culture to discussions of such issues as the impact of "homeland politics" on immigrant communities in Germany, the everyday problems of "guest-workers" as a result of linguistic, educational, and residential discrimination, and strategies to deal with the often rigid bureaucracy of the *Ausländeramt* [local government office for foreigner affairs]. Based on actual needs of immigrants, therefore, what began as a cultural form in the traditional sense has been transformed into a social unit helping members to *work through* the lived experience of "everyday culture" or "culture as a way of life." The notion of culture we find in the culture work of immigrants is thus not independent of the socio-political sphere, but *always already* constitutive of and constituted by it.

Such findings clearly contradict a wide-spread thesis in Germany that immigrant communities prefer to form "parallel societies" because their members refuse to "integrate." Instead, these immigrant cultural practices demonstrate their capacity to integrate *within the given limits* set by the society they are in. A similar point is made by Schirin Amir-Moazani, who argues that many second-generation immigrants' identification with Islam, despite their often high levels of education and competency in German, has developed largely within existing institutional frameworks in Germany. The two main Christian churches, for example, have always enjoyed a very privileged status, and the relatively easy institutionalization of Islam and home-language instruction in German state schools is the result of Muslims also laying claim to these basic principles rather than to a discourse of multiculturalism (Amir-Moazani 2006, 26). Ironically, the fact that Muslims in Germany are increasingly demanding their "rights" to practice their religion and maintain their home languages can be seen as a sign of their "cultural integration," although it is clearly not the kind of mainstreaming that German society has so far felt able to accept.

What are the ramifications of this discussion for Cultural Studies? Stuart Hall seriously doubts whether it is possible to "get anything like an adequate theoretical account of culture's relations and effects" due to what he terms *belated consciousness*: "the metaphor of the discursive, textuality, instantiates a necessary delay, a displacement, which, [I think,] is *always* implied in the concept of culture" (Hall 1996a, 271). But that is not to say that cultural studies, or for that matter, culture, is about anything and nothing:

> Although cultural studies as a project is open-ended, it can't be simply pluralist in that way … it has a will to connect; it does have some stake in the choices it makes. It does not matter whether cultural studies is this or that. It can't be just any old thing that chooses to march under a particular banner. It is a serious enterprise, or project, and that is inscribed in what is sometimes called the 'political' aspect of cultural studies. Not that there's one politics already inscribed in it. But that there is something at stake in cultural studies, in a way, I think, and hope, is not exactly true of many other very important intellectual and critical practices. (Hall 1996a, 263)

Hall's emphasis on the "political" is a commitment to decoding the ramifications of ideology and power, which are always already expressed in and through culture, but not in its traditional or conventional sense. When he speaks of culture, Hall means "the actual, grounded terrain of practices, representations, language and customs of any specific historical society … the contradictory forms of 'common sense,' which have taken root in and helped shaped popular life" (Hall 1996b, 439). This definition of culture as "lived experience" and "common sense" resonates strongly with the idea of "common culture" suggested by Raymond Williams in *Culture and Society*:

> A culture, while being lived, is always part of the unknown, in part unrealized. The making of a community is always an exploration, for consciousness cannot precede creation, and there is no formula for unknown experience. A good community, a living culture, will, because of this, not only make room for, but actively encourage all and any who can contribute to the advance in consciousness which is the common need. (Williams 1963, 234)

If we want multiculturalism to be more "political" in Stuart Hall's sense, or more "pedagogical" to use Henry Giroux's term, we have to make more space for this notion of "common culture" in the discourse. Following Lawrence Grossberg, we would then need to ask, "In what sense does a culture 'belong' to a group?" rather than focusing our energy on determining the relationship between identity and culture (Grossberg 1996, 88). This goes to the heart of what is "at stake" in multicultural societies and leads us to "a normative ethical [question]: to what extent can a society continue without a common, albeit constantly rearticulated and negotiated, culture?"

Taking this question very seriously with regard to Europe's future in the age of migration and globalization, Julia Kristeva believes that satisfactory answers cannot be generated by "the metaphysical duo reason versus faith on which scholasticism was once founded" (Kristeva 2006, 17). If we truly seek to understand our current "dark times," we should actually look more towards literature and writing as these "invite us to construct an interpretative, critical, and theoretical discourse in response to developments in the human and social sciences" (Kristeva 2006, 17). Unlike other discourses, literature and writing "constitute an experience of language transversal to identities (sexual, gender, national, ethnic, religious, ideological, etc.)" and thus present "a laboratory of new forms of humanism" (Kristeva 2006, 17). However, without a notion of freedom that both respects the diversity of cultural models and is not driven by the "calculating logic that leads to consumerism," we will not be able to validate emergent paradigms, such as humanism redefined as "hospitality" (Kristeva 2004, 18).

Arguably, the writings of Yoko Tawada, who has lived in Germany since 1982, engage exactly Kristeva's concerns, albeit from a semiotic/linguistic perspective. A prize-winning author in both Japan and Germany, Tawada publishes in both languages, although not all of her Japanese publications have been translated into German or vice versa, and, in fact, the language in the original manuscript may be different from the eventual language of publication. Although Tawada has been a recipient of the Alfred Chamisso Prize, usually awarded to immigrant authors writing in German, her semiotic approach to language and reality undermines any easy categorization of her work as immigrant literature or, to use the older term, foreigner literature. (Rösch 1998). In fact, so much of her writing challenges established paradigms of culture, identity, and language that some critics have characterized her as a "poetic ethnographer of her own and foreign worlds".[21] Certainly, the central theme in Tawada's work might well be called the "everyday aesthetics" of cultural and linguistic "foreign-ness," embodied typically in first-person female protagonists who are, like Tawada, Japanese women who have lived in Germany for some time. In the short story "Canned Foreign" (which has been published in English), for example, the narrator is on a bus when she suddenly realizes that she is being stared at:

> [S]he gazed at me intently and with interest, but she never attempted to read anything in my face. In those days, I often found that people became uneasy when they couldn't read my face like a text. It's strange the way the expression of a foreigner's face is often compared to a mask. Does this comparison conceal a wish to discover a familiar face behind a strange one? (Tawada 1989, 88)

Tawada first arrived in Germany from Japan in 1979 to study German literature at the University of Hamburg, later moving to the University of Zürich to complete her Ph.D. in 1998. Although primarily known for her creative writing, she has

---

21   Linda Baur, "Schreiben zwischen sinnlicher Sprachlust und sprachtheoretischem Interesse" [Writing between sensual language desire and linguistic theoretical interest], *Medien Observationen*, 2. http://www.medienobservationen.uni-muenchen.de/artikel/ literatur/ tawada.html.

also published numerous scholarly articles and translations. In fact, many of her short stories read like a series of intellectual and theoretical reflections on the ideological nexus between language and articulation, inseparable as they are from her place of enunciation as a "foreigner in Europe" who writes and speaks in a language she cannot claim as her "own":

> When I came to Europe, I had nothing to say about Europe because I didn't have a language which could be understood by my new fellow humans … The language in which I now speak about Europe is also a European language. Not just the language but a way of arguing and a certain tone also perhaps belong to Europe rather than to me. I regurgitate Europe in Europe. I can barely begin to speak about Europe without regurgitating it. That's why I'm going to stop speaking it. I have to come up with another way of dealing with it. (Tawada 1996a, 46)

What way, then, has Tawada found to deal with the problem of "foreign-ness" that is constitutive of and constituted by language? Interestingly, in Talisman, Literary Essays (1996), she suggests making language, foreign-ness, and Europe your "own" by literally ingesting the "other" into your body:

> Directly or indirectly, images always have to do with visual perception, but I want to perceive Europe no longer optically but with my tongue. If my tongue tastes Europe and speaks Europe, maybe I can cross the boundary between observer and object observed. Because what is eaten gets into your stomach and what is spoken makes it via the brain into the flesh. (Poetik-Dozentur Archiv 1998, 1)

This metaphor of alimentary consumption thus foregrounds, much along Julia Kristeva's line of a feminist materialism, an oral-sensory perception that relies on one's tongue – as both language and physical organ – to discriminate taste rather than vision, which, in the real sense of Franz Fanon's "burden of corporeal malediction," actually imprisons the body. This is shown, for instance, in "Canned Foreign" when the narrator rejects, physically as well as ideologically, the assumed "cultural difference" between Germany and Japan:

> I encountered these questions everywhere I went: mostly they began, "Is it true that the Japanese… " That is, most people wanted to know whether or not something they'd read in a newspaper or magazine was true. I was also often asked questions beginning, 'In Japan do people also…' I was never able to answer them, Every attempt I made to describe the difference between two cultures failed: this difference was painted on my skin like a foreign script which I could feel but not read, Every foreign sound, every foreign glance, every foreign taste struck my body as disagreeable until my body changed. (Tawada 1996b, 87)

On closer examination, however, the feeling of "foreign-ness" has less to do less with speaking an unfamiliar language than with a failure, on the one hand, to separate the sign from its meaning and, on the other, to recognize that *language speaks us* and not the other way around:

> Most of the words that came out of my mouth had nothing to do with how I felt. But at the same time I realized that my native tongue didn't have any words for how I felt either. It's just that this never occurred to me until I'd begun to live in a foreign language. Often it sickens me to hear people speak their native tongues fluently. It was as if they were unable to think and feel anything but what their language so readily served up to them. (Tawada 1998, 87)

"Native" and "foreign" thus complement each other to create a new understanding of language itself; indeed, here lies precisely the possibility of creating a new semiotics of communication or what Stuart Hall and Raymond Williams have called "common culture." In another of Tawada's stories, "By the River Spree" (2007), written in German and set, as the title indicates, in Berlin, the female protagonist/ narrator is stopped by a policeman as she walks through the main railway station because he thinks she is a foreigner. But rather than suspicion and conflict, what emerges from this incidental encounter between "native" and "foreign" is an unexpected pedagogical moment that allows us, albeit provisionally, to rethink European consciousness in a more radical sense than is made possible by either Habermas' "constitutional patriotism" or Tibi's "Leitkultur":

> "I'm not a tourist, I'm ... " I suddenly didn't know what to say next. Anyone with a U.S. passport is American, but someone with a European passport isn't necessarily European. You're born either European or as something else, and you can't become European after the fact. That's why I never applied for a European passport. So what's to be done with a police officer who wants to protect me from thieves? "I'm not a tourist. I live here. What do you call people who live in Europe? I asked. "I don't know," he said, a little unsure of himself, "immigrants?" (Tawada 2007, 14)

References

Amir-Moazami, S. 2006. Buried Alive: Multiculturalism in Germany. *ISIM Review* 16: 22–23.

Ang, I. 1998. Notes on a Reluctant Eurocentrism. In *Trajectories: Inter-Asia Cultural Studies*, ed. K.-H. Chen and D. Morely, 87–108. London & New York: Routledge.

Appadurai, A. 1996. *Modernity at Large: Cultural Dimensions of Globalization.* Minnesota: University of Minnesota Press.

Baur, L. 1997. Schreiben zwischen sinnlicher Sprachlust und sprachtheoretischem Interesse. [Writing between sensual language desire and linguistic theoretical interest]. In *Medien Observationen*. Available at: http://www.medienobservationen.uni-muenchen.de/artikel/literatur/tawada.html.

Beck, U.1997. Was könnte an der Stelle einer VW-Export Nation treten? [What comes after the Volkswagen-export nation?]. In *Was ist Globalisierung?* [What is Globalization?] Frankfurt am Main: Suhrkamp.

Benda, E. 2000. Theo Sommer für Leitkultur. [Theo Sommer for *Leitkultur*]. Letter to the editors. *Frankfurter Allgemeine Zeitung*, November 9.

Bloom, A. 1988. *Closing of the American Mind*. New York: Simon & Schuster.

Cohn-Bendit, D. and T. Schmidt. 1992. *Heimat Babylon: Das Wagnis einer multikulturellen Democratie*. [Homeland Babylon: The Risk behind a Multicultural Democracy]. Hamburg: Hoffman & Campe.

D'Souza, D. 1991. *Illiberal Education: The Politics of Race and Sex on Campus*. New York: Free Press.

Eagleton, T. 2000. *The Idea of Culture*. Oxford; Blackwell.

Fukuyama, F. 1992. *The End of History and the Last Man*. New York: Free Press.

Giddens, A. 1992. *The Transformation of Intimacy: Sexuality, Love and Eroticism in Modern Societies*. Stanford: Stanford University Press.

Giddens, A. 1994. *Beyond Left and Right: The Future of Radical Politics*. Stanford: Stanford University Press.

Giroux, H. 2000. Public Pedagogy as Cultural Politics: Stuart Hall and the 'Crisis' of Culture. *Cultural Studies* 14(2): 341–60. Available at: http://www.tandf.co.uk/journals/routledge/ 09502386.html.

Giroux, H., D. Shumway, P. Smith, and J. Sosnoski. 2006. The Need for Cultural Studies: Resisting Intellectuals and Oppositional Public Spheres. November 11: 1–12, Available at: http://www.theory.eserver.org/need.html.

Grossberg, L. 1996. Identity and Cultural Studies: Is that all there is? In *Questions of Cultural Identity*, eds S. Hall and P. du Gray, 88–107. London: Sage.

Grossberg, L. 1997. Cultural studies: What's in a name? In *Bringing It All Back Home: Essays on Cultural Studies*, 245–70. Durham: Duke University Press.

Göktürk, D. et al. (eds) 2007. *Germany in Transit: Nation and Migration 1955–2005*. Berkeley: University of California Press.

Hall, S. 1996a. Cultural Studies and its Theoretical Legacies. In *The Stuart Hall Reader*, eds K.-H. Chen and D. Morely, 262–75. London & New York: Routledge.

Hall, S. 1996b. Gramsci's Relevance for the Study of Race and Ethnicity. In *The Stuart Hall Reader*, eds K.-H. Chen and D. Morely, 411–40. London & New York: Routledge.

Hall, S. 1997. The Centrality of Culture: Notes on the Cultural Revolutions of our Time. In *Media and Cultural Regulation*, ed. K. Thompson, 208–36. London: Sage Publications.

Hari, J. 2007. How Multiculturalism is Betraying Women. *The Independent*. June 4. Available at: http://comment.independent.co.uk/columnists_a_l/johann_hari/article2496657.ece.

Hentges, G. 2006. „Integrationskurse" – Integration? Das Zuwanunderungsgesetz und seine Folgen. [„Integration" courses – integration? The consequences of the immigration law]. *Forum Wissenscahft* (3). Available at: http://www.bdwi.de/forum/archiv/archiv/277883.html.

Hornung, A. 1998. The Transatlantic Ties of Cultural Pluralism – Germany and the United States: Horace M. Kallen and Daniel Cohn-Bendit. In *Multiculturalism in Transit: A German-American Exchange*, ed. K. Milich, 213–28. New York: Berghahn Books.

Huntington, S.P. 1997. *Clash of Civilizations and the Remaking of World Order*. New York: Touchstone.

Kallen, H. 1924. *Culture and Democracy in the United States: Studies in the Group Psychology of the American Peoples*. New York: Boni and Liveright.

Kallen, H. 1956. Cultural *Pluralism and the American Idea: An Essay in Social Philosophy*. Philadelphia: University of Pennsylvania Press.

Kivisto, P. 2002. Multiculturalism in a Global Society. Oxford: Blackwell Publishing.

Kristeva, J. 2004. *Thinking about Liberty in Dark Times*. Lecture presented at the Holberg Prize seminar, December 2. Available at: www.holbergprisen.no/images/materiell/2004_kristeva_english.pdf#page=11.

Kristeva, J. 2006. Thinking in Dark times. *Professions – MLA Journal* 13–21.

Klopp, B. 2002. *Multiculturalism in Germany: Immigrant Integration and the Transformation of Citizenship*. London: Praeger Publishers.

Kymlicka, W. 1995. *Multicultural Citizenship: A Liberal Theory of Minority Rights*. New York: Oxford University Press.

Lammert, N. (ed.) 2006. *Verfassung, Patroitismus, Leitkultur: Was unsere Gesellschaft zusammenhält*. [Constitution, Patriotism, Core Culture: What holds our Society together]. Hamburg: Hoffman und Campe Verlag.

Lau, M. 2006. Islam-Kritiker Bassam Tibi verlässt Deutschland. [Islam critic Bassam Tibi is leaving Germany]. *Die Welt*, September 9.

Malzahn, C.C. 2006. Germany's Second Reunification. *Spiegel On-line*, April 6. Available at: http://www.spiegel.de/international/0.1518,410102,00.html.

Merz, F. 2000. Einwanderung und Identität. [Immigration and identity]. *Die Welt*, October 25.

Milich K. (ed.) 1998. *Multiculturalism in Transit: A German-American Exchange*. New York: Berghahn Books.

Moar, J. 2005. Becoming German. Available at: http:// www.becoming-german.de.

Parekh, B. 2000. *Rethinking Multiculturalism: Cultural Diversity and Political Theory*. Cambridge: Harvard University Press.

Parekh, B. 2005. Dialogues between Cultures. In *Democracy, Nationalism and Multiculturalism*, eds R. Máiz and F. Requejo, 13–14. London & New York: Frank Class Publications.

Poetik-Dozentur Archiv. 1998. *Yoko Tawada*, Frühjahr [spring]. Available at: http://www.germ-serv.de/poetikvl/tawada.htm.

Rösch, H. 1998. Migrationsliteratur im interkulturellen Diskurs. [Immigrantliterature in an intercultural context]. Paper presented at the Technical University Dresden. Available at: http://www.tu-berlin.de/fb2/fadi/hr/Dresden.

Rötzer, F. 2004. Anpassung an eine deutsche Leitkultur? [Adapting to a German core culture?]. *Telepolis.* November 21. Available at: http://www.heise.de/tp/r4/artikel/18/18854/1.html.

Schlesinger, A. 1998. *The Disuniting of America*: *Reflections on a Multicultural Society.* New York: W. W. Norton.

Sommer, T. 2000. Einwanderung ja, Ghettos nein: Warum Friedrich Merz sich zu Unrecht auf mich beruft. [Immigration yes, ghettos no: Why Friedrich Merz is wrong to refer to me]. *Die Zeit.* No. 47.

Tawada, Y. 1989. Canned Foreign. In *Where Europe Begins*, trans. S. Bernofsky, 85–90. New York: New Directions Books.

Tawada, Y. 1996a. Eigentlich darf man es niemanden sagen, aber Europa gibt es nicht. [Nobody is supposed to say it, but Europe does not exist]. In *Talisman*, 45–51. Tübingen: Konkursbuch Verlag Claudia Gehrke.

Tawada, Y. 1996b. *Talisman: Yoko Tawada.* Tübingen: Konkursbuch.

Tawada, Y. 2007. An der Spree. In *Sprachpolizei und Spielpolyglotte* [Language police and Play polyglot]. 11–25. Verlag Claudia Gehrke.

Taylor, C. 1992. *Multiculturalism and 'The Politics of Recognition'.* Princeton: Princeton University Press.

Terkesssidis, M. 2001. Kulturarbeit in der Einwanderungsgesellschaft: Zur kulturellen Praxis von MigrantInnen. [Culture work in immigrant societies: Notes on the cultural practice of migrants]. *IG Kultur Österreich.* Available at: http://igkultur.at/igkultur/kulturrisse/1158853565/ 1158855927.

Tibi, B. 2000. *Europa Ohne Identität? Leitkultur Oder Wertebeliebigkeit* 2 Auflage. [Europe without identity? Core culture or value relativism 2nd ed.]. Aalen: BertelsmannVerlag.

Wefing, H. 2006. Seyran Ates: Ätsch, ich darf stolz sein. [Seyran Ates: Whatever, I am allowed to be proud]. Frankfurter Allgemeine Zeitung, FAZ.net. Available at: http://www.faz.net/s/Rub117C535CDF414415BB243B181B8B60AE/Doc~EE18C49A9383E4692A0BFF5F4F4745894~ATpl~Ecommon~Scontent.html.

Wikan, U. 2006. The Honor Culture. *Axeess*, January. Available at: http://www.axess.se/english/2005/01/ theme wikan.php.

Williams, R. 1958. *Culture and Society 1780–1950.* London. Reprinted Harmondsworth 1963.

Zizek, S. 1991. *Looking Awry. An Introduction to Jacques Lacan through Popular Culture*. Cambridge, MA and London: MIT Press.

Chapter 13

A *Gemütlich* Segregation: Multiculturalism and the Iceman's Curse in Italy

Stefano Fait

In Italy, as in France, Germany and Austria, hyphenated identities are uncommon. It is generally assumed that a cohesive civil religion is incompatible with an emphasis on ethnic and cultural distinctiveness as discussed in the Adsett chapter. But what happens when this assimilationist logic, stressing what people have in common, comes face to face with an ethnic identity which celebrates difference?

South Tyrol/Upper Adige, the northernmost trilingual Italian region, on the alpine border with Austria, has often been celebrated as a model of how ethnic rivalries can be contained. However, the post-war agreement really was a 'cold peace' which rested on a peculiar reinterpretation of the 'separate but equal' doctrine. The campaign slogan adopted by the party representing the German-speaking majority used to be: "the clearer we make the distinction between us, the better we will get on with each other", roughly corresponding to the English saying "good fences make good neighbours". This compromise, together with a lavishly subsidized, but also vibrant, local economy – South Tyrol's per capita income exceeds the national average by 40 percent, and ranks among the highest in the world – has ensured that the interests of otherwise competing and antagonistic groups would not diverge too sharply. But it has come at a price: ethnic identities and interests matter sensibly more than individual identities and rights. An arrangement originally designed to protect ethnic Ladins and Germans – a majority in the region but a minority nationally – from the encroachments of the Italian State, has produced a 'fenced society'. Most people live side by side but separately (*nebeneinander*), often in self-enclosed, ethnically homogeneous enclaves, guarding their 'irreducible uniqueness'. Mixture (*Vermischung*), mixed marriages (*Mischehen*) and mixed schools (*gemischte Schulen*) are deemed undesirable; even nursery schools are ethnically segregated. This is the result of a clash of two distinct inflections of nationalism.

European nationalism did not come in a package with individualism and secularism, and the transformation of the agrarian world produced sensibly different outcomes. The moral and cultural consensus expressed by the nationalized masses could find a sense of cohesion and shared identity in opposite directions. In part, this is because modern European secular narratives have been shaped by both the Enlightenment and positivistic belief in the malleability of human nature and society and by the Romantic passion for ethnicity and localism and its critique of social fragmentation and dehumanizing mechanism. Under the influence of Romantic aspirations, national identities have been literally invented through the selective removal of memories of past hybridism and syncretism.

Historically, this dualism gave rise to two divergent traditions of accommodating cultural and ethnic diversity within a nation-state. The first is an assimilationist and contractual model, adopted in Western Europe, and mostly derived from the Roman and Roman Catholic ecumenical traditions, and from the Enlightenment and liberal individualist and cosmopolitan values. Its explicit aim is to gradually absorb diversity within its legal framework and the hegemonic national culture. Nationality thus coincides with civic, voluntary affiliation, and membership is determined by acquired traits such as a common language and shared cultural traditions. The second tradition is a particularistic and separatist model, where minorities are not encouraged to integrate into the larger society because their cultural identities are held to be not entirely reconcilable with the values and norms of the host society, and because their members are presumed to be too firmly anchored to their cultural baggage. Arguably this is what we have seen in the case of Germany and Austria in previous chapters, and in Eastern Europe. Within this model, nationality is an ethno-cultural, ascribed affiliation relying on genealogical criteria.

This difference in policy had important consequences. Both the German and the Italian unification processes began during the Napoleonic wars and came to fruition in the early 1870s. But German Romantic nationalism was impregnated with ruralism, ethnicism, and anti-cosmopolitism and drew heavily on a symbolic repertoire of peasants alienated by the ills of modern urban life. Conversely, Italian nationalism developed along the lines of ever-widening circles of integration and abstract superimpositions, and an emphasis on a common language, tradition, history, and on highly formalized juridical and political units that were inevitably inimical to ethnic particularism. The postulate of a 'natural causation' of politics and society was consistently rejected even by the far right, and nationalism was seldom associated with *völkish* themes (Absalom 1995). Thus, for instance, Italian encyclopedias and dictionaries consistently stressed the voluntaristic aspects of nationality and excluded 'race' as a constitutive, unifying factor (Gentile 2006).

In brief, German nationalism was more inclined to make a fetish of ethnic identity, that is, to treat it as something superior to humans, possessing an intrinsic, almost sacred value, whereas Italian nationalism often manifested an alarming state idolatry, which would fester with Mussolini's rise to power. Besides having a remarkable heuristic value as an analytical tool, this divide can be clearly seen in Trentino-South Tyrol (TST), where different ethnic groups managed to peacefully co-exist until the age of European nationalism. Until 1919 a province of the Austro-Hungarian Empire, TST was assigned to Italy by the treaty of Saint Germain, even though its German-speaking inhabitants – an ethnic majority in South Tyrol – longed for their reintegration into the Austrian homeland and especially for the unification with North Tyrol, still part of Austria.

When Mussolini came to power, he was determined to force upon the nation a sense of national identity, in order to make it disciplined and efficient, in spite of the existing linguistic and regional divisions. This meant imposing an absolute linguistic and cultural unity for the whole of Italy, which had been unified less than sixty years earlier. This would include the French-speaking Aosta Valley, the Slovenian-speaking minority, and the German-speaking South Tyrol. He then undertook an ethnocidal scheme of Italianization of South Tyrol, encouraging thousands of Italian workers to settle down in its towns,[1] disbanding cultural and recreational associations, hiring only monolingual Italian-speaking civil servants and barring access by local elites to positions of responsibility, forbidding the teaching and use of German language in public, and having place names, given names and even gravestone inscriptions translated in Italian.

Eventually, in 1939, Hitler and Mussolini devised a radical solution to this problem: 'voluntary' ethnic self-cleansing. South Tyroleans were asked to choose between staying in South Tyrol and renounce their cultural heritage and declaring themselves ethnic Germans (*Volksdeutsche*) and be resettled somewhere in the German Reich. Approximately 170,000 – 90 percent of Germanophones and 61 percent of Ladins – opted for the Reich and were called 'Optants' (*Optanten*). The *Dableiber*, those who refused to leave their land, and there were as many as 70,000 of them, were regarded as traitors by the others. This collective trauma left a legacy of pain among South Tyroleans.[2]

After the war, some of those who had been resettled in the former German Reich began to return home, but South Tyrol was not restored to Austria. Rome was instead urged to grant self-government to its German-speaking and Ladin-speaking minorities, which it did, in 1948, but in a way that would make sure that South Tyrol would not be able to secede, and which deeply enraged South Tyroleans. The special status was extended to the Trentini, their Italian-speaking neighbours to the South, and a new region was created, called 'Trentino – Upper Adige',[3] in which German speakers would once again be a minority with little control over their own destiny. Then came mass demonstrations, bombing attacks, the first victims, and troops were sent to police the province: the spectre of Northern Ireland loomed large in the national debate. Eventually, Rome agreed to discuss a set of far more meaningful measures of self-government for the ethnic minorities,

---

1   Until then, only 4 to 5 percent of the local population was ethnic Italian. German speakers and Italian speakers commonly identify themselves as, respectively, Südtiroler (South Tyroleans) and Alto Atesini (which has no English equivalent). In 2001, 69.15 percent of residents were South Tyroleans, 26.47 percent were Alto Atesini, and 4.37 percent were Ladins.

2   Incidentally, neither dictator really thought that this would settle the question once and for all: Mussolini, fearing a German invasion, approved the creation of a defensive line, the Vallo Alpino Littorio, to protect the northern border.

3   'Upper Adige' is the Italian and French name for South Tyrol, which is called *Südtirol* in German.

the so-called 'second autonomy package', which was originally signed in 1969 and put in place in 1972, although it took twenty years of fierce negotiations to implement all the measures (137) that it contained (*Paketabschluss*).

It was in those years, late 1960s – early 1970s, that two American anthropologists, John W. Cole and Eric R. Wolf, did ethnographic fieldwork in TST. They detected a number of distinctive cultural traits which set Italian-speaking and German-speaking peasants apart, despite living in the same ecological niche, to which they had adapted in much the same way. They ranged from settlement and field layouts (dispersed in South Tyrol and nucleated in Trentino); professional aspirations; economic and social arrangements (independence and self-government vs. interdependence and community-orientation, rural life vs. urban life); and, migration patterns (Italian-speaking emigrants maintained close ties with their homeland, whereas German-speaking emigrants burned the bridges behind them). But the most striking divergence was in kinship and family structures. In Tyrolean families, the first born son (*Wirth*) would inherit the estate (primogeniture) and the younger siblings would have to leave (*weichen*). Alternatively, some of them were allowed to remain at the farm, and work as farmhands (*Knechte*, which also means 'slaves'). Conversely, ethnic Italian families in TST divided the estate and the patrimony in equal parts among all siblings. Farmers would not regard themselves as rulers of an estate, but as stewards. Communities tended to be inclusive, democratic, reciprocal, and flexible, and families and distant relatives would enjoy broad social networks (Wolf and Cole 1999).

From this brief overview of ethnic relationships in TST, one can readily discern that this can easily result in a brand of multiculturalism in which power struggles between ethnic groups and interest groups may cause the right of peoples to self-determination to become a vehicle for the fetishization of group identities. Indeed, in South Tyrol, TST's northern autonomous province, every ten years, the ethnic census requires local residents, including foreign residents, to identify with one of the three available ethnic designations[4] – dubbed 'ethnic cages' by the critics of this system – which will determine welfare entitlements (e.g. social housing) and public employment quotas available to each group, in proportion to their numerical strength. The political implications of this census are obvious. Eastern Europeans living in the region are the most likely to self-identify as German-speakers in the ethnic census, for German was the official language of the Habsburg Empire, and was commonly spoken across south-eastern Europe. The recent decision on the part of the ethnic German ruling party to impose restrictions on migrant workers who are not from Eastern Europe, shows that ethnic allegiance overrides all other considerations.

---

4   The 1981 *Sprachgruppenzugehörigkeitserklärung* clause requires residents to officially declare that they are either German-, Italian- or Ladin-speakers, and to accept that they will be relegated to the designated ethnic category for the next ten years.

As a result, 20 percent of residents who would rather not identify with any of the official ethnicities or, given the choice, would check off more than one, have no choice but to select one. In other words, individuals are to a large extent defined by their membership in an ethnic group. Ethnic identities matter sensibly more than individual rights and, even though things are improving,[5] many, perhaps most people still live side by side but separately, in self-enclosed, ethnically homogeneous enclaves, guarding their 'irreducible uniqueness', and stigmatizing those who have dared to cross the clearly defined boundaries. People from different ethnic backgrounds, it is argued by the German-speaking political leaders, should meet "as little as possible and as much as necessary" (*so wenig als möglich, so viel als notwendig*). The imperative of 'boundary maintenance' is inexorable: society must be ordered in 'ethnic drawers' (*ethnische Schubladen*) (Staffler 1999), which means that individuals are forced into ethnic straitjackets that define them by their ascribed roles. Unfortunately, it is exceedingly difficult to initiate a reversal of perspective when social interactions and economic transactions are based on ethnically homogeneous pre-existing networks of trust. This is a problem that has been extensively examined by Patti Tamara Lenard in her chapter on immigration and trust.

This ideal Heimat,[6] for all its protections from the outside world and its perpetual reproduction of a 'geography of avoidance'[7], seems to be economically unfeasible and politically unwise in an increasingly integrated continental economy and in times of mass immigration. The underlying premise of this model of multicultural coexistence is that ethnic groups should be highly integrated, self-referential and static, or else South Tyrol would quickly find itself on the brink of *Verelsässerung*, that is, total assimilation, like Alsace, in France (*Elsass* in German).

As a result of all this, today Upper Adige is "the one area in Central Europe where there is not a dominated but a dominant minority" (Pallaver 1990, 70). But the outcome of this institutionalized compensatory differential treatment and measures taken to promote the autonomous development of each ethnic group – whether manifested in sport, media, religion, education, the labour market, the house market, social amenities, recreational facilities, etc. – can be usefully compared to J.S. Furnivall's (1948, 304) disillusioned description of South East Asian colonial societies:

> It is in the strictest sense a medley, for they mix but do not combine. Each group holds by its own religion, its own culture and language, its own ideas and ways.

---

5   According to the Provincial Bureau of Statistics (IPS 2006), 23.1 percent of the population is not concerned about interethnic relations. In 1991, the corresponding figure was 8.2 percent.

6   "To contemplate Heimat means to imagine an uncontaminated space, a realm of innocence and immediacy." (Rentschler 1993, 37).

7   Made of parallel cognitive worlds where ethnic groups live and develop as independently as possible.

As individuals they meet, but only in the marketplace, in buying and selling. There is a plural society, with different sections of the community living side by side, but separately, within the same political unit.

Life in the South Tyrol of ethnic quotas (*ethnischer Proporz*) can also be contrasted with the Cantle Report's (2001, Section 2.1) depiction of the inner cities of Northern England:

The extent, to which these physical divisions were compounded by so many other aspects of our daily lives, was very evident. Separate educational arrangements, community and voluntary bodies, employment, places of worship, language, social and cultural networks, means that many communities operate on the basis of a series of parallel lives. These lives often do not seem to touch at any point, let al.one overlap and promote any meaningful interchanges.

Bones of Contention

Symbols, systems of signification, and narrative accounts are tied together in complex ways, and even scientists sometimes end up enmeshed in the cobweb of identity politics. Between 1878 and 1900, in a political climate ideologically charged due to border disputes between Austria and Italy, Meran medical anthropologist Franz Tappeiner (1816–1902) and his colleagues used craniometric measurements and skin and hair sampling to argue that Trentini[8] closely resembled the dolichocephalous 'Germanic type'. Their colleagues in Trent, Giovanni Canestrini (1835–1900) and Lamberto Moschen (1853–1932), countered that, according to their own findings, Trentini should be classified together with their Italian neighbours to the south.[9] Paolo Mantegazza, one of the leading Italian anthropologists, while clarifying that his critical remarks should not be intended as a personal attack on an esteemed colleague and friend, remarked that he could not believe that "the hyper-craniological faith could be stretched to the point of fanaticism" (Mantegazza 1884, 355–6). Both sides refused to acknowledge the physical resemblance of South Tyroleans and Trentini, who had lived side by side and intermarried for centuries. This is a forgotten tidbit of local history which shows that even scientific practices may become objects of fierce struggle and impassioned debate over disputed classifications. This is far more likely when there is an ongoing conflict between ethnic groups vying for control of resources and power.

---

8   At that time, one of the Italian-speaking minorities of the Austrian-Hungarian empire.

9   In those years, the Italian-speaking elites were almost unanimously in favour of self-determination and exasperated by the intransigence of Vienna.

About a hundred years later, in 1991, German hikers discovered a well-preserved corpse, still half buried in a glacier on the South Tyrolean border with Austria. It turned out that the corpse was not that of a mountaineer, but of a man who lived in the region thousands of years ago and who was christened 'Oetzi the Iceman', because people initially thought that he had been found in the Austrian Oetz Valley. Since 1998, despite the protests of those who found this decision appalling and degrading, Oetzi has been on display in a refrigerated chamber at the South Tyrol Museum of Archaeology in Bolzano/Bozen, the capital town of South Tyrol, and has immediately become an object of desire. Hundreds of tourists from across the world[10] line up every day to catch a glimpse of the mummy through a small stainless steel window. As the oldest preserved human being, he has acquired a true celebrity status and, from an invaluable treasure for palaeontologists, he has turned into a huge business venture, spawning a veritable 'Ice Man industry', with countless commercial ramifications, from books and documentaries, to tours, holiday packages, and escorted hikes to the site of discovery, to special recipes, dishes, and menus, to merchandise. His image appears on cups, t-shirts, postcards, key chains, calendars, notepads, mouse pads, backpacks, etc. Now even Hollywood stars are joining the Oetzi-cult. It is reported that Brad Pitt got a new tattoo of Oetzi on his left forearm, perhaps because the Iceman himself had 60 tattoos, allegedly for shamanic/therapeutic reasons.

Now, because the body was found on the Italian-Austrian border, a legal battle ensued between Italy and Austria over the ownership of Oetzi, which soon became a clash between North and South Tyrol, Innsbruck and Bozen. Bolzano eventually won the dispute when a topographic survey established that the resting place lay inside South Tyrol, less than a hundred yards from the border. For the first time since the annexation, South Tyroleans had reason to rejoice for not being part of Austria: their special status meant that every archaeological finding would fall under the provincial jurisdiction.[11] This also meant that the ancient man initially dubbed by the media *Homo Tirolensis*, and portrayed as the first Tyrolean, really was *Homo Tirolensis Meridionalis* ('South Tyrolean Man'), with potentially serious implications for the future relations of the two ethnically related, but politically separated neighbours. Many Austrian Tyroleans thought that they had been robbed. After all, his name was Oetzi, like the Austrian Oetz valley, not Schnalsi, as he should have been called, if he had been found in the South Tyrolean Senales valley. This was but the latest of a string of altercations between Tyroleans, with the northerners accusing the southerners of taking unfair advantage of Italian multicultural policies to pursue their own interests to the detriment of their Austrian 'cousins'.

---

10   Over 300,000 visitors the first year and an average of more than 240,000 visitors a year since then.

11   This provision bears some resemblance to the U.S. Native American Graves Protection and Repatriation Act.

This story is important because it highlights the limits of identity politics when the need to emphasize diversity leads to the iconization of symbols of difference, even if it is the body of a deceased man, turned into a relic. Oetzi has been turned into a South Tyrolean saint, the object of a secular, spontaneous devotion. A hunter, a travelling salesman, a shaman, an outlaw, or a warrior, no one really knows who this man was. Nevertheless, his body, preserved forever in a sarcophagus monitored by multiple sensors, together with his goatskin leggings, axe, grass cape, longbow, arrows, fire-making kit, and backpack, is now part of a mythologizing process, which closely resembles the cultification of Lenin.

This is unsurprising, given that the cultural construction of ethnicity is grounded in objects, symbols, institutions, places, and habits. The perpetuation of undiluted cultures and ethnicities has much in common with the preservation of this warrior hero, media icon, and ancestral patriarch. The 5,300-year-old mummy is in many ways an allegory of how local power struggles have led to the fetishization of group identities. When certain ethnic identity markers are less readily accessible, or their content is thinning, or they are questioned, or no longer as distinctive as they used to be, and therefore less relevant –this is precisely what is going on in South Tyrol, as the new generations appear to be less interested in ethnicity – then it becomes necessary to develop and introduce some new ones (Wrong 1997). In other words, apart from the ordinary symbolic manipulation for commercial purposes, the hype surrounding Oetzi is possibly an indication of a decline of real cultural differences, or at least of a much less polarized division between South Tyroleans and *Alto Atesini*. This has forced ethno-political entrepreneurs to find new ways to mobilize intra-group solidarity. This secular relic is therefore a promise of immortality for the current multi-ethnic arrangement of the province, the guarantee that South Tyroleans will forever continue to exist as a distinct ethnic group. As the body of the mythical ancestor[12] has stood the course of time, so will the South Tyrolean identity (Bergonzi and Heiss 2004). What is even more interesting is that all this is occurring as North and South Tyroleans, who share virtually the same tradition and language, are undergoing a process of schismogenesis (Bateson 1958). Partitioned into two subgroups by the border, and therefore lacking those checks and restraints that prevent progressive differentiation, the division is becoming dialectically heightened to the point that it is spinning out of control and leading them to increasing rivalry and hostility. This could lead, eventually, to the breakdown of pan-Tyrolean ethnic solidarity, similar to the way in which, in the post-war years, Austrians distanced themselves from pan-Germanism as seen in Chapter 11. An event that would appear all the more baffling, given the otherwise stubborn commitment to the 'one Tyrol' ideology (*Landeseinheit*), which finds eloquent expression in the old folksong 'There is only one Tyrol' (*Tirol isch lei oans*). Ultimately, the nature of the alleged Iceman curse, which has thus far claimed the lives of seven persons somehow related to

---

12   In reality, the actual ancestors of South Tyroleans crossed the Alps only between the sixth and the eleventh century A.D.

the discovery of Oetzi or to research conducted on his body, might well be that those coming in close and prolonged contact with Oetzi are bound to be torn apart from their loved ones, and this is just as true for ethnic groups.

But there is another sense in which identity politics has major commercial implications. These days, DNA-screenings are performed on a number of peoples, particularly if they live in remote places, in which case they are known as founder populations, that is, human groups descending from a small number of ancestors (founders). They represent an enormous opportunity for clinicians, because their genetic variations become amplified, with a higher allele frequency. Instead, the rest of their genome remains substantially the same, given that very few mutations are introduced from the outside ('genetic noise'). These studies can only be useful if both the environment and lifestyles have remained unchanged, playing a minor role in genetic variation, and isolated populations come closer to the ideal conditions. This should facilitate the highly profitable and immensely helpful medical research into the genetic determinants of common disorders.

The Alps, with their narrow valleys and scattered settlements would appear to be extremely promising for genetic analysis of complex traits. And, indeed, there is an ongoing population research project, called GenNova, which is being conducted by the Institute of Genetic Medicine at the European Academy[13] in Bolzano/Bozen – which also hosts an 'Institute for Mummies and the Iceman' – in partnership with the universities of Harvard, Munich and Lübeck. Their homepage[14] says that 'several of South Tyrol's remote Alpine valleys and villages, especially some Ladin communities and other communities of the Val Pusteria, Valle Isarco and Val Venosta, have basically maintained the same geographical conditions, small-scale economic structures and above all, limited mobility since their settlement in the Neolithic period, leading to genetic-environmental 'microisolation'. Such small, visible pockets of microisolated populations, together with unique genealogical and medical documentation, make South Tyrol an ideal location for research in the field of genetic medicine.

Understandably, German-speaking media reports of this project often betray the crypto-colonial fascination with the "virgin", "the pristine", the 'Otherness' of peoples "living close to nature". Now even genetics appear to be committed to the preservation of the ethnic Garden of Eden, where South Tyroleans are most themselves, at their most pristine, unsullied and immune for centuries from the diluting influences of foreign cultures and genotypes (Pinggera et al. 2006). These communities have ostensibly marched through history in ordered ranks, keeping their ethnic heritage intact and becoming sites of moral values where pristine native culture intersects with a primordial landscape. However, critics have questioned the value of this kind of research, on the ground that population geneticists ignore the significant body of ethnographic literature pointing to the

---

13   https://www.eurac.edu/index.

14   http://www.eurac.edu/Org/GeneticMedicine/forschungsstandort_suedtirol.htm (last accessed on December 9, 2007).

mobility of the human species and to the contingency and plasticity of human cultural expressions and of group-boundaries. They believe that scientists have fallen prey to the so-called 'classificatory fallacy' (or 'essentialist fallacy'), in that they have mistaken artificially constructed and constantly negotiated and contested categories for natural categories.

Indeed, in deeply divided multicultural societies like South Tyrol, it is not always easy to disentangle scientific reasoning from preconceived notions of self-identity, and professional agendas from political agendas. For instance, let us consider Germanic kinship and inheritance systems. Traditionally, Germanic ethnic aggregations (*Stämme*) comprised a few thousand families and defined their identity in relation to a common ancestor and to their consanguinity (endogamy) (Gasparri 1998). It was customary for the members of peasant patriarchal clans to be unilaterally related to each other and to trace their genealogy back to the alleged founder of the lineage, that is, to their common ancestor. The patriarch was the highest religious, political, and legal authority of the clan and decided when it was time to transfer his power to the first-born son, together with the knowledge of the body of norms and practices of the lineage, according to the inheritance right called *Anerbenrecht*. It is therefore far more natural for South Tyroleans than for Alto Atesini to think of their heritage as part of this 'ancestral inheritance' (*Ahnenerbe*). Because we cannot assume a basic literacy in genetics and biological evolution for most South Tyrolean readers, many might erroneously understand genealogies in terms of genetic continuity – some sort of Eternal Recurrence – and regard their existence as an epiphenomenon of perpetual bloodlines. This would in turn exacerbate the existing tendency toward the fetishization of culture and identity, or neotraditionalism, whereby ethnicity is seen as timeless, bounded, discrete, and organic, the permanent and inalterable property of a primordial ethnic group.

Indeed, the implicit assumption is common, that the authentic South Tyrol is rural and that genuine South Tyroleans are healthy and sturdy mountain farmers. Those who have to leave the countryside for urban settings are presumed to be eager to reconnect with their rural roots, whenever possible. This belief recreates and commercializes a mystique of the natural and redeeming authenticity and purity of the Alps as a getaway from the pressure of urban daily life and from the corrupting influence of modernity, especially Italian modernity. The Alps are then viewed as an ideal space of subversive nostalgia, for those longing for a more genuine identity. It is through this psychological transference that environmental conservation (*Naturschutz*) and 'homeland protection' (*Heimatschutz*) become closely intertwined in the South Tyrolean self-narrative.

Advertising campaigns for tourism promotion make the link between environmental management and the multiple meanings and uses of the 'touristification' of heritage even more apparent. In the South Tyrolean tourism industry it is not unusual to encounter traces of ethno-nationalistic rhetoric such as the expression "the obstinate love of the people for their homeland" (*hartnäckige Heimatliebe der Menschen*) or quotes such as, "every man has a homeland and should love and honour that patch of land where he was born" (*Jeder Mensch hat eine Heimat und soll das Fleckchen Erde, wo er geboren ist, in Lieb' und Ehren halten*). These words, found in a tourist brochure, were taken from a poem by the nineteenth-century German poet and writer Julius Wolff, and were used by the South-Tyrolean Dairy Association as a caption for the photo of two blond children drinking milk while sitting in the mountain grass.

Within the ethno-environmentalist model "Homeland and environment" (*Heimat und Umwelt*), *Heimat* is the ubiquitous and constitutive feature of a defensive strategy against the globalized and secularized "outside world" which combines landscape preservation, economic protectionism, and the attempt to restore the perceived harmony of the past and the moral qualities associated with the countryside. Yet South Tyroleans should not be seen as passive recipients of the effects of this manipulation of signs and signifiers. They also play active roles in the dynamic conversion of the particular into the universal and back again, and they deliberately try to market a particular approach to modernity and multiculturalism, transformed into a fetishized commodity. In other words, today's South Tyrol is also a brand name closely identified with authenticity. By the same token, South Tyroleans, as they dress in traditional garb, play traditional instruments, sing folksongs, and try to anticipate the tourist's expectations are, as it were, human billboards, with a corporate identity who seek to generate brand loyalty among tourists/consumers while catering for the demands of the local tourist industry.

What is truly fascinating is that, far from restricting the jurisdiction of commoditization, as in Igor Kopytoff's model (Appadurai 1999), South Tyroleans are resolutely and purposefully committed to its expansion, as the only viable remedy to the increasing depopulation of mountain areas, and as a way to express their lifestyle. Self-objectification and self-commoditization via the resurrection, invention, and staging of folkways are palatable because they provide hard currency and symbolic capital, and revive practices that would otherwise have no place in everyday life. In this way, South Tyroleans can assert their group identity and teach traditional values, ideals and norms of behaviour to the new generations. The focus is on building a sense of continuity with the past and integrity in the present, and retaining an appearance of authenticity, spontaneity, worth, genuineness, and plausibility, that is, of collective identity. At least for young people, who are gradually losing the sense of ethnic self-preservation (*Selbsterhaltungsgefühl*), being South Tyrolean also means voluntarily consuming one's own identity, choosing to be part of a 'tribe', but only insofar as it is in their economic, social and political interest to do so (Maffesoli 1996).

I therefore have to disagree with Oliver Schmidtke's contention that "the pragmatism of a primarily managerial approach to a common market and the highly emotional reference to the endangered Heimat are not very compatible" (Schmidtke 1996, 298). South Tyrolean identity has served to protect and expand business opportunities. What is more, a fast-shrinking global marketplace causes distinctiveness to become commercially attractive, and at the same time it intensifies regional competition, fostering economic and cultural chauvinism. Hence, identity politics should be seen, at least to some extent, as a natural outgrowth of mass consumerism and the struggle for symbolic hegemony. It follows that there is no inherent tension between commercialism and traditionalism, and between exchange-value and use-value. Cultural preservation and business are simply two sides of the same coin, and the commercial exploitation of objects and practices (including a people's genome) may lead to native essentialism – the idea that group members have a primordial attachment to their traditional ways of life and worldviews – which, incidentally, seems to enjoy a broad appeal, and not only in South Tyrol (Brumann 1999).

Dominant Minorities

It is only fair to say that the alpine region has never been welcoming to foreigners, newcomers and underrepresented minorities. Witch-hunting was endemic in the isolated rural societies of the Alps and their foothill (Trevor-Roper 1969) and minorities such as Gypsies, Jews, Karrner, Hutterites, Sinti and Roma, have been systematically discriminated against, harassed and persecuted by institutionalized lynch mobs for centuries in Switzerland, Austria, Trentino-South Tyrol, and Slovenia. They were regarded as 'imperfectly assimilated' or 'inassimilable', and treated as 'matter out of place'. These itinerant, cosmopolitan, boundary-transgressing ethnic groups violated the deeply entrenched taboos and imperatives of societies where priority was placed "on keeping people judiciously apart, on maintaining delicate balances that made possible long-term accommodation" (Barber 1974, 256). This is precisely the state of affairs in Upper Adige.

Alexander Langer, a South Tyrolean green politician, journalist, and writer, ostracized in his own community for his hostility to ethnic segregation and for his alleged betrayal of his own ethnic group, committed suicide in 1995. In a short autobiography, he recalled the day that he was late for school and saw other children that he had never seen before, entering the school from a different entrance, which he had never heard of: "it wasn't my entrance, I did not know them, the whole place was different, and there were fewer children". It was then that he realized that an entire side of the school was reserved for children from a different ethnic background, with their teachers and their recreational area, their gate, and their schedule. This early experience made Langer's resolve to denounce and combat social segmentation, ethnic segregation, and separate education unshakeable. But even after his death, this state of affairs has not improved significantly. His dream of a society whose main slogan would be "the more contact we have, the better we will get on with each other" has not come true. The official motto of this formal democracy is still "to count, to weight, and to divide" (*zählen, wägen, teilen*) (Baur et al. 1998).

Under Mussolini's dictatorship, the only way for ethnic German children to study German was through a network of illegal, underground schools in farm-houses called *Katakombenschulen*. Today, it's the other way round, and there are ethnic German parents who must hire Italian teachers for their children *sub rosa*, because South Tyrolean and Alto Atesini pupils are not supposed to mix and learn about each other's culture. Integration cannot go too far, for Italians must continue to play the role of the 'perpetual foreigners-within' as Nicolacopoulos and Vassilacopoulos describe in their chapter. In the words of Siegfried Brugger, a former South Tyrolean People's (SVP) chairman, "we need no new type of South Tyroleans, who are a mish-mash, with a little bit German, a little Ladin, a little Italian. This is a political approach which is old-fashioned and has been superseded" (Quoted in Pallaver 2005, 203).

The South Tyrolean People's Party is a *Sammelpartei*, that is, a party with a cross-class electoral appeal representing an ethnically homogeneous constituency. It was founded in 1945 and has since managed to secure the votes of nearly all South Tyroleans and Ladins, invariably gaining the absolute majority of votes and seats in local elections. Oliver Schmidtke reports that, in the 1990s, a group of people, all wearing their folk costumes, appeared on an election campaign poster in support of the SVP, with the slogan "We South Tyroleans" (*Wir Südtiroler*). Schmidtke correctly argues that the poster seems to suggest that those who share that identity should cast their vote for the SVP (Schmidtke 1996). However, the obverse could also be posited: those who express a preference for the SVP are expected to dress, act, look, and feel like *Südtiroler*, at least once in a while. "My ethnicity right or wrong" (*Mir sein mir*) is still the dominant attitude in this corner of Europe. After all, in a less ethnically divided society, the party would lose considerable ground, because the very reason for the existence of the "guardians of the homeland" (*Heimatschützer*) would disappear, and a crisis of legitimacy would ensue (Pallaver 2005).

This is why the SVP maintains a peculiar attitude to autonomy, and concentrates its efforts in perpetuating inter-ethnic divisions and prioritizing social cohesion and ethnic conflict (*Volkstumkampf*) over individual rights (Rossi 1980). This approach is noticeably reminiscent of the collectivist "Liberty of the Ancients", understood as "active and constant participation in collective power", and is a far cry from the modern notion of liberty as private independence against the subjection to arbitrary power (Constant 1988). Freedom as intended in South Tyrol is a group right, not an individual right, a subject Andrew Robinson in Chapter 3 reflects on the importance of both personal autonomy and communal identifications in the pursuit of a meaningful life.

In order to preserve the "community of fate" (*Schicksalsgemeinschaft*) which keeps all South Tyroleans bond to one another and to the party, the SVP has invested heavily in ethnically based and party-linked social and cultural associations, knowing that, in the long run, they would ensure the propagation and hegemony of the party's ideology (Schmidtke 1996). In this respect, we should highlight the fact that, as part of the compensatory package, more than 90 percent of the tax revenue generated in South Tyrol is then returned to the province and that 70 percent of the budget is spent on the fixed costs of the 'hypertrophic' public sector which provides ethnically differentiated goods and services. This translates into a tremendous amount of financial backing for the party's essential purpose of preserving the status quo by avoiding conflict through compromises rather than through integration. Akin to Suzanna Reiss' (Chapter 5) and Reza Hasmath's (Chapter 6) trenchant analysis in Canada and China, South Tyrol's provincial government budgetary provision for 2008 has allocated €380,000 (~ US$518,000) to cultural investments such as the concert of the folk music band *Kastelruther Spatzen* and a folk music festival to be held next year.[15]

It is small wonder that given this almost embarrassing 'liberality', which benefits all ethnic groups, albeit not equally, open interethnic conflicts only resurface during times of economic and political crisis and are instead silenced in periods of economic expansion (Obkircher 2006). Still, a social system in which resources are distributed among ethnic groups according to their numerical size is more likely to succumb to envy and greed; because if one group obtains more goods and prestige, the other groups will correspondingly perceive themselves as losing worth. It can only work when the cake is large enough for all to share, and nobody knows what the future has in store for Italy and Europe (Wakenhut 1999).

Viewed in this light, one has to admit that the modernizing process in South Tyrol has, at least contingently, deepened the ethnic rift, instead of bridging it, possibly because ethnicity is vague enough a concept that it can be used to forge consensus around shared material interests, while concealing ulterior motives that might actually be contrary to the public interest. I do not believe that multiculturalism is necessarily bound to be "a formula for manufacturing conflict" (Barry 2001), but the fact remains that South Tyrolean identity politics is premised on a victim status that has outlasted its usefulness, and now prevents local people from accustoming themselves to hold multiple, fluid, hybrid.identities and affiliations.

References

Absalom, R. 1995. *Italy since 1800. A Nation in the Balance?* London and New York: Longman.

Appadurai, A. (ed.) 1999. *The Social Life of Things. Commodities in Cultural Perspective*. Cambridge: Cambridge University Press.

Barber, B.R. 1974. *The Death of Communal Liberty: A History of Freedom in a Swiss Mountain Canton*. Princeton: Princeton University Press.

Barry, B.M. 2001. *Culture and Equality: An Egalitarian Critique of Multiculturalism*. Cambridge. Mass.: Harvard University Press.

Bateson, G. 1958. *Naven: A Survey of the Problems Suggested by a Composite Picture of the Culture of a New Guinea Tribe Drawn from Three Points of View*. Stanford. CA: Stanford University Press.

Baur, S. et al. 1998. *Zwischen Herkunft und Zukunft*. Meran: Alpha and Beta.

---

15   http://www.questotrentino.it/2007/16/quante_cose.htm (last accessed on December 9, 2007).

Bergonzi, V. and H. Heiss. 2004. 'Progressi e Limiti del Regionalismo'. L'Alto Adige/Südtirol dopo la Seconda Guerra Mondiale. *Memoria e Ricerca*, 1: 79–100.

Brumann, C. 1999. Writing for Culture. Why a Successful Concept Should Not Be Discarded. *Current Anthropology* 40 (supplement): S1–S27.

Cantle Report. 2001. *Community Cohesion: A Report of the Independent Review Team*. Chaired by Ted Cantle. London: The Home Office.

Constant, B. 1988. The Liberty of the Ancients Compared with that of the Moderns. In *Benjamin Constant: Political writings*, ed. B. Fontana. Cambridge: Cambridge University Press.

Furnivall, J.S. 1948. *Colonial Policy and Practice: A Comparative Study of Burma and Netherlands India*. London: Cambridge University Press.

Gasparri, S. 1998. *Prima delle Nazioni. Popoli. Etnie· e Regni fra Antichità e Medioevo*. Roma: Carocci.

Gentile, E. 2006. *La Grande Italia. Il Mito della Nazione nel XX secolo*. Laterza: Roma-Bari.

Istituto Provinciale di Statistica (IPS). 2006. *Barometro Linguistico dell'Alto Adige*. Bolzano: Provincia di Bolzano.

Langer, A. 1986. *Minima Personalia*. in 'Belfagor-Rassegna di varia umanità'. 41(3).

Maffesoli, M. 1996. *The Time of the Tribes. The Decline of Individualism in Mass Society*. London: Sage Publications Ltd.

Mantegazza, P. 1884. 'L'Antropologia del Tirolo'. *La Natura* 1: 355–6.

Obkircher, R. 2006. Tensioni Etniche e Situazione Socio-Economica in Sudtirolo. *Archivio Trentino* 2: 125–35.

Pallaver, G. 1990. South Tyrol: The 'Package' and its Ratification. in Politics and Society in Germany, Austria and Switzerland. 2(1/2): 70–79.

Pallaver, G. 2005. 'The Südtiroler Volkspartei and its Ethnopopulism'. In *Challenges to Consensual Politics: Democracy, Identity and Populist Protest in the Alpine Region*, eds D. Caramani and Y. Mény, 187–208. Brussels: Peter Lang.

Pinggera, G.K. et al.. 2006. *Medizinisch-genetische Forschung in Südtirol; 1: Gene und Geschichte – in Stilfs – Langtaufers – Martell*. Bolzano/Bozen: EURAC.

Rentschler, E. 1993. There's No Place Like Home: Luis Trenker's *The Prodigal Son* (1934). *New German Critique* 60(3): 33–56.

Rossi, P. 1990. *The Political Ecology of Ethnicity: The Case of the South Tyrol*. M.A. thesis in Political Science: UBC, Vancouver, Canada.

Schmidtke, O. 1996. *Politics of Identity: Ethnicity, Territories and the Political Opportunity Structure in Modern Italian society*. Sinzheim: PUV.

Staffler, G. 1999. *Migration und Ethnizität in Südtirol. Zur sozialen Konstruktion von Fremdheit und Ethnizität in einer pluriethnischen Gesellschaft*. Diplomarbeit. Philosophie. Universität Wien.

Trevor-Roper, H.R. 1969. *European Witch Craze of the Sixteenth and Seventeenth Centuries and Other Essays*. New York: Harper and Row.

Wakenhut, R. 1999. *Ethnische Identität und Jugend*. Opladen: Leske und Budrich.

Wolf, E.R. and J.W. Cole. 1999. *The Hidden Frontier: Ecology and Ethnicity in an Alpine Valley*. Berkeley: University of California Press.

Wrong, D.H. 1997. Cultural relativism as ideology. *Critical Review* 11(2): 291–300.

Index

RESEARCH IN MIGRATION AND ETHNIC RELATIONS SERIES

Full series list